THE TRAIL
IS THE TEACHER

CLAY BONNYMAN EVANS

THE TRAIL
IS THE TEACHER

living and learning on the
Appalachian Trail

ISBN: 987-1-7353968-1-1

Published by

PONY TALES
BOOKS

Cover design, illustration & interior formatting:
Mark Thomas / Coverness.com

For Patches, Eazy-E, and Lava Monster,
who taught me what it means to be part of a trail family.

TABLE OF CONTENTS

ONE: THE BEST TEACHER IN THE WORLD

September 2016: Maine

Of the many the thru-hiking accounts I've read, most open with either a) a scene of transcendent beauty/personal revelation or b) a moment of excruciating pain/extreme challenge. Think of the opening scene in the movie *Wild*, in which Reese Witherspoon, playing hiker Cheryl Strayed, hurls a bloody hiking boot into a deep gorge with a scream of rage.

But after completing my own, unconventional, somewhat unexpected Appalachian Trail thru-hike, no singular moment of mysticism or misery elbowed its way upstage. Instead, I kept coming back to a hiker I first met about 600 miles up the trail, in southern Virginia.

The members of my unexpected crew—you'll meet them later—and I were cooking dinner with other hikers at Jenkins Shelter (mile 578.6; all trail mileages are taken from *The AT Guide Northbound 2016* by David "Awol" Miller) when a petite young woman tottered up, burdened by an enormous pack. She was trailed by a grimacing older man, who made quick, angry work of pitching his tent, then disappeared inside without a word.

The girl set down her pack and started chattering nervously. Fine blond hair, cut short, framed her narrow face and her blue eyes were friendly, but fretful. There was something quavery and frail about her that reminded me of a baby bird that had fallen from the nest. I was surprised when she said she was 23 and a college graduate. Her companion, First Step, was a kind of chaperone, a former college professor she'd recruited because her parents wouldn't let her hike the trail alone. Her trail name was Two Pack.

Over the next few hours, she talked almost nonstop, and I wasn't the only one who had a hard time imagining how she had managed to survive nearly 600 miles of the trail. She seemed to know very little about camping or cooking. She lay the rain fly to her tent on muddy ground to "dry" as a light drizzle prickled down from a gray-cotton sky; a friendly, slightly muddy, husky staying at the shelter quickly circled several times and plopped down on the convenient ground cover for a rest.

And when she pulled her boots and socks off, she revealed narrow, pale, blister-ravaged feet whose toes seemed strangely stacked atop one another, almost crumpled.

With her companion AWOL in his tent, shelter denizens took pity on her, helping her cook and offering advice. I shooed away the dog and helped her hang her rain fly, and tried not to stare at her battered Picasso feet while handing her a thick roll of miracle-working Leukotape for that violent-looking crop of bloody blisters.

"I guess I'm being too negative," Two Pack said, explaining First Step's lack of sociability. "I'm not appreciating him enough. I should be more grateful."

Though she usually pitched a tent, that night she nested securely among the many-colored lumps of a full shelter, like a baby bunny in a warm, comfy nest.

*

The next morning when I rose at 5:45 I saw through a misty gloom that First Step had already struck camp and bailed, abandoning his fragile charge. When she woke a short while later, she was literally shaking, freaked out and worried that he was gone for good. In classic, laconic hiker style, many of us offered words of encouragement.

"Well," someone said, "now you can do what you wanted to do in the first place: Hike the AT on your own."

A couple of hours up the trail, our crew passed a guilty-looking First Step, who wanted to know how Two Pack was doing. Cool, even a little remote—you don't just bail on people like that—we said she was fine; she was awake and gearing up to head out when we left. She would sink or swim now, on her own.

"I bet a thousand bucks," I said as we walked on, "she won't finish the trail."

Nobody disagreed.

*

Four months later, I had become a southbounder—or rather, a flip-flopper, having jumped off in Vermont and gotten back on at Katahdin to finish my trek. I had just rock-hopped across the nearly dry Piscataquis River on a warm, late-August day, slipping at the last minute and soaking one shoe.

But I was feeling good, having just knocked out the first 90 miles of the 100-Mile Wilderness in four days. Now I was sitting on a rock, wringing out my sock, when a fast-moving woman in purple breezed by, grunted a hello, and picked her way quickly across the stones. She was soon followed by two companions, the first of whom I immediately recognized.

"No way!" I shouted, jumping up, genuinely feeling more elation than when I'd summited Katahdin just a few days before. "Two Pack!"

She clearly didn't recognize me. Her once doubtful blue eyes now seemed steely, almost grim with the same thousand-yard stare I'd seen on the faces of so many northbounders (aka NOBOs) who were plunging through the wilderness like hounds on a scent.

"My name's Pony. We met somewhere in Virginia, way back in May," I said, reaching out for a fist bump. "I gave you some Leukotape. Your companion bailed on you that morning...."

"Oh yeah," she said slowly, a smile briefly softening her galvanized expression. "You were with some other guys, right? Younger guys? You guys were doing big miles.... Yeah, I remember you now."

"I hope this doesn't hurt your feelings," I said, "but I was absolutely sure there was no way you would ever finish. I'm super psyched to see you all the way up here! You definitely get my vote for most inspirational story on the AT this year."

"Well ... thanks," Two Pack said. But her companion was hollering from across the creek and she was already moving up the trail. "I've had a lot of people tell me I've grown a lot on the AT."

But I could see she didn't need a compliment from me or anyone else. She had gotten up that chilly, foggy May morning in Virginia and, taking the advice of other hikers, just started walking. I learned later that her erstwhile chaperone bailed out in Pearisburg — but she just kept going. Now, some 1,500 miles later, she'd be catching her first glimpses of Katahdin within a few days. One step at a time, sometimes on painful feet, she had walked right past all her doubters — her parents, her former professor, my crew — to prove that she was tough and resourceful and resilient.

Of course, she didn't do it alone. Nobody does. Other hikers helped her out, and so did the trail itself, the best teacher in the world.

TWO: SNOW

March 2016: Great Smoky Mountains National Park

S tanding on Charlie's Bunion in Great Smoky Mountains National Park, I experienced my first spectacular non-view along the Appalachian Trail. Completely enveloped in fog, my cheeks needled by cold rain driven by a harsh March wind, I could see nothing but gray.

Later that night, I hunkered down inside my 20-degree sleeping bag, huddled next to a dozen other lumps lined up in Tri-Corner Knob Shelter. The blue-tarp windbreak strung across the entrance provided marginal defense against the icebox air outside, which one hiker had measured at 17 degrees. I slept fitfully, chilly despite armoring myself with every layer I had, my earplugs insufficient to mute the buzzsaw snoring of the old man next to me.

I wouldn't even be here, I thought, if my lovely wife Jody and I hadn't decided to trade the discomforts of Rocky Mountain winters for life on a balmy Southern beach. And just 12 hours earlier, I'd been warm and dry at the Grand Prix Motel in one of America's cheesiest towns, Gatlinburg, Tennessee, having decided to cut short my shakedown hike and bail out ahead of a wintry blast, predicted to hit the next morning.

But when I woke the sun was shining from an open blue sky, and hiker guilt began to gnaw at me like a mouse trying to get at a Snickers wrapper. The 500-mile Colorado Trail had schooled me well eight months earlier, but now I found myself having to reabsorb my lessons in Remedial Hiking 101, courtesy of the AT: *Never make a decision at the end of the day; Don't waste your hike trying to outsmart the weather;* and *Stop being such a lazy-ass!*

I had looked forward to descending to Gatlinburg's gaudy, animatronic-haunted strip for a leisurely breakfast surrounded by tourists who, on average, seemed to weigh three times more than the scraggly hikers who'd found their way to town. Instead, shamed by the sun, I gobbled a couple of Pop Tarts, stumped back to the road into the park and put up a thumb.

I hate hitching. Grizzled older men are not, I can say with confidence, widely prized as companions by many drivers. Car after car breezed past. Meanwhile, two young female hikers passed by offering cheery greetings. They walked 50 yards up the road, where the mere sight of their bare thumbs nearly caused a collision. Thirty fruitless minutes later, as I pondered going back to Plan A—which was actually Plan B, so I guess this was Plan C—and calling it quits, I heard a shout from a large white pickup headed into town.

"Hang on, Pony! We'll be back in five minutes!"

It was Mountain Momma and Godspeed, two trail angels who had given me a ride from Newfound Gap (plus a Coke, chips and a sandwich) the afternoon before.

"Thought you were done after yesterday," Godspeed said after I tossed my pack in back and climbed in.

"Yeah. But then I saw how nice it was this morning...."

Fifteen minutes later I started up the trail, still infused with morning optimism despite feeling the first tiny droplets of cold rain on my face.

*

My Appalachian Trail ambitions started small. I'd fallen in love with the stinking, sweating, marching, freeing, mesmerizing life that is thru-hiking while hiking the CT, and now that we'd relocated to the South, I realized the most renowned of long trails was just a few hours' drive away. My first plan was simply to sample the trail with a week or 10 days of spring hiking.

But when a writing project unexpectedly fell apart, the void in my calendar yawned enticingly. Now I proposed to Jody that I'd hike from mid- or late-March to the week before Memorial Day, when I was scheduled to give a talk at the National World War II Museum in New Orleans. I thought I might get 700 or 750 miles, roughly a third of the AT, and if I loved it, I would finish in subsequent years.

And so I slipped into that zombified state that is, for me, the obsession of planning a long hike: Incessantly poking through my gear, poring over guidebooks and maps—David "Awol" Miller's excellent "2016 Northbound AT Guide" and maps published by the Appalachian Trail Conservancy—reading blogs and gradually replacing daily beach runs with pack-laden walks.

Then in early February, I received a text from my cousin Helen, 19, who was "wwoofing"—working on farms in New Zealand through Worldwide Opportunities on Organic Farms—and planning to hike the AT upon her return.

"I've tried to find hiking partners but they keep falling through, so I'm mostly going to be hiking solo," she wrote. "However, my parents and I thought it would be a good idea to have a partner for the first week ... Would you be interested in hiking with me for a week and showing me the ropes?"

I'd always been mostly a solo hiker myself. But Helen was smart and fun, and I love the way the trail makes no distinctions, forging connections between people of different ages, backgrounds and circumstances—a retired firefighter and a college cross-country runner; a lonely 18-year-old girl and a 30-something, professional couple; trail "families" that spanned decades and nationalities and languages ... why not two second cousins separated by 35 years?

But this meant a change in plans. I'd hoped to start at Springer Mountain in Georgia, the southern terminus of the trail, in mid-March, but Helen couldn't start until the second week of April.

The smart thing, of course, would be to push my start date back three weeks. But waiting would have cut my commute time to and from the trail in half and spared me the expense and hassle of finding a shuttle—you know, good stuff.

And patience is not a virtue of which I've often been accused.

THREE: TUMBLING DOWN

*March 2016: Winding Stair Gap
to Nantahala Outdoor Center*

I spent the night of March 12 crammed in the back of our trusty '93 Subaru in the officially closed Big Creek camping area near the north boundary of Great Smoky Mountains National Park.

I'd already experienced the first of many "Charlie Brown" trail moments—stupid stuff that wouldn't have happened, if only I'd been paying more attention. In this case, a small plastic bottle of olive oil had come unscrewed and oozed out of a Ziploc bag, greasing up my food bag to make it even more attractive to bears.

While relieving myself long after midnight, an enormous, dark shadow loomed out of the mist in front of me. Snapping on my headlamp I saw six shining green eyes. Though hunted to extinction in Tennessee by 1850, elk were reintroduced in the 1990s, and this massive, gorgeous bull and his two female companions represented about 1 percent of the state's population.

*

Standing in a light rain at Winding Stair Gap, I watched my pricey shuttle disappear down the road the following afternoon. After checking my straps and retying my Hoka One One Mafate Speed trail runners, I was ready to begin my 130-mile shakedown cruise to the north end of the Smokys.

"Hell yeah, we're doin' the Appa-fuckin-lachian Trail ... Here we go, *hell* yeah!"

I turned to see three hefty young hikers shuffling across U.S. 64, enormous packs swaying. They high-fived and charged toward a gravel road adjacent to the trail. I could still hear them hollering as I descended a couple of rough stone steps and took my first steps on the AT. I caught up to them a few minutes later as they took a smoke break on the steep lower reaches of the climb toward Siler Bald.

"All the way to Maine," the woman bringing up the rear replied when I asked where they were headed. Her cheeks were mottled but she wore a big smile. "We just decided to start here instead of Georgia, to avoid the crowds. We'll come back and do that later."

There was something deflating, even a little embarrassing, about having to describe my patchwork plan: hike for a week, head home to wait for Helen, then start at Springer and go as far as I could before Memorial Day. I had mentally targeted Daleville, Virginia (mile 727.5), about a third of the trail, as a good stopping point, but I really wanted to be able to say that I was going all the way, too.

I said so long and continued up that first, 1,200-foot climb, surprised at feeling winded. After all, these were not the Rockies or Sierra Nevada. The Appalachians—as we were literally taught in school in Colorado—are much older, *gentler* mountains, their sharp edges scoured away by the eons. And if overweight, cigarette-puffing hikers were feeling that confident, how hard could it be?

The trail was beautiful in a spare, spooky way, climbing through barren, witchy woods matted with slick brown leaves and spiked with straight, gray trunks, signs of autumn's annual massacre. Tiny gray, piping birds were the only signs of life.

I passed one more hiker, a chunky bearded kid who had plopped on the grass of Siler Bald. The "balds" of the south—not all actually bald—are, or once were, hilltops cleared of brush and trees to make way for grazing animals and provide clear views for scouts and lookouts. This guy looked a little shell-shocked after his first 125 miles on the AT.

"I didn't really expect it to be this hard," said the kid, sagging toward the dewy grass. "But I'm just going to take my time and see how far I go."

It was the right attitude. Benton MacKaye, who first proposed the trail in 1921, said there were only three good reasons to walk the trail: "To walk, to see, and to see what you see."

I arrived at Wayah Bald Shelter following a steep descent from its 5,300-foot namesake peak and my first thought was, *Everest base camp.* The area was jammed with hikers, and smoke, laughter and music billowed out from the three-sided lean-to. Tents and hammocks crowded every level inch of ground 30 yards out from the shelter. I managed to find an acceptable, if uneven, spot, and pitched my REI Quarter Dome 1 tent. I quickly changed into my trusty, 25-year-old Patagonia silkweight longjohns and a warm shirt. I walked two-tenths of a mile down a blue-blazed trail to get water then cooked up some ramen noodles.

As I walked past the shelter on my way to try my first AT privy before bed, I heard a woman declare, "I only do a few miles a day so I can get a spot in the shelter." The idea that minimal effort earned such a reward irked me, and such "six milers" became the first gremlins in my pantheon of early-trail "bozos."

"Party kids" soon joined the rogues' gallery.

Typical early trail night, constant waking, shifting position, I wrote in my journal. *The night was windy and roaring, and the groovers were up late whooping.*

It was dark when I woke, but by the time I started walking, raw, red sunlight was clawing through the barren trees, hinting of rain. I happily rambled up and over several small peaks for the next few hours, appreciating the smooth, leaf-littered path beneath my already aching feet.

But the friendly tread turned trickster as I sang, "Down, down to goblin town!" on the 7-mile, 3,000-foot descent to the Nantahala River valley. In 500 miles on the CT I'd fallen exactly once, but in less than three hours I took three acrobatic tumbles, each time vividly demonstrating an even more ridiculous way to eat dirt. The final fall sent me rolling a good 20 yards down a steep, leaf-littered slope, where I lay thinking about those "I've fallen and I can't get up!" commercials. *Old man!* I cursed myself in my journal that night.

The rain I'd expected all day finally began falling just as I reached an empty Rufus Morgan Shelter, but I decided to continue on to the Nantahala Outdoor Center, where I paid $22 to stay in the hiker bunkhouse. After dinner and a Dirty Girl Blonde lager at the NOC restaurant, I took one more fall, into bed.

How can I be this tired after just 27.6 miles? I wondered as I nodded off.

But those gentle old Appalachians were just getting started.

FOUR: ZOMBIES AND NORO AND BEARS—OH MY!

March 2016: Nantahala Outdoor Center
to Birch Gap Campsite

A cool fog haunted the hollows as I left the Nantahala Outdoor Center bunkhouse and began the long, 3,300-foot grind toward 5,000-foot Cheoah Bald. By the time I summited, the temperature was nudging toward 80 degrees. The 360 views on top revealed endless brown hills ever-so-faintly dusted with the green of incipient spring.

My legs are built for going uphill. Many Bonnymans sport short legs with big calves, glutes and quads—a necessity, my great-grandfather used to say, for plowing the stony fields of the Scottish Highlands. And that trait is the source of my trail name: I described my hiking style—short and stout, I put down my head and go all day—to Slow Man, an old guy on the Colorado Trail who urged everyone to slow down. "So, you're like a little mountain pack pony," he said. Thus, I became Pony.

But that 8-mile march up from the NOC continued the erosion of my Rocky

Mountain pride. If there was a high point ahead, the AT was all but certain to go there, via the shortest, steepest possible route. *Switchbacks? We don't need no stinkin' switchbacks!*

Well, at least the afternoon looked easy: a 1,500-foot descent, and just one more short climb to my destination, Brown Fork Gap Shelter (mile 153.1).

The hike into Stecoah Gap, a steep, leaf-slippery slog, wasn't easy, but it was nothing compared to that final climb, dubbed "Jacob's Ladder" by hikers. As I stood warily eyeing the route, a young guy in sweat-drenched technical pants cruised past with a brief hello and attacked the ridge. I fell in behind him and we reached the top together.

"Holy cow," I said. "That's a crazy steep hill."

"Yeah. Might be the steepest part of the trail so far," said the kid, Chickenfoot.

Actually, it is merely the *second* steepest half-mile of the trail to that point (NOBO), behind "The Jump-up" to Swim Bald, which hadn't made the same impression, and only the *62nd* steepest half-mile segment on the entire AT, according to data geeks on whiteblaze.net who have tallied such things. What's more, of the 75 steepest half miles, just 10 occur south of the Mason-Dixon line, all 25 of the steepest *miles* occur up north, in Massachusetts (1), Vermont (1), New Hampshire (12) and Maine (11). Luckily, I didn't know that yet.

Chickenfoot attempted the AT in 2015, but said he got caught up in a "party bubble.

"It took me six months just to get to Harpers Ferry," he said.

This time, he was strictly solo, pulling 20- to 40-plus-mile days, taking zeroes every chance he got. When I turned off for the shelter just after 3 p.m., he continued, saying he planned to hike another 25 miles that day.

I reached Brown Fork Gap early enough to claim a shelter spot. The eight others who joined me (along with several nearby tenters) were young, but thankfully not party kids. For the first time since stepping off the CT, I got to revel in one of the trail's greatest pleasures: Bringing together people who would never spend time together in "the World."

The group included two brothers from Knoxville, Goose and Sonic, both collegiate runners, their friend Spidey and the newest member of their uber-speedy quartet, Atticus, who was hiking the AT to mark the end of his German military service.

The headline in camp that night was norovirus. Both Great Smoky Mountains National Park and Appalachian Trail Conservancy officials had sent email alarms that the dreaded virus—feces-borne, spread by contact with unwashed hands, and able to linger on hard surfaces for days, it caused relentless vomiting and diarrhea—had been reported on the trail. Rumor had it that the famous Fontana Hilton, a two-story shelter reputed to be one of the best on the trail, was ground zero.

I slept poorly once again, thanks to roaring wind and an acute case of "mousanoia." Hikers have cleverly rigged up rodent-resistant "mouse mobiles" in many shelters—bits of stick tied to bits of string, with a soda can affixed—to hang packs out of reach of ubiquitous shelter mice. Despite complete confidence in my Ursack/OPsack setup, I hung my pack, then spent hours being jerked awake by the sound of tiny claws scrabbling on aluminum.

*

Notwithstanding a rapidly accumulating sleep deficit, I managed to keep my face out of the dirt during the long, sloping downhill to Fontana Dam. Although the dam beckons enticingly for many miles, it takes forever to get any closer, thanks to a series of new switchbacks.

The Appalachian Trail continues to grow every year, thanks to rerouting. I heard hikers grumbling about long series of switchbacks, but of course, they'd grouse if it was nutty steep, too. And trail sections properly rebuilt by more than 30 local and regional clubs help prevent damage to the trail from erosion. Still, it can be disheartening to stare at your destination for more than an hour as you continue to stump down the hill.

The day was gorgeous and warm by the time I reached the marina, where I flopped down for lunch with a cluster of hikers, including the young quartet of Corncob, Rhodo, and the "Kentucky Cruisers," Jellyankles and Cheeetah. A recreational boater on his way home meandered over and handed us a treasure trove of calories, including peanut-butter crackers, cookies, baloney, cheese, bread and even raw broccoli (which, desperate for greens, I split with the Cruisers). My first trail magic.

They turned out to be the last humans I'd see until after dark, leaving me feeling as if I'd entered a post-apocalyptic world. The Fontana Hilton looked fantastic—roomy and clean, with a beautiful view of the lake—but it was empty. "DO NOT STAY HERE!!!" screamed one logbook entry. "THIS IS GROUND ZERO FOR NORO!!" The dam visitor center was closed. Making my way across the concrete monolith, I pondered what I'd do if hordes of zombies began stumbling toward me from both sides. Jump to my death below, I guess, since I had no weapon sturdier than my mom's Leki trekking poles.

The 2,200-foot climb to the tottering skeleton of the old Shuckstack fire tower was brutally hot and long. But when I climbed the rickety structure, wind through broken windows and holes in the plywood floor left me shivering. I didn't realize it at the time, but I was dehydrated.

I felt like I was seeing evidence of a once-great civilization now falling into ruin today, I wrote that night.

Despite feeling a little woozy and sick, somehow, I'd hiked nearly 20 miles. By the time I arrived at Birch Spring Gap, a campsite with bear cables and a trickling little spring — and site of a shelter torn down due to bear activity — I enjoyed a few moments of evening sun, low and red, before the barren little hollow became eerily still and cold as a grave. I ate instant mashed potatoes and jerky, then nursed a hesitant little fire into existence, seeking the companionship of flame.

The stars were pricking sharply through the bare trees when two headlamps came bobbing down the blue-blaze to the site. Two young, bedraggled hikers grunted hello before pitching their tents on the opposite hill. One came back, water bottles in hand, and stood briefly by my pitiful fire, introducing himself as Rush.

He and his buddy, Tesla, just 16 and 17, were thru-hiking. According to Rush, Tesla was "patient zero" of the Hilton noro outbreak and this was their first day back on trail after a couple of days recuperating in a nearby town.

The five miles up to Birch Gap had drained Tesla, but at least he was no longer violently ejecting fluids from every orifice.

Although there was no wind that night, I bolted awake three or four times, my dreams full of the sounds of snuffling bears. I'm really not a "bearanoid" hiker, and there were no bears; I was still weeks away from seeing my first bruin. I did learn later that the park has a standing bear warning for Birch Spring Gap, but the tale I heard later of a woman chased down the mountain— at night, wearing just one boot—by a Birch Gap bear, is, so far as I can tell, a myth.

FIVE: SMOKY HIGHS AND LOWS

March 2016: Birch Spring Gap to the Pigeon River

T he weather was perfect for hiking the next day, with temperatures in the 60s, clear skies and a light breeze. I rolled out of Birch Spring Gap not long after sunrise and made good progress up to the Smoky Mountain ridgeline, but spent much of the day in full-blown "noronoia," thanks to a funky belly. I veered off trail on a blue blaze around 1 p.m. to check out Spence Field Shelter, where I was officially "permitted" to stay (and where, just two months later, a bear took a bite of a hiker's leg through a tent, causing the park to close the shelter).

In the Smokys, hikers must register and pay a camping fee and stay only at designated campgrounds and shelters, where tents aren't allowed. Thru-hikers are waived from declaring their exact itinerary but must surrender shelter spots to registered campers, whereupon they are allowed to pitch a tent. The definition of thru-hiker, according to the park, is anyone who is hiking the 70.5 trail miles through the park as well as 50 miles on either side.

I took that rule much too literally. Because I was not hiking 50 miles north of the park until April, I stupidly decided to apply for the more restrictive non-thru permit. But now I'd arrived at Spence Field after just 11 miles, with hours of daylight to spare, and I wasn't about to waste a beautiful day—especially since two women day-hikers at the shelter told me that a "huge, nasty" storm was on the way. So, I went outlaw.

The six miles to the next shelter (including a summit of good, ol' Rocky Top) were tough going. *Rough, rocky, rooty and steep, with lots of PUDs* (pointless ups and downs), I wrote that night, thankfully oblivious to how much rockier, rootier and steeper the AT would later become.

But I enjoyed the camaraderie that night at Derrick Knob Shelter. I met two unusual hikers, Optimistic Dreamer and Babychicken (whom I would come to refer to collectively as "Optimistic Chicken"). O.D. was a quiet, almost grim guy in his 40s who had SOBO thru-hiked the AT in 2015, summiting Springer Mountain, incredibly, on *New Year's Eve,* then turned right around for a 2016 NOBO "yo-yo." He began his long trek after the death of his baby son, father and two brothers in short succession; far up the trail, I would read more than a few of his anguished shelter logbook entries—"Why me?"—from his SOBO journey.

Babychicken was his determined, bookish companion, a mother who had decided to hike the trail after her husband abruptly left her. She co-owned an unusual company, Novel Adventures, which arranged travel for mostly middle-aged women to experience their favorite books, especially Diana Gabaldon's Scottish "Outlander" series. I talked endlessly about books with Babychicken and marveled at the pair's fancy (for hikers) meals, including summer sausage fried in globs of butter and honey. As different as they seemed, by mile 189.3, they were tightly twined partners, and they stuck hard in memory.

Though I give him credit for honesty, I was less fond of another older guy bedding down for the night.

"I just want you all to know, I do snore," said The Snorer (not his real trail name). Oh, man, did he. Like a grizzly bear with a chainsaw. All. Night. Long. Once again, I slept poorly.

Thanks to the Snorer and a persistent pre-dawn owl, I was up and out by 7 a.m. for another gorgeous hiking day. The skies were a perfect, unsullied blue as I marched up toward Clingman's Dome (mile 199.5), at 6,667 feet the high point of the AT. I reveled in the cool scent of spruce trees on the ascent, and for the first time the Appalachians reminded me of my native Colorado mountains. Spring hadn't really sprung, but I was starting to see more than just tiny birds—squirrels and spring-brown snowshoe hare.

A bitterly cold breeze was blowing by the time I reached the top of the observation tower. I hunched down and ate tortillas and peanut butter with a couple of bicyclists and two hikers, including Greyhound, who I would see again nearly 2,000 miles up the trail. Descending the ramp, I ran into Chloë de Camara, my first ATC ridgerunner—staff members who hike certain sections of the trail keeping tabs, helping hikers and promoting Leave No Trace principles.

Blue-eyed and rather hard-charging, Chloe grilled me as she (appropriately) did every hiker.

"Trail name? Northbound? Thru-hiker?" she asked briskly, clipboard in hand, cheeks red from the chilly breeze. "And you put the white copy of your permit in the box when you entered the park, right? You've got your copy?"

"Oh yeah. Yup," I said with forced confidence. In fact, I'd lost the non-thru permit I *did* have (in case any park officials are reading, it was 2016 permit #B158242), and, of course, I'd already violated the terms of my non-thru permit. I felt like a POW on the loose in enemy territory, terrified that she would soon demand, "Your papers, please!" in a German accent, and I'd be carted off to hiker jail and slapped with a $5,000 fine. She didn't, and I scurried off into the spruce trees on my scofflaw way.

But I wasn't going to need the permit anyway: I'd decided to hike seven miles into Newfound Gap, hitch to Gatlinburg, and end my AT shakedown cruise before the "huge, nasty" winter storm hit. When I finished hiking with my cousin in April, I told myself, I would start from the gap instead of northern terminus of the Smokys as I'd planned. But I knew in my heart I was just wimping out.

Not that the run down from Clingman's was a stroll in the park. As I noted in my journal that night from the wuss-out comforts of the Grand Prix Motel, *"Net downhill" is fine. But on this trail, that doesn't seem to translate to "easier." I still had 700 feet of hefty climbing and my heart was pounding. That, plus "town miles"*—in an astonishing violation of the laws of physics, the last few miles into town are *always* longer than normal trail miles—*made for a long day.*

But I also experienced trail magic at Newfound Gap, having been skunked for the previous 500 miles of the Colorado Trail and 100 miles on the AT. Two good-hearted local Christians, Mountain Momma and Godspeed, offered make-your-own sandwiches, soda pop and chips to passing hikers.

"We serve the hiking community because we love God, His creation, and people. It is our hope and prayer that you find ultimate peace while on this pilgrimage," they write on their business card. "Our wish is that your blisters be few and your memories filled with adventure and joy. May God bless your journey."

They also gave me a ride to the Grand Prix. I told them I was done for now, but I'd be back in April, starting at Springer.

Good to have a break, but frustrating to break the rhythm, I wrote that night. *I've enjoyed trail life this week. Now three weeks of waiting, then hiking with Helen. It seems like way too long.*

*

Interlude: Gatlinburg: A clash of civilizations, where skinny hikers desperate for calories swim upstream against an endlessly flowing river of enormously overweight tourists, white kids performing lame raps on street corners, cheesy hillbilly animatronic "attractions," huge jangling sports bars, the constant grumble and grind of glass-packed pickups the size of armored personnel vehicles.... A different world.

*

But, as I wrote earlier, I just couldn't face the shame of not hiking when the next morning dawned beautiful and sunny. Feeling stupid and guilty, I packed up and walked out to the road up to Newfound Gap. Ignored by every passing vehicle, I owe deep thanks to Mountain Momma and Godspeed, who picked me up and had me back on trail by 11:30 ... precisely when the storm I'd done my best to bail out on arrived.

Not long after I started walking, a tiny, pinprick snow began to fall and the entire mountain became enveloped in a cold fog. The view from Charlie's Bunion, an iconic Smokys vista, was just gray nothing, like a television, tuned to a dead channel (apologies to William Gibson).

But honestly, I didn't mind. The weather was bracing, not torturous, and the selfies I took in the sprinkle of hard snow and heavy fog, show a very happy hiker. More than anything, I was pleased that Mother Nature had fooled me into not bailing out like a big, fat wimp.

After 15 miles and climbing some 3,100 feet through rain, fog, light snow, hail, and occasional glimpses of pale sun, I reached Tricorner Knob Shelter at around 5 p.m., where I was relieved to claim what appeared to be the last human-sized slot in a very-crowded shelter.

Temperatures plunged to 17 degrees that night, pushing the limits of my warm-weather gear and 20-degree REI Igneo sleeping bag. I rolled and rocked all night again. *Well,* I wrote in my journal, *that was a chilly night. I slapped earplugs in early and often against the astonishing buzzsaw snoring of the guy next to me, to no avail....*

Snoring having rattled my brain, I was up very early and marching through an icy, foggy tree tunnel in near dark. But the trail was relatively easy, and I rolled quickly along a ridgeline in my down puffy and long pants against weather that shifted from wind and fog to sun and light snow.

As I neared the northern end of the park and the end of my first leg, I came upon Chickenfoot, the big-mile hiker who had psychologically dragged my butt up Jacob's Ladder, hunched against the bole of an old, dead tree. He said he'd zeroed in Gatlinburg, started late, and drifted into Tricorner about 2 a.m., where he cooked "dinner" before heading up the trail. He'd tried to sleep without busting out his bag or tent, huddled next to a tree a mile north of the shelter.

"I didn't sleep much," he said.

When we parted, he was planning to hike another 20 or 25 miles. I took his trash, then humped another three miles downhill, hitting the Pigeon River by late afternoon. From there, I hitched back to the Big Creek Ranger Station, then slogged about a mile through cold rain to the horse camping area where I'd left my car.

I didn't know it yet, but those first 130 miles or so had given me an Appalachian Trail experience in miniature. The possibilities of camaraderie, every kind of weather, from 80-degrees and sunny to 17 degrees and snowing, the relentless progress of the trail up and over every dadgum mountain it can find, the beauty, the pain, and the indescribable joy of living simply, every day.

I'd walked through the Smokys, allegedly the hardest part of the trail in the South (in all honesty, I'd found the trail south of the park just as challenging), but it was beginning to dawn on me that this might just be the hardest thing I'd ever do. But driving toward Asheville in a driving rain, I was already pining for the trail and counting the hours until I could return.

SIX:
TRAILUS INTERRUPTUS

March-April 2016: Hilton Head Island
to Hawk Mountain Shelter

H ere's how my wife Jody describes me during my breaks from the AT: "You were just so not here. You were lost in the world of the trail. It was like having a pig in the house," she says. "It wasn't like having a dog, because I would at least be able to interact with the dog. Yeah, the pig would respond if called, and it didn't cause trouble. But it wasn't human, and it wasn't fun."

I'd left my heart on a bridge over the Pigeon River beneath a pale March sun, yearning northward. While home, I managed to meet several writing deadlines, but otherwise, I was just about worthless for the next month. I can only hope the last days of my life feel so long.

My 19-year-old cousin Helen had invited me to start the trail with her in early April, once she dispensed with two weeks of jury duty. I was haunted by visions of her being sucked into a months-long murder trial, but if she managed to wriggle free, it was looking like we could start walking April 8.

Hiking as much of the AT as possible would be the last adventure in Helen's "gap year" before starting at Rice University, following several months in Argentina and working on Hare Krishna farms in New Zealand through World-Wide Opportunities on Organic Farms, aka WWOOFing.

I was excited to walk with Helen, who is smart, funny and admirably laid back. I love how the trail is blind to distinctions of age and circumstance, and two cousins, 35 years apart in age, would make an intriguing trail story. I also thought walking with her might would give me an opportunity to overcome my deeply etched trail impulse to go, go, *go!*

While in limbo, I spent time going over my gear. I was happy with my most important choices: my garish, aqua Hoka One One Mafate Speed trail shoes; REI Quarter Dome 1 tent; Therma-a-Rest Z Lite Sol sleeping pad (minus a couple panels, to save weight); Snow Peak Gigapower stove with auto lighter; Leki Jannu trekking poles, (allegedly designed for women and swiped from my elderly mother, who could no longer use them); REI Igneo 20-degree down sleeping bag; Aqua Mira water purification drops; my beloved ULA Catalyst pack; and a Kindle Paperwhite e-reader, for me an indispensable luxury.

I managed to shave off a few ounces, but my base weight was still 19 pounds. That situation would improve once I sent cold-weather gear home.

With a week of jury duty availability to go, Helen texted to tell me her cousin Reid, a recent graduate from the College of Charleston from her mom's side of the family, would be joining us. Restless and eager to hit the trail as I was, he decided to start hiking April 3 and retrace his steps to Springer Mountain to meet up with us six days later.

But unlike me, Reid was all about simply walking the trail, no expectations, no deadlines, no totting up miles or calculating speed to two decimal points.

"I'm all about the journey, not the destination," he said later. "I like to stop and climb up rocks and hang out. I don't want to rush this experience."

Thankfully, Helen escaped serving on a jury, and on April 8, I drove a rented car to Ellijay, Georgia, where Helen and her mom Jean picked me up. That night we stayed with our cousin Anne, her husband Chris, and their four boys, ages 6 to 14. The house, built by Chris, lay hidden in the steep, wooded hills of northern Georgia, and the yard was aflutter with a dog, meowing cats, and many chickens and ducks.

Before dinner the oldest boy, Forrest, insisted we hike up a ridge behind the house. Churning up that steep, leaf-littered slope, my quads reminded me that whatever adventures the AT had in store for me, it wasn't going to be easy.

*

When we met Reid at the Forest Service parking lot below Springer Mountain the next morning, he handed some extraneous gear, including a brawny hunting knife and a hatchet, into Jean's safekeeping. But between his books—source of his eventual trail name, The Librarian—a hammock, a tent and other gear, he was still humping a 50-pound pack.

Anne, the boys and Jean joined us for the easy, two-mile round-trip hike from the parking lot back to the Springer summit. The skies were clear, but I donned my winter gear against the bitter wind that razored up the mountain.

I stamped away the cold through many summit photos and extended goodbyes down below, and we finally hit the trail at 11 a.m. The walk to Hawk Mountain Shelter (mile 8.1) was easy, but I could see right away that Helen would soon be knocking off 15- and 20-mile days.

There were lots of people at the two-level shelter when we arrived, including four big, noisy middle-aged guys and a friendly, purple-haired young woman from Quebec. The mood was high as we exchanged stories against a background of hissing stoves.

"My parents took us camping a lot when we were kids," said the pretty Quebecois, "but I *hated* it. Every time I complained about something—dirt in my food, being cold, having to poop in the woods—my father would yell, 'It's camping!'" I said that should be her trail name, and she seemed to be considering it.

"Mah home is *right here on the Appalachian Trail*," boomed a friendly, barrel-chested older guy wearing an expensive yellow shell, whom I silently named Big Bird. "Mah wahf just kicked me out of the house."

Temperatures dropped below freezing that night, and thanks to the wind, a light case of butt-chafe (which I treated with the miracle cure: Vagisil. Incidentally, when Jody found the discarded box in the recycling bin, she couldn't help but wonder what kind of company I'd been keeping.) and what I described in my journal as, *four grizzly bears with asthma rippin' and roarin' like chainsaws*, I barely slept.

New rule, I scribbled in my journal. *Check to see if any old fat guys are in shelter—if yes, PITCH TENT.*

SEVEN: HIKE YOUR OWN HIKE

April 2016: Hawk Mountain Shelter to Low Gap Shelter

I t was still dark when I crawled out of my bag at Hawk Mountain Shelter. A thin rime of frost coated the picnic table as I heated water for oatmeal and coffee. Hovering over the tiny flame, I tried to rub the warmth back into my hands while I chatted with It's Camping.

Because Reid had sent a resupply box to tiny Suches, Georgia, we decided to stop at Gooch Gap (mile 17.8) that day, hitch into town and camp or stay at one of two hostels. I waited until Helen and Reid got up, then told them I'd wait for them down the trail.

Despite faint green hints on high branches, spring was still in abeyance on the southernmost reaches of the AT. The stillness of sleeping trees was interrupted only occasionally by the flitting of tiny, nondescript gray birds and a volley of conversation between two barred owls—*Who, who, who cooks for you?*

I passed several hikers, including one poor guy on his knees to the side of the trail on Justus Mountain. "I'm sick. I just vomited. I think it's noro," he said, looking half-dead. I gave him a little water—and a wide berth.

At Gooch Gap I called to reserve three bunks at the Wolfpen Gap Country Store hostel in Suches. Helen and Reid were four miles back, so I got out my sleeping bag and started to read. When it started to rain, I scored a ride to town with a couple of day hikers.

There are scores of hostels and hiker bunkhouses along the Appalachian Trail. Some are legendary for catering to hikers' needs, but more than a few are run by people who are only out to make a buck. Such was Wolfpen Gap (which closed after the 2016 hiking season, probably for the best).

Upstairs from the ratty store with half-empty shelves, two stale-smelling rooms offered banks of two-by-four, plywood bunks adorned with a strip of creepily stained carpet for a "mattress." The bathroom was cramped and humid and the toilet was crusted with urine, speckled with brown spots and sprouting stray pubic hairs, as if some evil Jackson Pollock had used it as a porcelain canvas. A squishy, clammy bathmat lay before a shower stall streaked with rust marks and clotted with clumps of hair and lumps of soap. Even after I scrubbed the toilet and shower, as a public service, I held my breath while I pissed, certain that the very air was teeming with norovirus. And sure enough, a girl from San Angelo, Texas spent much of the night miserably yarking and shitting away in there.

Refusing to pay for overpriced congealed pizza or grease-soaked chicken lumps that had incubated in the store for who knows how long (thanks to arcane county liquor laws, we couldn't even buy a beer), I ate a hiker special— tuna, tortillas and peanut butter—before hitting the sack. Although exhausted, I slept badly, courtesy of a snorer in the next room and the soundtrack of that poor noro girl.

Helen and I got out of there as fast as we could in the morning. Alas for Reid, the post office didn't open until noon, but we agreed to meet him at the foot of Blood Mountain, feared by many NOBOS as the first "real" climb on the trail.

Walking through that misty morning with Helen, I was amused by the notion that she might need help from me or anyone else, frankly. Strong, smart, resourceful, flexible and friendly, she is truly one of the most natural thru-hikers I know. I laughed like crazy when she told me she'd overheard Big Bird on a cell phone at Cooper Gap, just four miles past the shelter where he'd declared the AT was his home, now that his wife had booted him out.

"Honey," he was saying, "I *swear* it'll be different this time…."

We reached Jarrard Gap (mile 26.7) by late afternoon under grim gray skies. Weather reports promised a cold, rainy night, but due to a curious requirement that overnight hikers carry a hard-shell, bear-resistant canister for just the next *five* miles to Neel Gap, we couldn't hunker down in shelters that lay a tantalizing 1.5 and 2.6 miles up the trail.

Helen—who had earlier that day had rejected Jellybags, my suggestion for a trail name; her mom had literally packed jelly into tiny, 1-inch square Ziplocs—and I pitched our twin REI Quarter Dome 1 tents, made dinner, and hung out as the looming storm turned the sky darker and darker.

"You know," she said, "it's OK if you want to take off tomorrow."

Gor' bless my cousin. She could see that I was chafing under the slow pace —and I could see that she needed no guidance from me.

"Really? Thanks," I said. "I really loved walking with you today"—we'd talked about everything under the sun—"but I do get sort of … impatient."

"Really?" Helen said, with her usual friendly smile. "*You?*"

When Reid rolled into camp a couple hours later, he walked us a few yards down the trail to a clot of thick, black bear hair. I picked it up, sniffed it (I smell everything; why ignore this perfectly good source of information?) and discovered that, just as my wife always asserts, bears are rather pungent. If not for Reid, I wouldn't have seen it at all.

The soothing white noise of rain on my tent all night gave me a good night's sleep at last. Waking early, I broke camp in the dark, tossing my wet tent into a plastic garbage bag until later, when I could hang it to dry. Walking silently past Reid's hammock and Helen's tent, I felt a little guilty (and a little embarrassed) that my lofty fantasy of hiking with a trail family had been deflated by my impatience in just three days. On the other hand, I *was* just following the First Commandment of the trail: *Hike your own hike.*

A surprisingly pleasant, warm rain was falling as I descended Blood Mountain—an anthill compared to the coming mountains of Georgia, North Carolina and the Smokys—and I was happily soaked when I reached Mountain Crossings at Neel Gap (mile 31.7). The trail literally passes through the place, via a short, stone-walled passage. It's rumored that a quarter to a third of would-be AT thru-hikers call it quits here (and it's confirmed that countless others plunk down lots of money for better, lighter gear; location, location, location, as they say...). But I just bought Gatorade, Pop-Tarts, candy and jerky—a thru-hiker cornucopia—and headed up the hill.

As it happened, I'd met the former long-time owner of Mountain Crossings, Winton Porter, through a mutual friend on the beach in Hilton Head (Laurie, aka Sundance, whose son "Constantine" was also out on the AT in 2016). Porter's book, "Just Passin' Thru: A Vintage Store, the Appalachian Trail, and a Cast of Unforgettable Characters," amply details the hope and desperation of hikers who arrive, often shell-shocked, after the first 30 miles of the AT.

"I could usually tell, with about 95 percent accuracy," he told me, "who was going to make it, and who wasn't."

I left Neel Gap in a warm fog but occasionally the mist thinned enough and a weak sun broke through, providing hazy views of endless trees from Cowrock Mountain and Wolf Laurel Top. Late in the day, I tumbled down to a paved parking lot at Tesnatee Gap to find a dozen hikers lounging in chairs set up by a Christian fellowship offering chips, candy, soda pop and water.

Christians, it turns out, are a reliable source of trail magic in the South. It seems to me they do ministry just right: Offering sustenance to strangers to show the strength of their faith and contents of their hearts, rather than preaching.

After a half-mile slog up Wildcat Mountain—a 500-foot ass-kicker, though far wilder Wildcats lurked more than a thousand miles north—and a few more miles, I called it a day at Low Gap Shelter. Only one kid was in the shelter, but there were a dozen or more tents scattered nearby. A flock of party kids had built a fire and the celebration was already underway.

A hiker whom I'll call Weasel soon showed up. Although my cousin Helen later told me she hadn't picked up on it, I'd found him slightly creepy when it came to young women; maybe I was wrong. At any rate, he plopped down in the shelter and started to hit on a young woman named Rachel, or so it appeared to me. When she didn't respond, he said he was heading on to camp somewhere or go to the next shelter.

I wandered up the hill to meet my fellow hikers, but quickly perceived that I was considered a creepy old party crasher. I also witnessed the mob descending into junior-high barbarism to drive Rachel from the herd. One guy mocked her loudly for asking about "narcovirus," while another stared dully when she told him a goofy joke: "What are you, like, in fifth grade?"

Exiled from the tribe, Rachel rolled out her sleeping pad in the shelter, joining me and Luke, a quiet kid from Indiana. She made a hasty dinner and buried herself in her sleeping bag. I washed the gummy remains of pasta from her Jetboil cooking cup, thinking my shred of service might cheer her slightly in the morning.

It was the first time I'd seen that kind of nastiness intrude upon the supportive ethic of the trail. I consoled myself with the thought that most of those thoughtless party kids would grow bored and bail off the AT soon enough.

"I see a lot of hikers who have no idea what's in front of them," says the legendary 77-year-old hiker Billy Goat, who has been hiking one trail or other 150 days a year three decades. "They just want to drink beer and smoke pot, like the (trail's) nothing but one big party."

Yes, the trail changes everybody, I wrote in my journal. *But it also amplifies who you truly are.*

EIGHT: HAPPY HIPPIE HAPPENING

April 2016: Low Gap to Franklin, N.C.

A brisk breeze was blowing when I lit out of Low Gap early the next morning, but intermittent sun and clouds made for excellent hiking weather the rest of the day.

Not wanting company, I spent the first several miles scanning ahead for any sign of Weasel. Sure enough, I spied his blue jacket about four miles up the trail, ducking in and out of his tent off to the right of the trail. To my relief, I managed to scurry past while he was on his knees, fiddling with something.

Exultant, I spent much of the morning singing Dan Fogelberg (good, older Fogelberg, not the treacly late-career stuff) and cowboy songs. Just as I was reaching the crown of 4,430-foot Tray Mountain, I came upon an older woman whose blue Deuter pack was adorned with a yellow flower. I asked about the flower.

She said she had hiked about 1,200 miles of the Pacific Crest Trail the year before after the death of her husband. Ready to quit one breezy day in the

Sierra Nevada, she told me, she felt something tapping at her ankle: a small, yellow flower nodding in the wind. She took it as a sign from her husband to keep walking.

"So, what's your trail name?" I asked as I turned to start down the mountain.

"Blue Butterfly," she said.

"Gotcha," I said. Then, before I could stop myself, I gave voice to a thought that had popped into my head. "I thought maybe it was Soulflower."

*

Though I'd planned to walk 23 miles to Deep Gap Shelter, I was waylaid at Tray Mountain Shelter (mile 58.6) so I could assist Jody remotely with writing and editing an obituary (a small service we have done for several years). By the time I'd finished it was late afternoon and I decided to stay.

As I sat on a rock, waiting for my next email and surveying sweeping views in three directions, a big hiker from Boston, OSHA, and his ukulele-packing friend (I neglected to write down his name) stopped by for lunch and a "safety meeting," which they invited me to attend.

"Safety meeting?"

OSHA—the origin of his trail name would soon become apparent— wordlessly explained by pulling out a small pipe and a gray-green knob of weed (the preferred 21st-century term, though *I* still think of it as "pot"). I enjoyed the euphemism, but declined to join in.

*

I stopped briefly at Dick's Creek Gap (69.5) the next morning to take a photograph for my friend Kristen, who had buried her beloved dog Owen nearby a decade earlier.

Many NOBOs find a haven at the Top of Georgia Hostel and Hiking Center a half-mile west on U.S. 76, famous in part for the "shakedowns"—winnowing of unnecessary pack weight—by proprietor Bob "Sir-Packs-a-Lot" Gabrielson. I did not partake, but later heard varying opinions on his advice (I could never remember his name, and lazily defaulted to my own version, "Super-Pack-Head-Bob").

Just past Dick's Creek Gap, I heard someone approaching as I was peeing to the side of the trail. I danced and shook and managed to put myself in order by the time Blue Butterfly reached me.

"I want to thank you, Pony," she said. "I thought about it, and I'm going to keep the name Soulflower. I was Blue Butterfly then, but now I truly believe this is my name."

*

Hiking the AT, I learned to embrace every opportunity to celebrate and mark my progress and catch every view. Unlike the high Rockies and Sierra, which offer spectacular eye-candy on an hourly basis, the AT is known for its endless "green tunnel"—miles upon miles of hiking through trees. I began to look forward to more than just the next view—a border crossing, a century mile point, the next road or trail crossings, where magic just might lurk.

At mile 78.5, I came to a battered wooden sign nailed to a tree reading, simply, *N.C./GA.* I could now tell myself I'd completed 1/14th of the states traversed by the AT. My sense of elation and triumph was only slightly dampened by the steep, half-mile slog up to Courthouse Bald that followed.

I thoroughly enjoyed the company at crowded Muskrat Creek Shelter (mile 81.4) that night. The crew included Leave No Tracy, whose boyfriend at the time, Odie, was the brains behind the annual AT Hiker Yearbook; Nemo, a loquacious guy with Elton John-style glasses who literally danced up the trail and who often packed a bottle of wine and a pound of gourmet chocolate; Hula Bear, who was never without her light-up hula hoop and her dog, Kita-bear; and The Dude, a gregarious Houston accountant.

I realized that night that I wasn't eating enough. Eventually on a thru-hike, bodies tend to wake up from a sluggish metabolism and ignite the infamous "hiker hunger," but as on my Colorado Trail hike, in these early miles I was losing weight like crazy—and I was nearly out of food.

*

The big bugaboo for the next day was the short, final pitch of Albert Mountain, one of the very few southern stretches of the trail that approaches the steepness further north. But thanks to human-constructed stone steps, the climb went quickly (I was also inspired to put some distance between me and the rednecks firing guns from the parking area below). Someone had scrawled "100 miles" on the tower, another psychological horizon: Only 2,089 miles to go!

When I arrived at Long Branch Shelter (mile 102.5) in late afternoon, I was surprised to find a section-hiker I'd met earlier. I'd had a short day to Tray Mountain (15.4 miles) thanks to the long-distance work situation, but had covered 43.9 miles the next two days to reach Long Branch, and I knew I'd passed him at his camp the morning after I'd last seen him.

"Wow," I said. "You must be doing big miles."

"Not really," he said. "Around 17 a day."

(Note: In the original version of this chapter, I wrote that I suspected this hiker—whom I'd referred to by a made-up trail name—of "yellow blazing," and segued into a description of that term. He contacted me in September 2017, vigorously objecting to my portrayal of him and saying he did not yellow blaze any part of the trail. Given the subjectivity of my—or anyone's—impressions, I have edited this section. However, I have kept the observations about the concept of "yellow blazing" below.)

"Yellow blazing," a reference to the yellow lines on highways, refers to hikers who skip parts of the trail with mechanical assistance. Although "purists" insist the only *true* AT thru-hike is one in which the hiker walks past *every* white blaze, carrying the full weight of her pack, in truth many 2,000-milers end up yellow blazing at least a few miles.

I'm no purist, but I certainly understand the logic: If a hiker doesn't walk every single step of the trail, how much skipping is allowed? Ten miles? Twenty? A hundred? That said, most hikers frown upon yellow blazing just to avoid a tough section, and *lying* about yellow blazing is widely considered one of the few true sins of the trail.

As I sat finishing up dinner, a middle-aged hiker stopped by to cook dinner. His name was Wishing Bone, and he was from the People's Republic of China. As it was already evening, I assumed he'd be staying the night, but after eating, he began packing up to move on.

"My visa is only for six months," he said cheerily, "so I must go along quickly." He was averaging well over 25 miles a day.

Aside: More than a year later, I drove to Salida, Colorado to meet up with another AT friend, Sour Patch, whom you'll meet later, at the local hostel, before heading further south to climb several 14,000-foot peaks. After spending the night at the hostel, I gave Sour Patch and another hiker a ride up to Monarch Crest, then made two more trips to ferry hikers back to the Colorado Trail. On my final trip down, I saw a hiker craning over a map at the side of the road where the trail crosses U.S. 50.

"Do you need a ride?" I said after pulling over. The middle-aged Asian man who hopped in my car seemed vaguely familiar. It was Wishing Bone, this time on a shorter visa. He didn't remember me, but we talked all the way into Salida about the AT.

*

In no mood for hitchhiking, and completely out of food, I hustled to reach Winding Stair Gap the next morning to meet a 9 a.m. shuttle run by Haven's Budget Inn in beautiful, downtown Franklin, North Carolina. I tumbled into the gap at 9:08, and the shuttle arrived seven minutes later.

The driver was Ron Haven—*Long-time local 800-pound gorilla,* I wrote, *owns hostel and hotel in Franklin and runs shuttle*—and seated just behind him was a, red-faced, barrel-chested, John Goodman-looking guy with pounds of AT bling dangling from his neck. His announced himself as Baltimore Jack and began enthusiastically discoursing on the trail, offering unsolicited tidbits of advice and answering questions for the entire winding, 15-minute descent into town. He didn't look like a hiker to me, but he sure seemed to know his stuff.

My guess is that Haven, a long-time conservative commissioner in Macon County, doesn't much approve of the vagabond appearance and lifestyle of most AT hikers. But as owner of the Hiawassee Budget Inn and Franklin motel, as well as a $20/night bunkroom across the street, he sure didn't mind them as customers. He repeatedly emphasized that the shuttle was free, whether or not you stayed at his place, but given that it was the only stop, and considering hikers' well-known aversion to "sideways miles," it was no surprise that everyone that morning decided to bunk at his place.

Baltimore Jack told those of us planning to stay at the hostel that he'd meet us there in 10 minutes to sign us in. When he showed up, it was obvious he'd taken time out for a little nip.

Walking back from the grocery store after having bought too much food—food supply is a skill I have not mastered; my food bag always feels overstuffed or I'm running on empty before I hit town—I saw two young hippie women hula hooping.

"Hey," I called out cheerily, "my wife makes hula hoops."

"Cool," said the one wearing flowy, stripy balloon pants. "Are you a thru-hiker?"

"Yup."

"Cool!" said the other, her hair a wild nest of bronze curls. They stopped hooping and walked over to me. "Hey, man, you should come to our party tonight. It's for all hikers, up at Gooder Grove … do you know where that is?"

It was the new hostel in town, a 10-minute walk up the hill and into the trees from Haven's place.

"I'm Jane Owl," said the one with the hair, holding out a fist for a bump, "and she's Flow. We're going to have beer and music and all kinds of food. You should come."

Around 5, I headed out with Stretch and Badger to check out the party. As we were walking up Philips Street, a white van stopped next to us.

"Are you guys headed to the party? I'm Zen, I own the place," said the driver, a dark-haired young guy with glasses. We said we were. "We're going to get the keg. When you get up there, tell them to give you a bottle of Highland Gaelic Ale. See you there!"

Zen (aka Colin Gooder) had invited part of a trail-walking hippie troupe from Oklahoma—Flow and Jane Owl, Yosh the Oracle, Doctor See and Rhythm, and The Green Lady—to play music and make vegetarian food (a clever hiker later dubbed them the "Oklahomies.") It was quite a party. There was a keg of IPA from nearby Lazy Hiker Brewing, hot dogs, hamburgers, fruit, chips, cookies, brownies and more for those not into the excellent vegetarian Oklahomie fare. Safety meetings abounded and multiple dogs, including

Grove residents Bodhi, Josie and Ambrose, milked constant attention from canine-starved hikers.

Zen showed me around the place, including a downstairs area he was renovating to put up more hikers and install a hot tub.

"I'm trying to build the business," he said. "But I have to get a shuttle going. Right now, Ron Haven scoops up all the hikers for himself."

Zen invited me to bring my pack up and stay the night for free. He gave me a ride down to the hostel, where I packed up my gear. "You leaving us?" Baltimore Jack said as I passed by the office.

Despite my initial impressions of him, I'd had a couple of short, interesting conversations with this enthusiastic guy. I especially appreciated his candor about snoring: "I'm a snorer. I know I'm a snorer. So I don't stay in shelters."

"Yeah," I told Baltimore Jack "Met some new friends."

He wished me luck and I headed out. I would not realize until a few weeks later that I'd been talking to a genuine AT legend.

Sitting around a huge bonfire in the trees while the hippies played music, I talked for a long time to The Dude, whom I'd met at Muskrat Creek Shelter. I soon understood why so many hikers found him similar to his namesake, the big, laid-back character played by Jeff Bridges in the Coen brothers' cult film, *The Big Lebowski*. Eventually, he and I walked into town to meet Leave No Tracy, a young hiker named Pending and a section hiker named Tony at the brewery. I wandered back to the Grove and fell into bed about 11 p.m., sober, stuffed and happy, but the party went on without me until near sunrise.

I'm glad I stayed here, I wrote that night.

But the next day a shuttle would carry me 140 miles up the trail and I doubted I'd see any of these excellent people again.

NINE: SMOKE AND WISHES

April 2016: I-40 to Overmountain Shelter

T hanks to a late shuttle—the driver had taken a leisurely lunch after church—it was nearly 4 p.m. by the time I crossed the Pigeon River Bridge (mile 239.5). It was 45 degrees warmer than when I'd finished up here in March, and wildfires to the north had turned the air a hazy, somnolent yellow.

A missed turn led me to the famous Standing Bear Farm hostel. I turned back and soon was sweating the 3,000-foot climb to the beautiful, grassy top of Snowbird Mountain. I'd originally planned to camp on Max Patch, the most beloved bald on the southern AT, but because of the shuttle delay, I didn't even get to Groundhog Creek Shelter (mile 247.5) until just before 7 p.m. It was the worst shelter I'd seen so far.

Old and sagging, I observed in my journal. *Privy practically in the middle of camp, filled to the brim. Animals have gnawed away half the toilet seat.*

It was also the first shelter I'd had entirely to myself (not counting a bug-eyed little brown mouse, who scrabbled all night but remained oblivious to my food bag; thank you, Ursack). But I cooked dinner next to a group of eight friendly, card-playing young tenters who planned to rise early to catch the sunrise on Max Patch.

Thanks to my little friend, I was up early myself, and started up the trail in the dark. Outside the cone of my headlamp beam, the forest was alive with sound, owls talking, skitterings and skirmishes in the underbrush, and even the crunching footfall of some much larger creature deep in the shadows. Sunlight, stained bloody gold by a cold layer of smoke, finally fingered through the bare trees around 7. I came upon the only two hikers who had answered the summons of a 3 a.m. alarm, Kaleidoscope, a young woman from Ecuador, and a kid who was soon leaving the trail for a Ph.D. interview; they weren't going to make it up the hill for sunrise, nor was I.

Standing atop Max Patch, I cursed my shuttle driver's after-church luncheon. Tenters and yawning cowboy campers were packing up after a clear, cold, windless night of stargazing and sunrise worshiping, and I knew I'd missed something special.

I'd made up my mind that I was going to hike 26 miles into the trail haven of Hot Springs, North Carolina. As the day grew warmer, wildfires that had lain down overnight—cooler temperatures equal higher humidity, which tamps down flames—raged anew. I've always loved the smell of wood smoke, but that day it was thick enough to turn my throat gritty and sore as I chugged up 4,500 feet of climbing.

I leapfrogged two fast-moving hikers, a young bearded guy from Virginia named Patches and a tall Californian, Sequoia, until they finally passed me in late afternoon. Hot, frog-croaking and tired, I paid $10 to pitch my tent on the spreading lawn of the Laughing Heart Lodge in Hot Springs, right next to Sequoia.

After stuffing myself at the Spring Creek Tavern—including an outstanding Kolsch-style beer from Ashville's French Broad brewery and, even better, chocolate cake—I took a shower and joined the conversation on the Laughing Heart porch. The fact that I generally sleep with my food bag (where required, as in the Smokys, I hung my bag; when a locker was available, I made use of it) earned the ire a belligerent hiker whom I'll call Bad News.

I explained to her that my system, a Kevlar Ursack with an odor-proof OPsak (an air-tight, water-tight, "sealable plastic bag is made from special film that is 17,000 times more odor resistant than HDPE," an industrial-strength plastic, according to Ursack), works so well that even shelter mice don't know there's food under my knees.

"Bullshit!" Bad News barked, jabbing her cigarette in my direction. "You're killing bears when you don't hang!"

I understood what she was talking about: When bears learn that food bags are easy prey, they become conditioned to seek them out. When that happens, "nuisance" bears—though it seems to me that *we* are the nuisance—are too often killed by authorities.

But my system was far less likely to attract a bear than most of the lazy-ass hangs I had seen along the trail. Dangling a bag from a spindly branch 6 feet off the ground—and I'd seen plenty hung lower—is like inviting every bruin in the neighborhood to the world's easiest piñata party.

I bowed out of the conversation when Bad News—with whom I would have another run in many miles later—wouldn't drop it. But I did later overhear her muttering, "OK. So I guess it *is* Kevlar," after she'd taken time to look Ursack up on her phone.

*

I escaped Hot Springs the next morning, just two days before that section of trail was closed for nearly a week due to the wildfires. After another hot, smoky day, I pitched a tent at Hemlock Hollow, a remote, vaguely *Deliverance*-esque little camp near Greenville, Tenn. I met a hiker named Grey Ghost who had just spent several days off trail due to infected blood blisters; he still looked like he was walking on broken glass. I was grateful that I'd had no blisters on the AT so far; amazingly, I never would.

Still, my feet were feeling the punishment of some 65 miles and 12,000 feet of climbing (with nearly as much descent) in three days. Just as I'd briefly imagined I could outfox the weather, I had at one point fancied that I could avoid "the agony of da feet"; but this is one form of suffering virtually every thru-hiker must learn to tolerate. After a long day, the soles of my feet felt like they'd been pulverized with a meat-tenderizing mallet by a very large and sadistic masseur; yet somehow, they always felt renewed by morning. I remained blissfully ignorant of how much *more* sadistic the rocks of Pennsylvania, New Hampshire and Maine would turn out to be.

The following day—*Dude, it's 4/20!* I scribbled, though I didn't intend to partake—I hiked through Jones Meadow, looked over Whiterock Cliff, crossed numerous small streams, and traversed a long, rocky ridgeline on my way to Sugarloaf Gap (mile 310.9).

Although the profile in Awol's guide didn't look too arduous, the 25 miles between Sugarloaf Gap and No Business Knob Shelter added up to more than 4,500 feet. The weather was fickle, veering from cloudy to sunny, with plenty of wind, forcing numerous changes of clothing and making me cranky. A Pepsi and snacks, courtesy of trail angels at Spivey Gap, improved my mood—and eased worries over a nearly empty food bag.

I love sleeping in my tent. But I am a fundamentally lazy hiker, and whenever rain threatened overnight, I did my best to get to a shelter; who wants to mess with drying out a tent? No Business was small and packed, but a storm was coming, and kindly hikers squeezed and shuffled to make room for me. Rain rattled the roof all night long.

I headed out early the next morning during a break in the storm. Walking through the fog and wet trees, I had long, beautiful views of the Nolichucky River below. To my good fortune, I reached Uncle Johnny's Nolichucky Hostel outside Erwin, Tenn. at 9:15, just ahead of a torrential downpour that would deliver a steady stream of drowned-rat hikers for the rest of the day.

Uncle Johnny was an old trail hand (sadly, he died in February 2018). Between his tie-dye shirt, floppy fishing hat, grizzly white beard and his lumbering, friendly dog, a one-eyed Rottweiler mix named Jerry Garcia, he was the very stereotype of an aging hippy. The hostel, which runs a shuttle to businesses and restaurants three times daily (I always wonder if there's payola), offered varied accommodations, from tenting to cheap bunks to newer, better appointed private rooms. I opted for the dingy bunkroom.

I enjoyed talking to hikers at the hostel, as usual, but my feet were itchy before the day was out, as usual. And while I wasn't exactly bored, I found myself wishing for a serious change of scenery; I'd had enough of rhododendron tunnels, mountain laurels and bare southern trees. And as much as I enjoy hiking alone—it's almost all I've ever done—I was surprised to feel the slightest twinge of, not exactly loneliness, but a totally unprecedented desire for company.

What the hell? I wrote. *Must be coming down with something.*

But the next day I saw few hikers (I credited a free church barbecue in Erwin). Except for two sisters from Massachusetts, Legs and Verge, who waved hello as I walked past Curley Maple Gap Shelter (mile 346.4), I saw no one as I ground out the 3,500-foot, half-marathon climb to the summit of 5,200-foot Unaka Mountain. The trail climbs through lush, temperate rain forest over many rocks and rills, arriving at a crown dense with evergreen magic. It was beautiful, even when shrouded in a chilly fog.

After a long, clammy descent—*I'm sick of clouds and rain and fog—sun tomorrow please!*—I pitched my tent in an abandoned apple orchard just past Iron Mountain Gap. The place was lonely, beautiful and peaceful (never mind the rumpus of wild hogs squealing somewhere down the hill to the west). In late afternoon, Legs, Verge and their friends Sweets and Jingle rolled in. A little later, a newlywed couple named Tumbleweed and Shiv arrived—a thru-hike of the AT isn't *my* idea of a romantic getaway, but hey, Hike Your Own Honeymoon.

I learned that Legs' and Verge's parents, Bombadil and Goldberry, were somewhere ahead on the trail, also thru-hiking. And I watched, fascinated, as Tumbleweed, an organic farmer, skipped out into the field and returned with wild violets, ramps and onions to toss onto a frying concoction of *fresh* vegetables. I was relieved that I hadn't eaten my little lump of hyper-processed instant mashed potatoes in front of such dedicated (and healthy) gourmands.

Magic was plentiful down South, and the next day was the best yet. I stumbled onto the dirt road at Hughes Gap where Kansas, a woman who thru-hiked in 2014, was offering an unbelievable spread—deviled eggs, barbecue sandwiches, pop, candy, cheese, cupcakes, brownies, chips, hummus, carrots and celery, and more. I seldom stop for long during the day, but I had a hard time pulling myself away from this bounty.

On top of that, my wish for fresh landscapes came spectacularly true in the gorgeous Roan Highlands of Tennessee, some 2,500 feet above the gap. The weather was warm and breezy, just right for a stroll up a series of long, bald ridges adorned in grasses caught between winter yellow and spring green. I was thrilled to see a troupe of turkeys slinking off into the shade of the spruce-fir forest and sang out a curious assortment of songs on the long descent to Overmountain Shelter—the old cowboy tune "Strawberry Roan," Simon and Garfunkel's "America," an incredible song about "life after death" (but probably not like you're thinking), "Bristlecone Pine," and (brains are strange indeed), Hall and Oates' "Kiss on My List," which I don't even like.

Overmountain is one of the iconic shelters on the AT (sadly, it was closed in 2019 due to concerns about structural integrity). Built in the 1970s, it's a two-story barn that was converted into a shelter by the Tennessee Eastman Hiking Club in 1983. But I'd heard it was overrun with mice, and the weather was so spectacular, sunny and warm, that I and a dozen other hikers—the biggest crowd I'd seen in a while—decided to pitch tents or cowboy camp on the adjacent lawn. Among the crowd were an intriguing couple from Wisconsin, Birkie and Roo, and Tumbleweed and Shiv (whose marital bliss seemed slightly on the rocks at that point; strong as they were, I wondered if they would make it to Katahdin).

There also was Patches, 23, who had flown past me on the way into Erwin, and his friend Lava Monster, 27, a long-distance runner whose first trail name had been Ultra. These two high-rollers had rumbled through the Smokys together, 70-plus miles and some 12,000 feet of climbing, in just three days. I definitely couldn't match their speed, but somehow, I was keeping pace with them day to day.

I slept beautifully beneath the stars, waking up to the sounds of coyotes in the valley and turkeys gobbling in the woods. I left before 6 a.m., when everyone was still sleeping, passing several dew-drenched cowboy campers. Alone, as usual.

TEN: ON THE ROAD TO DAMASCUS

April 2016: Overmountain Shelter to Damascus, Va.

L eaving Overmountain Shelter, I hiked alone up and over two beautiful balds that reminded me of the Scottish Highlands. The sun was out, the breeze was just right to keep me cool, and my heart soared as I came to a sign at the end of a small clearing at Doll Flats: *Leaving N.C.* Two states down!

Just as I reached U.S. 19E, which led to Roan Mountain, Tenn. on the west and Elk Park, N.C. to the east, I heard someone call my name. I turned back to see Lava Monster and Patches motoring along at their usual rocket pace.

"We made a point of getting up early this morning," Lava said, "but you were *still* gone!"

Slowly, but surely, these two young speedsters were beginning to understand how such an old man could possibly keep pace with them day to day.

"Well, I wake up with the birds, sometimes before," I explained. "And there's not much point in lying around in my tent."

They invited me to hitch into Elk Park with them for a late-morning breakfast at the Sissy's Ole Country House restaurant, a hiker favorite that serves Southern vittles in heaping portions. But I had already decided to walk a third of a mile the other direction to bolster my food bag at the Mountain Harbour hiker hostel. Besides, I explained, I hated hitchhiking. So, we went in our separate directions, seeking fuel.

Although the terrain was gentle, smoke and sun made for a long, hot afternoon. I had planned to "stealth camp"—pitch a tent in a non-designated camping area (perfectly legal along most of the AT)—but reached the Upper Laurel Branch stream without having found a good spot. A fast-moving couple with a sweet, tired-looking pit bull named Matilda, pointed out a faded blue blaze that led two-tenths of a mile upstream to Vango Abby Memorial Hostel, named after the late Ron "Vango" Frey and his beloved dog.

I made a snap decision and took the blue blaze. Walking along the beaver-dammed stream, the faint sound of music rippled through the woods. The first thing I saw upon entering a clearing was a tall, bearded, bespectacled guy playing Elton John's "Rocket Man" on a porch piano. A Confederate battle flag hung limply from a high pole … above a Bernie Sanders yard sign. Four young hikers were lounging out front wearing terry cloth bathrobes, waiting for their laundry to finish.

"Welcome to paradise," one said. "You'll love this place."

Piano-playing Scotty, an engineer and Trekkie with 14,000 trail miles to his credit, has run the place since Vango died. A trail angel paid for construction of a sizable bunkhouse with a kitchen with a private "Astronaut" suite above. A bunk was just $10 and soda and frozen pizzas were just as reasonable. Scotty and I talked about *Star Trek*, Ray Bradbury and movies before I showered and did my laundry.

Birkie and Roo soon arrived and took the upstairs room and Patches and Lava rolled in and pitched tents beneath the flagpole. Later, the five of us stayed up late (for hikers; so, like, 9 p.m.) talking, laughing and feasting on pizza, Ben & Jerry's and Coke.

Happy to be here, I wrote. *And—surprise!—happy for the company.*

*

The year 2003 bears the dubious distinction of being one of the rainiest years ever on the Appalachian Trail, with hikers reporting wet conditions on anywhere from half to two-thirds of every day during peak season, including a run of more than three weeks in May.

I experienced my share of rain on the trail—including a three-week run of wet weather in south and central Virginia—but in truth, the 2016 season will be better remembered as a drought year with many wildfires. The morning I left Vango Abby I literally walked through the still-smoldering remains of the Railroad Grade fire, a suspected arson blaze that consumed nearly 1,500 acres.

I had started off at 7 a.m. expecting an easy day. But an endless run of PUDs (pointless ups and downs) and a late-day march up Pond Mountain would add up to 3,500 feet of climbing on a day that turned hot and dry by noon. But the variation in terrain was a welcome relief, and at the bottom of an absurdly steep series of stone steps, I enjoyed dunking my head at Laurel Falls, where my mother had fallen and broken her elbow during a summer-camp expedition as a child.

During the 2,000-foot descent of Pond Mountain, I realized how much I had begun to despise the sound of traffic whenever I approached a road. The perpetual whine struck my ears as not just irritating, but aggressive, compared to the quiet of the woods. But there were perks to roads: I crossed busy U.S. 321 to find a cooler full of icy Cokes, courtesy of a guy named Mountain Man.

Dumping my pack at a picnic area for the Watauga Point Recreation Area, I stripped off my sweat-soaked clothes. As I was laying them out on the lawn to dry, a small SUV drove up.

"Hey, Pony!" It was Kansas, the '14 thru-hiker who had provided the incredible spread just before Unaka Mountain three days earlier. She was driving back to Virginia when she saw me crossing the road and wanted to know if I wanted what was left of her trail magic. Just then, Patches and Lava rolled in, and the three of us Hoovered up candy, fruit, chips, soda and more from Kansas' rolling magic pantry.

"Double magic," I said as the three of us sprawled in the sun following a fast, frigid dip in Watauga Lake. "Who gets that?"

Several hikers had endured a harrowing incident at Watauga Lake Shelter a couple of weeks earlier, in which bears actually *entered* the shelter and shredded tents in search of food. Optimistic Dreamer later described it as a night-long siege. Nobody slept, and the men took turns stoking a fire to keep the bears at bay. As a result, not only was the shelter closed, but hikers were not even allowed to stop for the next four miles (the ATC tore the shelter down in 2018, resigned to the fact that the bears were not giving up). Although it was late afternoon, the three of us plunged ahead through the "bear freakout zone" and, for the first time, made camp together.

But I was up at 4:30 the next morning and headed up the trail alone. Again, what appeared to be an "easy" day from the elevation profile in Awol's AT Guide, wasn't.

Following the slog up Pond Mountain, I'd coined the term End of the Day Motherfucker (or EoDMofo), to describe the seeming inevitability of one last, brutal climb before reaching camp. Nearly 500 miles in, I was beginning to grasp the true nature of this trail and the "gentle, old" Appalachian Mountains.

There are NO 'flat' or 'easy' days on the AT, I wrote later. *At least not when you are hiking more than 20 miles.*

And, inspired by "the lads," as I had begun to think of Lava and Patches, we were piling up serious miles. Following a 25-plus mile day, we'd decided to push through 27.4 miles and 4,000 feet of climbing, which would put us less than 10 miles from tiny Damascus, Virginia, home of the famous annual Trail Days gathering and a much-celebrated waypoint.

Somehow, I stayed out front of Lava and Patches all day. The scenery was beautiful, ranging from long ridges to grassy meadows with old stone walls. I arrived at Abingdon Gap Shelter (mile 458.6) at 3:20 and the lads came tramping in an hour and a half later. Giddy at the prospect of a giant breakfast, we vowed to reach town before 10 a.m., and settled in for a memorable night.

As I rolled out my sleeping pad, a lump that had appeared to be a pile of cast-off clothing in the corner of the shelter released an audible fart. A large, pale young guy emerged from the heap, yawning and asking what day it was. He introduced himself as David.

Later, a lively young couple, Terrible Lizard and Les Mayo (who turned out not to be an actual couple), showed up, full of smart, snappy banter that would have made the Marx Brothers proud. Terrible Lizard got her name when she accidentally scooped up a small red eft—a juvenile eastern newt, commonly seen on the trail— while filling her water bottle.

"Yeah, yeah, I know, it's not a lizard," said Terrible Lizard, a scientist. "But 'Terrible Newt' just doesn't have the same ring."

This prompted a running conversation between us about women scientists and how they are portrayed in movies. Terrible Lizard railed against the insipid new movie, "Jurassic World," in which the main female character stumbles around in heels and makeup, as compared to the original, which featured a badass female hacker and a field scientist who dressed in boots and gear suitable for … wait for it … a scientist. As I traveled north, I would come to appreciate this pair's sharp and sardonic shelter logbook entries, such as wildly exaggerated "bear counts" that mocked breathless hiker bear tallies (and eventually segued into a "shark count").

Eazy-E, a fast, compact New York hiker pushing a 30-plus mile day to get into Damascus, stopped by the shelter to make dinner before soldiering on.

While the rest of us cooked dinner, David shamelessly begged for everything—coffee, food, tobacco, water—leading us to dub him The Mooch. Lava, encouraged by what he'd seen of my unfiltered manner, egged me on to bestow the name upon him, to his face. I declined, in part because he seemed more homeless than hiker.

Near the end of dinner, Lava headed off into the woods downhill, small plastic spade in hand; the shelter had no privy. When he returned, he laid the dirt-covered tool right next to where I was eating.

"You know," I said casually, "it's interesting. In *theory*, a hiker's trowel never actually *touches* feces; only dirt. And yet, you can't help feeling an aversion to it when it's laid upon the table where you are cooking dinner.…"

Lava's cheeks flushed to the approximate shade of a red eft as he sheepishly removed the offending instrument. To my disappointment, he refused the new trail name I suggested: Shit Shovel. (Sometime later, when I told this story to his lovely wife, Heather, she said, "I'm so not surprised. That's *so* Andrew," her husband's Real World name.)

After dark, we had front-row seats to a spectacular storm that split purple-black skies with jags of lightning and sent a river of marble-sized hail coursing beneath the shelter. After the tempest had passed, we heard a woman's voice singing up the trail. When a headlamp came into view, we hollered out a greeting. Lady Catherine had already walked more than 20 miles and braved the hail in the dark, but she said she was plunging on, 10 miles in the dark to Damascus.

The lads rose early the next day and we started together. I soon lost sight of them in the warm fog, but they waited for me up the trail, and after that, we flew in formation. Giddily (and literally) jogging the last three or four miles, we spilled into sleepy Damascus at 9:20. We checked into Crazy Larry's, one of several hostel options in town, before taking care of the real business: stuffing our faces at the excellent Mojo's Trailside Café & Coffee House.

I always feel a sense of release when I hit town. My body lets down its defenses just a bit, as if to ask, "Uh … does this mean we're *done* with all this foolishness?" This time, the ball and big toe of my right foot were extremely sore; I didn't realize it yet, but the trail would permanently change my feet. In addition, my right knee and a ligament in my left ankle felt "twingy."

But as always, it didn't take long to start feeling antsy about doing my "chores"—food shopping and laundry. And by late afternoon I was champing at the bit to hit the trail.

"You are," Patches would tell me on a sunny August day, less than a mile from the end of the trail, "the most *restless* hiker I've ever met!"

But I didn't resist when the lads roped me into one more breakfast at Mojo's the next morning. We rolled out of Damascus late, exactly 24 hours after we'd arrived. As always, the pleasures and pains of town faded quickly into the reality of the trail. Only this time, all the good company was right there with me.

ELEVEN: FOUR'S COMPANY, A SNORER'S A CROWD

April-May 2016: Damascus to Partnership Shelter

Repeating our pattern, the lads got out front of me not long after we left Damascus, then I passed them when they stopped for lunch.

That afternoon, Eazy-E, the fast hiker who had stopped to eat dinner at Abingdon Shelter before continuing his 30-mile day into Damascus, motored past me on a flat, forested stretch of trail. Just minutes later, I caught up to him at a huge metal bear box stocked with soda and sugary snacks by a local church.

We introduced ourselves, but after mainlining as much sugar as possible in a couple of minutes, I rolled on. The trail wandered through peaceful pastures that smelled faintly of cattle dung—to me, a pleasant, earthy odor that spun me back to my cowboying days. As the trail left the fields and began to rise through the trees, I sensed someone on my heels.

Turning, I saw it was Eazy-E. Compactly muscled, wearing a cap, sunglasses, and a neatly trimmed dark beard, he wore the look of a man on a mission.

"You're faster than I am," I said as he approached. "Feel free to pass."

"Not so sure about that," he said, flashing a quick smile, "since you always seem to be ahead of me."

"I just don't stop much. That's how I got my trail name."

"I noticed," Eazy said. "I'm sure I'll be seeing you again."

Virginia continued to offer a rich variation of terrain that included not just rhododendron and mountain laurel tunnels of the three previous states, but also farms, meadows and long, exposed ridges. On the approach to spruce-crowned Whitetop Mountain, Virginia's second-highest peak, I walked through wind-tossed grasses and open fields with hazy purple valleys stretching away to either side. Sunny, breezy and cool, the weather was Goldilocks perfect for hiking.

After more than 20 miles and nearly 5,000 feet of climbing, I skirted Whitetop and came to a gushing spring with spectacular views to the east. I explored a half mile up the trail, but decided to pitch my tent by the spring. Eazy, Patches and Lava and an older hiker and Navy veteran, Umgahwah, eventually joined me.

We finally learned a little more about Eazy. He had been pouring it on to put miles between him and Bambi, following the dissolution of their month-long trail romance. Bambi, rumored to be the "hottest" hiker on the AT that season—I suspected I'd seen her early one morning as I passed by a shelter—was a flaming blonde beauty surrounded by a frantic flurry of male hikers desperate to "help" her.

"Yeah," Eazy said carefully, "that would be her."

He'd enjoyed the romance, he said, but eventually she'd let slip that a guy she knew was coming out to meet her on the trail, and he'd felt deceived. Deciding to focus on hiking, he headed on, and since leaving Bambi had been knocking out 25- to 30-mile days.

That day, in a different kind of trail magic, we gained a fourth companion.

*

The last day of April would turn out to be one of my most memorable on the southern stretches of the AT. After skirting 300 feet below Virginia's high point, 5,729-foot Mount Rogers, we entered Grayson Highlands State Park, duly celebrated for its population of feral ponies.

But before that, I inadvertently led Lava and Patches (Eazy had risen and hit the trail before me; there went *that* advantage) on a mile-and-a-half detour. The AT is well-marked for almost all of its 2,189 miles, yet it's surprisingly easy to get lost in your head and veer from the white-blazed path without noticing. Feeling like a doddering old fool, I half expected my new companions to bail on me after I led them astray.

"Pretty sure we were all to blame on that one," Lava said later.

True, none of us noticed the error until Patches finally asked when we'd seen the last blaze. I still felt stupid … and we managed to get off track twice more that day, though not nearly as far.

The morning skies were blue, but by the time we came upon our first ponies (besides one scrawny fellow), it was cloudy and cool and dark skies hung like a waiting army to the west. I hustled down from the high, exposed pony country, but couldn't outpace the storm, and soon I began to feel tiny drops of cold rain on my legs, hands and face.

As I approached the sprawling, corral-like enclosure at Massie Gap (mile 500.9), a non-hiker—I was getting pretty good at making such distinctions—in a red baseball gap lumbered toward me from a parked pickup.

"Are you a thru-hiker?" he hollered through the rising wind. "If you are, there's *magic* right down there. Go on through the gate and head left to those tents."

Magic is most magical when it's needed the most, and I'd been running low on chow. Pushing through the gate, I approached the encampment of pavilion-style tents, where more than a dozen hikers sat laughing and eating around an enormous fire. A tall guy wearing a Buddy the Elf costume held out his fist for bumping and I knew he was a hiker (never shake hands with a filthy hiker). He introduced himself as Mathrage, a teacher who had thru-hiked the AT in 2004.

"Eat and drink as much as you want. Take as much as you want with you. That's why we're here," he said. "I'm serious. As much as you want."

This was no ordinary trail sorcery. Mathrage gathers friends the last weekend of April each year at the gap, setting up camp for the whole weekend to provide hikers with hundreds of dollars of free food, warmth and good cheer. They cook meals throughout the day on a huge grill, from breakfast burritos to tacos to barbecue, and keep a seemingly bottomless larder of chips, snacks, soda, beer, and all the fixins you could want.

Patches and Lava rolled a few minutes later, but Eazy wasn't there. We stuffed our faces in the warmth of a burning log some three feet in diameter. I enjoyed eavesdropping on Mathrage, as he explained his personal taxonomy of AT hikers: "big-dick" hikers, driven by speed, pursuit of miles and a sense of competition; "party animals," whose favorite piece of gear is a pipe; social butterflies, who above all revel in fellowship; and various other species.

I could have stayed there for hours, as many hikers had already. But I'd only walked 10 miles, and with thoughts of outrunning the worst of the storm, I stuffed a couple of beers, a soda, and snacks in my pack and headed out. The lads soon passed me, of course, but to my great relief, the storm didn't decide to cut loose until after we were safely ensconced at Hurricane Mountain Shelter (mile 513.2).

When we arrived, a friendly, bearded guy in his 40s, wearing a hat emblazoned with the words, "God is Good," was the lone occupant. A soft-spoken Southerner, Five Star was hiking the entire trail in Bedrock sandals so minimalist they would have impressed the famous sandal-running Tarahumara Indians of northern Mexico. When I asked, he described himself simply as "a follower of Jesus" who belonged to no religion.

(Fair warning: The next several paragraphs address religion, spirituality and atheism.)

Jennifer Pharr Davis, the remarkable Ashville, N.C. athlete who held the record for the fastest known supported hike of the AT until a few years ago, is a God-believer who has written that she encounters mostly unbelievers on the trail. I'm not so sure.

Certainly, overt religiosity is uncommon, but I never heard any outspoken atheism, either. Patches came from a big family that practiced Messianic Judaism—Christians who live according to some practices of the ancient

Jewish faith—and Lava, like me, came from a Catholic background. Religion came up in our conversations, but I never knew precisely what their beliefs were—and I didn't care; I still don't. Likewise, I never told them that I am an atheist.

The truth is, accepting my lack of belief (for no matter what anyone says, belief is not volitional) is what led me to the trail. I'd grown up Catholic, going to "CCD" (formerly Catechism) and church, and I adored visiting Christ in the Desert Monastery with my high-school girlfriend's family (to be honest, being smitten with beautiful girls is the only thing that kept me connected to church throughout my teenage years). And I have had great friendships with progressive priests and monks throughout my adult life.

But after decades of attempting to force myself into faith, exploring dozens of traditions as a journalist covering religion—every flavor of Christianity, Judaism, Islam, Hinduism, several strains of Buddhism, Wicca, Scientology, and more—reading countless books, and interviewing literally hundreds of people about their beliefs, I'd never encountered evidence sufficient to convince me of the existence of the supernatural, whether ghosts or God. Today I am an "agnostic atheist"—I still see no evidence for God or the supernatural, but as I cannot know everything, I don't claim knowledge that no such thing exists.

It took me years of personal work to shake vestigial fears of the punishing God of my youth. I first vaguely tried to believe in a "higher power," but even that strained my credulity. Eventually I settled on a pure metaphor: Life is like reading a novel. You can read it purely for the plot—i.e. just walk around and do stuff—but if you want to learn and grow, you have to pay attention to subtleties, symbols and metaphors.

Having depersonalized the idea, I was able to start pecking through the shell of fear that had held me hostage for most of my life. I came to accept that this is the only life I know for certain I have, and it can end at any moment. As Morgan Freeman's character put it in The Shawshank Redemption, it was time "to get busy living, or get busy dying." Accepting this part of myself at last, without guilt, I vowed to start living in the present rather than regretting the past and fearing the future.

That was my personal great awakening. I auditioned for and got a part in my favorite musical (*Jesus Christ Superstar,* believe it or not), traveled across the world to help recover the remains of my grandfather Alexander Bonnyman, Jr., a Medal of Honor recipient who had been lost for seven decades, and fell in love with long-distance hiking on the Colorado Trail.

I've had people point to trees, stars, the sea, to love and beauty, and ask how such things can have come into being without some guiding hand. But if anything, my unbelief has expanded my capacity for love, compassion, joy and wonder. Every day on the AT was a marvel that didn't require any further "meaning." The beauty, the pain, the friendship and the rain—every moment between Georgia and Maine—was exactly what it was. All I had to do was *pay attention.*

And yet I will always admire people like Five Star, who live their faith with quiet strength, peace and love.

(OK, you're safe now. Back to hiking.)

Alas for Five Star, our arrival was not to be the last of the day's insults to his solitude. A couple of hours later perhaps eight young hikers showed up, giddy, wet and full of laughter. Though friendly and fun, they were extremely loud and not overly attentive to the presence of others.

Leaning against the back of the shelter, the four of us watched the group we dubbed, variously, the Mickey Mouse Club or Chuck E. Cheese—names courtesy of Lava and Patches, respectively—like a line of sullen old buzzards. After about an hour, Five Star quietly began packing up.

"Oh, man. I feel bad that you're being driven away," I said, wondering if anything I'd said or done had contributed to his departure.

"I'm not being driven away," he said, smiling. "This is just what I've decided to do."

Years later, I reconnected with Five Star and I'm happy to report he's happily married to a woman he met on trail.

Eazy impressed me later when, sternly, but without condescension, he asked the kids to pipe down so others could sleep. They instantly complied, as if Dad had shushed a room full of giggling children.

Sometime after midnight, I woke to the sound of rain hammering on the tin roof.

*

If I look objectively at my 4,000 miles of thru hiking to date, I have to say I've been incredibly fortunate with weather. The CT taught me that if you aren't willing to get wet and cold, you might as well go home, but I really only experienced one brutal drenching over nearly 500 miles.

Overall, the problem for 2016 Appalachian Trail hikers was not *enough* rain, as most seasonal and even some previously reliable water sources went dry. But the storm that blew in while we sat around Mathrage's bonfire was the beginning of a weeks-long stretch of almost daily rain.

The skies uncorked on us for four or five hours after we left Hurricane Mountain, and I was reminded that no matter if you're wearing a $600 Arc'teryx jacket or $9.99 Frogg Toggs coat, *rain gear will not keep you dry in a sustained downpour.* That morning, I neglected Patches' advice (first shared with me by MoonBeam on the CT) to walk jacket-less through warm-weather rain. My old GoLite (RIP) jacket was sodden after 20 minutes.

Wet or not, it was a beautiful day as I walked alone through forests now fully adorned with emerald foliage and long meadows full of tiny white and yellow flowers. A grouse boomed off into the underbrush and I kept my eye out for countless red efts and tiny toads drawn out by the rain.

We planned to walk a "short day," 19 miles, to Partnership Shelter (mile 532.2), much loved by thru-hikers because you can have pizza delivered from nearby Marion, Va. But when we arrived at 1 p.m., Patches and Eazy decided to hitch to town. Lava and I crushed bills into their hands, knowing they'd return with mega-calories of junk food.

An hour or so later, we gorged on McDonald's—which I hadn't eaten in years—soda, beer, Oreos, and more. Later, a group of section hikers from Wisconsin (two couples and a teenage girl we dubbed The Swingers) gave us pizza. The fabled shower at Partnership was too cold for my tastes, though I did wash my head in a sink at the back of the shelter. Other hikers continued to arrive, including a chatty, appealingly geeky young woman named Olive Oil.

Late in the day, a burly guy in his late 50s showed up, unduly proud that he'd just completed the first eight miles of his SOBO section hike. He proceeded to loudly boast about the cabins he owned in Gatlinburg and continually tried to prod people into political conversations. As soon as one group of listeners found a way to escape his attentions, he'd find new victims and repeat his spiel almost word for word.

The Swingers took the upstairs at the barn-like shelter, while our crew, Olive Oil and the guy we christened The Gatlinburg Bore set up on the lower level. The Bore was lucky we didn't string him up for the bears after he destroyed any possibility of sleep with his mind-shattering snoring. This guy roared like a jake brake without cease from the time he hit the sack until morning.

I was unfortunate enough to be about a foot and a half away from his buzzsaw piehole. I vertically flipped during the night to give me five more feet of buffer, but it didn't help. At one point, I turned to see Eazy glaring like a vengeful demon, seemingly ready to leap over me and strangle the guy (I wouldn't have stopped him). Instead, he hauled his sleeping bag out to the lawn, until a steady rain drove him back to the picnic table.

All hikers snore sometimes. People can't help snoring. Even the slightest teen girl will emit the occasional Disney Princess snore. But this was a simple matter of courtesy. Back in Franklin, I'd heard no less an authority than Baltimore Jack present the obvious answer to the problem: "I know I snore. That's why I don't sleep in shelters."

Eventually we just got up, brains brittle with lack of sleep. I scanned the row of boots with my headlamp, trying to remember which pair belonged to the GBS—the Gatlinburg Bore and Snore.

"I'm going to piss in 'em, I swear," I whispered through gritted teeth. "No, wait—I'll *take a dump* in them!"

As they say, what happens on the AT, stays on the AT. And as they say, karma's a bitch.

Not that I believe in karma....

TWELVE:
THE HILLS ARE ALIVE

May 2016: Partnership Shelter to Lickskillet Hollow, Va.

The rain began in earnest not long after we left Partnership Shelter and didn't stop for the next two hours. This time I'd acquiesced to the MoonBeam-Patches "c'est la vie" approach: *No coat, walked it out,* I later recorded. *Got utterly soaked, but lo! everything dried on my body once the rain stopped.*

Virginia's varied terrain made for another long, gorgeous day of hiking as we traversed streams, railroad tracks, woodlands, hills and swoopy green meadows. The lads stopped to chow down at The Barn Restaurant, just off I-81. I straggled in a few minutes behind, slurped down a cup of coffee, and headed on, knowing they'd catch me soon enough.

By the time we were together again, the sun was beaming down on the rain-freshened hills of southern Virginia, reminding me of James Herriott's Yorkshire Dales and The Shire, homeland of hobbits in Tolkien's legendarium. Shortly after 2 p.m., on the slopes of Gullion Mountain (aka Little Brushy), we came upon a sign reading, "1/4 WAY POINT/1641<ME—GA>547."

Whenever I'm running a marathon or ultramarathon, swimming a mile, or engaged in other long(ish) distance activity, my brain becomes a complete geek and starts doing math to distract me. This mental tic has me constantly computing fractions and percentages—*OK, I've done 28 out of 72 laps, so that's 14/36ths or 7/18ths, so I'm ... uh ... [click, whirr, long division] ... 38.8 percent through the workout....*—I wasn't so obsessed on the AT (thanks, scenery), but I did take note when I'd walked 5 percent or 10 percent of the total miles, and 25 percent felt like a major milestone. *Wow,* I thought, *I've only got to walk three times the distance I've come so far.*

But hiker Dan "Wingfoot" Bruce, author of *The Thru-Hiker's Handbook* (the most popular AT guidebook before David "Awol" Miller came along), suggested that while hikers reaching New Hampshire have completed 80 percent of the miles, fully 50 percent of the effort still lies between them and Katahdin. I hadn't read Wingfoot, and it would take me at least a couple million more steps before I grasped that all my brain's fractions and percentages utterly failed to capture how much "farther" I really had to go.

*

We'd agreed to make a 26.3-mile, 4,000-foot day to Knot Maul Branch Shelter (which we *Star Wars* weenies dubbed Darth Maul Shelter, mile 558.5). But as we began climbing the long, grassy hills leading us into a three-mile EoDMoFo, we spontaneously began belting out all the lyrics we could remember from *The Sound of Music*, from the obvious—"The hiiillls are aliiiive...."—to the unmanly ("I am 16, going on 17....") and the ridiculous, "High on a hill was a lonely goatherd, etc. etc." I've since learned that the hills of Virginia bring out the same lunacy among many more AT wanderers than I would have guessed.

To this day, if I had to name a single day that most vividly portrays the glory and joy of my AT experience, that was it. Four dudes, a rap fan from New York, a Virginia kid from an evangelical family, a Catholic from Ohio and me, an atheist more than twice their age, all singing and laughing amid flowers beneath blue skies. If there is such a thing as heaven, I hope it's like this.

*

Sleep deprived and tuckered out, we flopped at the shelter in a giddy mood. Still haunted by the nightmare of the Gatlinburg Bore and Snore, I scribbled out and posted a sign reading, "Welcome to our humble shelter. If you SNORE intrusively, please consider the courtesy of tenting. The Management." A few non-hikers who saw a photo of me looking grumpy in front of the sign earnestly accused me of being an anti-snore-ite—*C'mon, man, people can't help it if they snore!*

To them I say, it's the courtesy, stupid! To quote Baltimore Jack, sage of the AT, once more, if you *know* you snore like a grizzly bear wrestling with a chain saw, DO NOT IMPOSE ON OTHERS.

We shared the shelter that night with Olive Oil, who was clearly a kick-ass hiker (and, I learned, a purist, as was I ... so far). Later, an older hiker named The Natural, along with his much-younger companion, Hashbrowns, and his sweet dog Maple Bacon Pi, showed up.

Passing Chestnut Knob Shelter (mile 567.9) the next day, I was sorry that I wouldn't be staying (though I would get the chance three years later). Fully enclosed and made of stone, it looked just like an old stone Yorkshire cow "byre." Ducking out of the rain for a quick bite, we met one of those intriguing odd couples of the trail, Two-Pack, a young woman who appeared to be no more than 16 or 17, and her hiking partner First Step, who looked about 60 (if those names sound familiar, it's because they appear in the prologue to this tale).

Eyeballing Awol's elevations, we expected an easy afternoon. Thanks to endless PUDs, rain, mud and wet rocks, it was not. Our stay that night at jam-packed Jenkins Shelter (mile 578.6) was made memorable not just by Two-Pack, but also two weekend hikers who struggled, literally for hours, to get a fire going. As Lava put it, "It's like they read in a book about how to build a fire, but had never actually done it."

While one kid collected soggy fuel from the surrounding area, the other began whacking away at a downed birch trunk with a large machete, despite the fact that there was (weirdly) a saw hanging in the shelter. When they extracted two Ball jars from their packs, one filled with a purple powder, the other with clear liquid, and walked gingerly over to the fire pit, it was like we'd strayed into some bizarro-Harry Potter world.

"What's that?" someone asked.

"Explosive," one kid said, sniffing at the purple powder.

"We have to keep 'em in separate packs," added the other, whose shirt suggested he might be a U.S. Air Force recruit.

Lacking only popcorn, we hung back and watched the unfolding absurdity, trying not to laugh out loud and imagining the whirling fireball that would result if they bumped into each other on trail. We were only slightly unsettled by the thought that their hapless efforts might reduce us all to cinders.

But even through alchemy they could not summon anything but a few feeble, ill-fated flames. Jack London was surely rolling in his grave as they fanned the machete and huffed noisily at steaming piles of moss and damp twigs, generating thick clouds of damp smoke that immediately billowed into the shelter. I was sure "Dad" (aka Eazy) would have to intervene before they choked us all, but finally, mercifully, they gave up.

Lava, who clearly—and not entirely inaccurately—seemed to see me as a 54-year-old version of that one smart-ass kid in grade school you could always egg on to do stupid stuff, dared me to approach the sooty, defeated duo and bestow upon them the trail names we'd jointly devised for them. I declined.

Firestarter and Burning Man, after all, *were* armed with a machete and, just maybe, enough explosive chemicals to blow the other hapless denizens of Jenkins Shelter to kingdom come, and if they didn't take kindly to the names....

*

May 4 was another memorable day.

First, Lava's lovely wife Heather was going to drive up from Knoxville to Lickskillet Hollow on remote VA 608 to deliver a hiker feast in honor of her sweetheart's 28th birthday.

That was also when I heard that Baltimore Jack, whom I'd met at Ron Haven's place in Franklin, N.C., died. It was not until his death that I learned he was not just some overweight dude who knew a bit about the trail, but a bona fide AT legend who had thru-hiked the trail eight times since 1995.

Not everyone loved Baltimore Jack. He espoused political beliefs that did not always square with those of freewheeling hiker trash. He also was savagely opinionated, never missing an opportunity, for example, to blast SOBO AT hiking and hikers. And while a friend of his, Miss Janet Hensley (another trail legend, though I was still 1,300 miles away from our first encounter) told me he'd died of a congenital heart defect, it was sadly clear that he also struggled with alcoholism.

Despite my first, ignorant impression of Jack as some kind of blowhard, the trail taught me that his opinions were all grounded in hard-won experience and a genuine desire to see thru-hikers succeed. He dissed SOBO hikes, for example, because Maine and New Hampshire are so brutally challenging that many SOBOs—who lack the conditioning gained by NOBOs over the first 1,700 miles of the trail—become discouraged and quit. Over my next few town stops, I read and listened to interviews with Baltimore Jack—World name, Leonard Adam Tarlin—and came to appreciate his wisdom.

Party animal that he was, I'm sure Jack would have appreciated the celebration we had that night. Heather brought us (cue "Twelve Nights of Christmas" music..."): six Wendy's burgers, four Little Caesar's Hot 'n' Ready pizzas, 14 beers, 12 sodas, two bags of Doritos, tortilla chips and guacamole, a huge package of golden Oreos (a trail favorite for me), Snickers and other candy to replenish sagging food bags, and, best of all, her homemade Oreo cheesecake.

Reclining on my Therm-a-Rest Z Lite pad, wearing glasses, a warm hat, 25-year-old Patagonia long johns, a rain jacket and dirt-smeared Crocs, I know I looked and smelled like a bum—but I felt like royalty.

"Pony was definitely the most talkative," Heather wrote in her blog about being a trail widow, *Spousesounds*, "and I now understood why Andrew (Lava) had named his stories 'Ponytales.'"

Yes, yes, a *talkative* bum ... I don't deny it.

But Heather had not come all that way merely to deliver a feast to four grimy dudes in the woods. In the morning, she would spirit our friend away for a friend's bachelor party; he wouldn't make it back to this happy little hollow until five days had passed. And since, as Heather wrote, our crew "had become something of a fearsome foursome, continually putting up big miles," we would very likely be 100 or more miles gone by then.

Patches had been with Lava, off and on, since the Smokys. I hadn't known him as long, but he was *family*. His understated humor, intelligence, authenticity and dry sardonicism was an integral part of our organism. Odd quadruple that we were, it worked. In the years following my AT hike, despite our age difference, he would become one of my best friends.

"I'm going to catch you guys," Lava vowed.

Physically, I knew he had the legs and grit to pull off day after day of 25 and 30 milers. But I would be getting off trail no later than May 18 for a run of unavoidable (and all good) Worldly obligations. By the time Lava got back on, he would have nine days, at most, to regain 100 or more miles on us. This might be the end of our time together.

"I ... felt a little sad knowing that these 3 would be continuing on," Heather wrote, "and that when Andrew returned to the trail, he would be hiking without them."

I, too, was mourning the loss. But when he drove off with Heather the next morning, Lava would turn out to be the lucky one.

THIRTEEN:
GOOD TIMES, BAD TIMES

When I was 15, two friends (14 and 15) and I took a bicycle tour from Yellowstone National Park to Calgary, Alberta, down the Okanagan Lake Valley of British Columbia, and across to Vancouver.

It was an incredible trip that taught me more about self-sufficiency and survival than anything I'd learned in life to that point, even in scouting. We had our share of travails, starting on day one when I got hypothermia in the freezing rain on 8,800-foot Dunraven Pass. Thanks to my friends and a public bathroom with heat-blasting hand dryers, I recovered … and vowed never to let it happen again.

On May 5, 2016, a menacing cold front engulfed almost all of the southern Appalachian Trail, dropping temperatures into the 30s and 40s and delivering not just rain, but wind, sleet and snow. That day came close to ruining my youthful vow to avoid hypothermia.

Patches got out front from the start. The morning's miles were relatively flat, crossing several streams and passing by Dismal Falls, the weather cool and gray. But a steady, cold rain was pelting down by late morning. This time, I donned my rain jacket, but it didn't matter. I was soaked, inside and out, in 15 minutes. By the time I reached the top of a 1,500-foot climb just past Wapiti Shelter (mile 616.3), the rain had turned to snow.

I sent good vibes to Heather for the three pieces of pizza I wolfed down for fuel, put on my warm hat and thin glove liners, and kept walking. I didn't seriously consider changing into dry clothes: Anything I put on was going to get soaked, anyway, and I knew the only way to stay warm was to keep moving as fast as possible.

The next several hours were brutal, as I stumbled over wet rocks and slogged through freezing mud, numb feet squishing inside sodden shoes and the sleeves of my jacket sucking all warmth from my bare arms like some nightmarish, alien parasite. Sleet and snow gnawed at my face, hands and legs, driven by a maniacal wind that continually found its way beneath the trees. My journal entry for that night, written with half-insensate fingers, was the shortest of my entire AT journey: *Forecast cold, wet. Didn't anticipate this. Sufferfest.*

There is disgruntlement among some old-school thru-hikers about uppity young'uns who listen to music while hiking the trail, very much in the, "Back in my day, we didn't have all that crap …" vein. But as with most such things, the concerns are not baseless. Hikers wearing earplugs cut themselves off from a crucial source of sensory input (try passing one and see how high she jumps), while those playing music (or words) out loud are inevitably intruding on someone—or some critter's—enjoyment of the serenity of the woods.

Although I don't use earplugs, I will sometimes listen to books, podcasts, and occasionally music, particularly if I'm having a tough day. I just slip my iPhone into a watertight plastic sleeve and secure it to my wrist or a pack strap. And on that miserable Cinco de Freezo, an mp3 audio version of J.R.R. Tolkien's *The Lord of the Rings* saved my ass. Frodo, Sam, Gandalf, Bill the Pony and the other members of the fellowship were also miserable and cold as a blizzard hurled them back from slopes of cruel Caradhras.

"The wind whistled and the snow became a blinding blizzard. ... The hobbits, bent nearly double, toiled along behind the taller folk, but it was clear they could not go much further..."

In the end, of course, they did go much further, nearly 1,000 miles further. They had no choice ... and neither did I. There was a fellowship to keep.

When I stumbled around the corner of Docs Knob Shelter, Patches gave a whoop. He'd rolled in a half hour earlier and had begun to wonder if I'd bailed out to the legendary—and no doubt warm—Woods Hole Shelter. My fingers were so numb that he had to help me unzip my rain jacket. Thankfully, the inside of my pack was dry, and once I'd put on warm, dry clothes, I buried myself in my sleeping bag beside Patches, who was doing the same.

Maybe I should have put on more clothes. Perhaps a sopping-wet down puffy would have provided more insulation than skin and sodden Gore-Tex, and long pants would have cut the wind. But I doubted that anything I had in my pack could have protected me from the onslaught. I envied Patches' Merino wool shirt, which insulated even when wet, and vowed to make one—with long sleeves—part of my kit.

An hour later, Eazy showed up, glaring and cursing like a maniac.

"What ... the ... FUCK?" he said, teeth chattering.

He soon joined our sleeping-bag huddle to watch the miserable sleet and rain turn into a small river in front of the shelter. Much to our astonishment, a heavy, hairy hiker, The Professor, showed up just before dark, every bit as soaked as we were, and decided to suffer for *nine* more miles on the promise of a dry bed in Pearisburg. Temperatures that night were at or near freezing, but I burrowed into my bag and stayed warm and dry.

Thanks to my anticipation of food, warmth and other comforts, the next morning's hike felt longer than it was. But when we hit the road, Patches and I were fortunate to catch a ride almost immediately from a young mother who took us to the post office, then up to the unsupervised, $10 "suggested donation" hostel at Holy Family Catholic Church.

Pearisburg's modest comforts seemed positively heavenly after our ordeal: an all-you-can-eat Chinese restaurant, a laundromat, good company, and a good night's sleep (beneath the eaves of the porch, where we moved our bedrolls after a hiker named Wild Card drove us out with snoring). The cynical Professor was there, as was a guy named Oak, who seemed more drifter than hiker, and Trekkeroni, an odd, bespectacled kid who carried a 65-pound pack. The kid's trail name reflected the fact that he routinely duct-taped two-pound pepperoni sticks to each of his hiking poles; these spicy-delicious death-spears were dangling from the rafters above Patches' head until he persuaded Trekkeroni into moving them.

Just eyeballing them, I doubted any of these intriguing characters would make it to Maine. But it was Eazy who shocked me the next morning when he announced he was taking a zero to manage persistent pain in his shins.

"Doing 150-mile weeks has been fun," he said, "but I need to recover."

As quickly as it had flowered, our little trail family had dropped two petals. A lesson in impermanence, courtesy of the AT.

And by the next day, Patches' stomach was giving him trouble. After a 1,100-foot EoDMoFo, we pulled up at Bailey Gap Shelter (mile 658) at mid-afternoon and he went straight to sleep. After a rainy start, the day had turned semi-pleasant, and I tried to soak up a little sun while chatting with a group of mostly older hikers, including Applejack, whom I'd met in the Smokys.

*

There's an old Jimmy Buffett song that contains the lines, "I've had good days and bad days and going half-mad days." Almost all of my days on trail are good ones, but the next wasn't one of them. Walking alone through wind, fog and rain, I continually dropped my poles, twisted straps trying to shrug on my pack and stumbled constantly, while changing weather continually forced me to don or shuck rain gear. Some 3,200 feet of climbing up Johns Creek Mountain and Bruisers Knob didn't help.

Worst of all was the first fall I'd taken since my three-tumble day going into the Nantahala Outdoor Center. Walking with my poles tucked under my arm, I tripped and timbered into the rocks, smashing both knees and jamming my wrists. There was only a little blood, but I would pay for the mishap for many days with increasingly sore knees. One stupid mistake, one random mishap, and your hike is over; the AT is fickle, and unforgiving. I vowed to be more careful.

But it finally stopped raining that afternoon and the trail wooed me back with meadows, pastures, creeks and bridges—*Thank you, Virginia, for providing more than just untidy oak-rhodo-laurel forests*, I wrote.

I took time to ponder just how far I'd come. Two or three days from now, I'd reach Daleville (mile 727.5), the original projected end point of my AT *section* hike. But I'd made good time, and now, if all went well, I should easily be able to cross the 800-mile mark.

And suddenly, in the midst of that discombobulated, knee-smashing, lonely, wet, crappy day, I was flooded with such an intense love for life on the trail—*this* trail, this maddening, painful, exhausting, wet, beautiful, liberating *Appalachian* Trail, and the friends I'd met—that it brought tears to my eyes.

My heart seized with momentary grief at the thought of bailing out after 800 or 850 miles and returning to the World until next year. Life gives no guarantees—how was I to know I'd even *have* a next year? Finishing this year would mean more hardship for Jody, more expense, more travel, more hassle and crazy logistics … but I knew that if I didn't try, it would break my heart.

*

That night at Sarver Hollow Shelter I told Patches my plan.

"Yeah," he said, "I was having a hard time believing that you were just going to quit like that."

A relentless whippoorwill—are there any other kind?—roused us out of bed long before sunrise the next morning.

Virginia's gifts just kept on giving, offering gorgeous ridgewalks, steep ascents, and interesting features, from a memorial to World War II hero Audie Murphy (mile 690.1) to the Dragons Tooth, a long, steep climb that ends in the first jewel in Virginia hiking's "triple crown" (with the other two just a day away on the AT).

I was surprised at how few deer I saw on the AT compared to Colorado, where they are as common as crows or rabbits. On that muggy, cloudy day, I saw eight deer, as well as a huge rattlesnake. Downclimbing the Dragons Tooth was the most technical—and therefore fun—challenge of the trail so far. And for the first time in days, there was no rain.

I caught up to Patches at the famous Four Pines Hostel near Catawba, located just up the road from the trail where it descends from the rocky heights above. A favorite of hikers, Joe Mitchell's hiker flophouse is a sprawling, tin-sided garage filled with cots, couches and mattresses that can sleep 30 or 40 hikers in a pinch. Two dogs, Lil Bit and Daisy, and a chunky cat named Buddy gave me a much-needed fur fix, and I enjoyed listening to the chickens, guinea hens, ducks and one old tom turkey hanging around the yard.

Joe and his oddball collection of hangers on—who were gearing up for their annual trek to make barbecue at the Trail Days celebration in Damascus—shuttle hikers to the famous Homeplace Restaurant for all-you-can-eat family-style meals for under $15. Alas, the Homeplace was closed the day we arrived; instead, I ate gross, greasy food from the quick-stop place down the road, giving myself a mild case of "town belly."

To my great surprise and pleasure, Optimistic Dreamer and Babychicken (aka Optimistic Chicken), whom I'd met in the Smokys, were there. When I mentioned that the stitching on one of my pack straps was unraveling, Babychicken whipped out a needle and thread and sewed it up tight. Magic comes in many forms....

*

Patches and I headed out early the next morning, eager to reach the single most photographed location on the AT, McAfee Knob, a rocky promontory jutting some 1,600 feet above the Catawba Valley below. Following that we'd hit the third "jewel" in Virginia's "triple crown," Tinker Cliffs, a gorgeous, half-mile cliffwalk, which, if anything, offered even more spectacular views.

We reached the knob at 11 a.m., only to find it completely shrouded in cloud and crawling with hikers. But the sun soon burned through and we stripped off our shirts and took what was, for us, a long and leisurely break for the next two hours, taking the obligatory photos, eating and just flopping around.

"Man," Patches said, "I'm pretty sure I've never seen you stay in one place this long unless you were sleeping."

We rolled on in early afternoon, marveling at Tinker Cliffs and eyeing an increasingly cloudy sky that looked like it might make things complicated later on. We'd planned to do a relatively short day and bunk at Lamberts Meadow Shelter.

But when we got there, something didn't feel quite right. There was part of a shredded Z Lite pad, full of puncture wounds, and bits of trash strewn around. Looking closer, we saw that someone had tacked an ALL CAPS message to one of the posts, describing the previous harrowing night, during which a bear had actually *entered* the shelter and stolen food bags. My friend Kristen even heard about the attack on public-radio news in Colorado.

We groaned. Obviously, we weren't going to stay there (and the shelter was soon closed for the season). The next shelter, the rather obscenely named Fullhardt Knob (the "t" is silent), was 14 miles off, beyond the town of Daleville.

Patches shrugged, we laughed, and decided to make the best of it. We saddled up, intending to bust out a 30-mile day to Fullhardt, and not even five minutes down the trail Patches stopped in front of me, put a finger to his lips, and pointed into the trees to our left. A black blur was disappearing into the trees—my first bear!

That put a spring in our step and convinced us that we'd done the right thing, and we had a jolly time rolling along through Virginia greenery. And then, maybe five miles outside of Daleville, the black storm that had threatened all day invaded the sky above, and just uncorked on us. With the possible exception of one brief storm in Pennsylvania, this was the most torrential downpour I would experience on the trail, and it lasted for a half an hour.

Soon, the trail was literally running like a creek. There was nothing to do but keep hammering ahead, and in the curious way of adversity in my life, we got more determined and enjoyed ourselves. At one point, we splashed past a young female hiker trying to ride out the storm by huddling next to an enormous boulder.

But the fun soon turned to stress as we found ourselves exposed on a long ridge with lightning slashing all around. We passed under high power lines that were audibly sizzling, and the last series of switchbacks seemed to take forever.

Out of the bears, I wrote later, *and into an electrical storm. Oh, AT, you smartass!*

Then, suddenly, we came to a road lined with restaurants, motels and other businesses, and the rain finally moved on. Standing there bedraggled, a little punch-drunk and, in my case, chilly and wet, we were startled when the young woman we'd seen popped out behind us.

"Hey," she said, without introduction. "You guys want to go in on a motel room with me?"

She made up our minds for us on the spot, and the three of us walked two minutes to a Howard Johnson's Express, which kindly gave us a hiker rate of $49.95 a night. Split three ways, it was a hell of a deal. Cinnamon, a Latina college student from Plano, Texas, made an excellent roommate, and I spotted her share of the night's rent. Several other hikers, including a German guy we knew named Goldrush, had also taken refuge at the HoJo's.

After hot showers, Cinnamon made us an intriguing offer: If we bought the makings, she would whip up motel-room, Tejano-style tacos, using a roast chicken, corn tortillas, cheese, avocadoes, tomatoes, onions and salsa. She also decided to buy a 12-pack of Oculto, a tequila-infused beer with Dia de Muertos-style packaging.

That, I wrote in my journal, *is the best meal I've had on this trail. And despite the rain, this was the coolest day on the trail yet.*

Patches and I gallantly said we'd share one of the queen beds so Cinnamon would have her own, but I think we disappointed her with our lame partying skills. I was stuffed to the gills and by the time I managed to finish one Oculto, I was nodding off. Last I saw, Patches and Cinnamon were reclined on her bed, watching the movie *Jupiter Rising* featuring Mila Kunis.

*

The next day, I woke about 4 a.m. with a stuffy nose and a headache. I immediately considered taking my first zero. But at breakfast with Patches (Cinnamon was still asleep), we talked to a couple, Diesel and Coldsnap, and I decided to hike after all.

The day was unexceptional, except for the fact that Patches' brother had hidden a can of Devil's Backbone CranGose beer at a specified place along the trail, a nifty bit of magic. I slurped down Nyquil, sucked Jolly Ranchers and was constantly coughing and blasting snot-rockets into the forest, but it was a losing battle. When we reached Wilson Creek Shelter after just 11 miles, I told Patches I was packing it in.

"But seriously, don't hold back for me," I said. "If you need to roll on, I completely understand. I'd miss you, but I get it."

The fact that he decided to hang with me when I knew he could have done another 15 or 20 remains, for me, one of the most touching moments on the trail. Here I was, this old fart, sick and tired, and this 23-year-old guy thought enough of my company to change his plans.

The shelter was jammed with an assortment of oddballs, not a one of them thru-hikers, including the unnecessarily defensive "dad guy" who kept telling everyone, "I did this trail before any of you even thought of it. I've got nothing to prove," and a bulky snorer who looked like Ray Bradbury. I conked out and slept the afternoon away, waking only briefly to pee.

When we woke early the next morning, I felt a little better. But as we packed up, Patches couldn't find the plastic bag that held his Awol guide and a Narnia book he'd been reading. We both completely unpacked, thinking perhaps it had gotten tangled in a sleeping bag or something, to no avail. We asked the Ray Bradbury guy, who was on Patches' other side, if he'd mind doing the same, but he didn't find it either.

"I don't get it," Patches said. "It was right by my head."

We looked all around the shelter, then started working our way around the outside, in wider and wider circles, looking for any sign of the bag. That's when some tenters emerged and told us they'd had a running battle with a gang of raccoons in the night.

"Aw, man," I said. "I know it sounds crazy, but I wonder if a raccoon popped up over the edge of the shelter and just snatched it, on the off chance it contained food." After all, I thought, coons had surely been conditioned to see colorful things inside plastic bags as potential groceries.

With that in mind, we spread out even further, and I even walked a third of a mile downhill to the spring. But we saw no trace of books or bag. Then, for the first and only time, I saw Patches get mad. He packed up and stormed off, moving fast. I would have been mad, too, but it was, after all, just a guidebook and cheap paperback. As I headed down the trail, I worried that he blamed me for his loss, since he wouldn't have been there if he hadn't stayed behind. I half expected that I wouldn't see him again, and spent the day feeling guilty.

But then, after 25.4 miles and the 2,000-foot EoDMoFo of Floyd Mountain, I reached Cornelius Creek Shelter, and there was my friend. He had calmed down considerably, and when I tentatively ventured that he could have my Awol guide, he shook his head.

"Thanks, Pony," he said. "But the reason I got so mad is that I had all my notes in that book, all my memories, and now they are gone."

Now I understood. I told him again how sorry I was and thanked him for sticking by me in my moment of weakness.

A chance for my friend to 'show his quality,' I wrote that night, alluding to a line in Peter Jackson's adaptation of *The Lord of the Rings. You have shown your quality, sir.*

*

That night, I felt melancholy. Patches had hung with me, but he was going to meet his brother and some of his friends the next day, and told me they'd only be hiking 10 miles a day for the next few days. Meanwhile, my own enforced break now loomed before me, making me long for the trail even as I was still on it.

But I was also excited. My stepson Dane was coming to visit. After that I would participate in a pre-Memorial Day ceremony with the governor of Tennessee in Nashville, then meet my family in New Orleans, where I would give a presentation at the National World War II Museum about my grandfather. Then in late June I would accompany my mother to a family reunion in the mountains of North Carolina, where I'd get to see Helen—who now sported the trail name Margarita—and we could swap stories.

I'm excited to go home, see Jody and do all the amazing things I've got coming up, I wrote. *But I'm feeling so torn! I'm not ready to get off.*

Poor Jody didn't know it yet, but I was now determined to come back to the trail in late June. That made leaving easier to bear, but didn't change the fact that when I did, I'd be solo again, and the friends who had made these last weeks the best I'd ever had on trail would be hundreds of miles away.

FOURTEEN: ALONE AGAIN

May 2016: Cornelius Creek Shelter to Waynesboro, Va.

A night of solid rain made for a hot, humid—but thankfully, net-downhill—morning, and as usual, Patches had quickly gotten out front.

I crossed the James River Foot Bridge ("the longest foot-only bridge on the AT," according to Awol, named after the late AT hiker and volunteer Bill Foot) at 1:45. Patches had left me a hastily scribbled note on the other side to say he'd hitched into Glasgow. He planned to meet his brother Ben at the parking area around 5, and wrote that he understood if I needed to head on.

Now I had a chance to show *my* quality. If I obeyed the impatient demon whispering in one ear, this would be it. The fellowship would be broken. I decided to wait. I not only wanted to see him again, but also didn't want him to wait by himself. After spreading my sweat-soaked clothes and shoes on rocks, I reclined on my Z Lite pad to soak up warm sunlight.

Patches was back within the hour and we spent a fine last afternoon together. Like many other AT hikers, we pretended not to see the warning signs and enjoyed a couple of 20-foot plunges from the footbridge into the cool green waters of the river below, then lolled nearly naked in the sunshine, and ate. Patches had brought me a 16-ounce IPA and some candy, and two older women, alarmed by our scrawny frames, gave us a liter of soda and an unopened 14.3-oz. package of peanut butter Oreos. We consumed it all immediately.

Just one other hiker came by over the next five hours, perhaps because so many people had made the pilgrimage back to Damascus for Trail Days. Candyman, coach of the rowing team at Williams College in Massachusetts, told me he was about ready to bail off the trail.

"I'm just lonely," he said. "I didn't expect that."

It was a fine afternoon, but when Patches' brother still hadn't arrived by 7:30, I decided to hike to Johns Hollow Shelter (mile 786) to make dinner and get ready for the next day. I found Candyman's tent and invited him to join the party when Patches arrived with his new crew, but he declined. It was well past dark by the time they rolled in, and I enjoyed the company (as well as far too many more Oreos) only for an hour before heading to bed.

It wasn't a great night. Tiny noseeums whined their way inside my sleeping bag and my stomach grumbled and groaned all night. I had tossed away caution a couple of days before and started drinking untreated water from mountaintop springs and creeks, per the advice of famous AT curmudgeon Warren Doyle, but now I wondered if I'd made a mistake. More likely it was just that I'd eaten three-quarters of a pound of Oreos and drank a Pabst Blue Ribbon in addition to the earlier IPA.

I woke early and was ready to go before the sun had peeked into the hollow. I tapped Patches on the shoulder and gave him the last 147 pages of my Awol guide, for the journey north. It was the least I could do upon saying farewell to a man I already loved as if I'd known him my whole life.

"I'm so glad I got to hike with you," I whispered as he gave me a sleepy embrace. "You are a good man."

I turned and walked to the trail without looking back, tears in my eyes.

*

The air was muggy and I felt feverish as I slogged 2,000 feet up to Big Rocky Row, then followed a long, meandering ridgeline with an expansive view of forest to the east. Walking along the shore of a pond in the afternoon, I spooked several deer, spied a rattlesnake and felt a thrill as I passed an 800-mile marker crafted by hikers from small stones.

I made good time, hoping to beat a wet cold front predicted to arrive by mid-afternoon. The air was still and full of portent as I passed Brown Mountain Creek Shelter (mile 804.3), but I decided I had time to tackle a 2,400-foot EoDMoFo to the summit of Bald Knob, where I planned to camp, before the rain hit. I also was eager to catch up to Wanderer, a correspondent for the *Sounds of the Trail* podcast, who I knew had to be just in front of me, based on shelter logbooks.

When I hit U.S. 60 less than two miles later, a hard, cold rain had begun to fall. Two bedraggled hikers stood mournfully next to a trail sign, trying to stay dry. Too stubborn to backtrack two miles to the shelter, I marched miserably on.

Long, wet, cold crank up a mountain with too many false summits. My forearms are freezing again! I scribbled in my journal that night. And I never did see Wanderer, who had been smarter than I and bailed into town ahead of the storm. But I would meet him eventually.

The rain gave way to a bitterly cold wind by the time I reached the summit which was not a bald at all. A tangle of thick undergrowth put flight to any thought of pitching a tent, and I was forced to continue.

Like many thru-hikers, I am not fond of "sideways miles"—any hiking that does not keep you moving up the trail. When I came to the sign for Cow Camp Gap Shelter (mile 810.5) I groaned: It was *six-tenths of a mile* off trail, but now I had no choice. This day wasn't quite as bad as Cinco de Freezo a week earlier, but if I didn't get out of my wet clothes and into a sleeping bag soon I'd find myself staring down the big H again—hypothermia.

I muttered curses when I approached the shelter and saw at least a dozen people milling around; with my frozen, sloth-like fingers, I doubted I could even pitch my tent. In foul weather, hikers will usually find room for everyone, and fortunately for me, the entire crowd was made up of a Boy Scout troop on its way down the mountain. Eventually another guy, Skibo, strung his hammock in the shelter—widely considered a faux pas, but since only two other section hikers showed up, it didn't matter.

Rain lashed the roof on and off throughout the night, driven by a maniacal wind. The air was bone-cracking cold by the time I woke in the dim dawn. There was ice on the trail and for the first time since the Smokys in March, I had to wear all my cold-weather gear to hike. The sun peeked out around noon, but the biting wind forced me to stay bundled all day. It didn't help that my food supply had dwindled to almost nothing; my body had long ago burned away all those Oreo calories.

By early afternoon I reached the 3,885-foot summit of The Priest. Just before that, I stopped to eat a few meager calories at The Priest Shelter (mile 827.3), where it is a longstanding tradition for hikers to "make a confession" in the logbook. Flipping through, I found more candor and fewer jokes than I'd anticipated: hikers confessing that they really *were* bums, on the trail (shhhh!) because they didn't want to be working; many *meas culpa* about lax bear precautions ("I haven't hung a bear bag since the Smokys"); violations of Leave No Trace principles—"I don't actually dig every cat hole six inches deep!"; admissions of yellow- or blue-blazing; and more.

"No confession for me," I wrote, in no mood for either jest or candor. "My Catholic days are over."

Nonetheless, The Priest seemed to bless me when a woman named Virginia Creeper and her daughter Kiwi stopped for lunch. Like me, they planned to make the long descent to the Tye River, then climb the first third of a 3,000-foot climb to Three Ridges Mountain before stopping at Harpers Creek Shelter, where they said they'd be happy to share some extra food with me.

Tumbling tiredly down a steep, rocky, rooty, 3,000-foot descent to the river, my nose ran like a faucet, necessitating constant farmer blowing, aka snotrockets, and loud honking into a bandana. About two-thirds the way down, I rounded a curve to find two day hikers peering out over the gorgeous, sunlit Tye River Valley.

"Was that you making all that racket away up in the woods?" the older man said in a British accent. "Surely your mother didn't teach you to blow like *that*?"

"Aye, mate, she did do," I said in a faux accent.

"Are you from England then?"

"Nope," I drawled, smiling at the memory of all my many exchanges with Patches. "Just like to talk in fake accents."

"Eh, well, you're not that good," the guy said.

"Fooled you for a minute there."

"Nah," he said, grinning. "I was just momentarily stunned by all that honking."

Down by the river, I hesitated for a moment. I could stick out my thumb and catch a ride to the Devil's Backbone Basecamp Brewpub, famous for its beer, chow and hospitality to hikers. There is even a well-built outdoor pavilion, complete with electrical outlets, where they can bunk for free after enjoying the far at the pub. It was sorely tempting, especially since I was half-starving and my food bag was nearly down to fumes.

In hindsight, I have no idea why I didn't go there and my journal offers no illumination. Unbeknownst to me, the prodigious Lava Monster was about to catch up with Patches, and if I had opted for that nero, I might have seen them again. Instead, I headed north and the 1,000-foot EoDMoFo and short, rocky descent to Harpers Creek Shelter (mile 834.3), making for a rough end to a long, battering day. On the way up, I passed an older woman who was clearly struggling on the steep trail with a younger hiker gently coaxing her on. When I reached the shelter, a solemn young thru-hiker named Kaio asked if I'd seen her Aunty Grace and friend Nikei.

A good two hours after I arrived, the two women came into camp. Nikei promptly dropped her pack, and headed back the way she'd come: She had sherpa'd Aunty Grace's pack and was headed back up the hill to retrieve her own. Aunty couldn't stop talking about how steep the trail was. A chatty young woman, Debbie, also had joined thru-hikers Kaio and Nikei for a week on the trail, anticipating her own future thru-hike.

These two solemn, religious young women had been hiking together since Springer, and now they were slowing down to spend a few days with Aunty Grace and Debbie.

"It's what you do for friends and family, right?" Kaio said.

＊

When I woke early the next morning I was exhausted, sniffling and feeling lonely. But my food bag was now literally empty—Virginia Creeper and Kiwi had never arrived—and with another nasty cold front predicted for the next day, I decided to push all the way to town. With some 5,000 feet of climbing and 27 miles ahead of me, it would be a long haul.

Better than starving in freezing rain, I wrote.

I was glad I'd had the good sense to knock out a third of the steep, grinding climb up Three Ridges Mountain. The sun played peekaboo as I steadily made my way up a series of switchbacks, but the air remained cool. Pushing hard, I managed to make the last 2,000 feet to the summit in just over an hour, happy to have finished the day's big climb.

But once again—and not for the last time—I learned the painful lesson that just because Awol's elevations *look* like smooth-sailing, it doesn't mean they are. The five miles of the AT from Reeds Gap along the western shoulder of Humpback Mountain offer a harsh preview of Pennsylvania's notorious rocks. There is little net elevation gain or loss, but the tread is almost entirely made up of blocky, mossy, slippery rock. The trail dips and rises constantly, six feet here, 12 feet there, making it all but impossible to get into any kind of rhythm. The final climb up to Humpback is more of the same, only steeper. There are gorgeous views here and there—it's still Virginia, after all—but for much of the way, it's green-tunnel city.

Just Charlie, a section hiker I would meet far up the trail, told me it wasn't always this way. He began hiking the AT in 1970 and 46 years later, was about to finish.

"There used to be a lot more road walking, and crossing farms and pastures," he told me. "But over the years, they have rerouted the trail to a ridge every time they get the chance, on the theory that roads and farms aren't 'wilderness.'

But I loved those parts of the trail; when you are hiking the whole thing, or long sections, you don't always need to be on a ridgetop or in the middle of the woods."

I, along with many other hikers I've met, agree with Just Charlie. There are other factors at play—for example, routing the trail through public lands to the greatest extent possible—but I suspect that trail designers over the years have not had thru-hikers in mind when rerouting the AT. And where I imagine many weekend hikers find road walks or farm fields dull and domestic, they are a welcome break from ridges, climbs and green tunnels for a thru-hiker.

But magic often appears when you need it most, and as I approached the summit of Humpback I came upon a couple eating on a rocky promontory. It was Bombadil and Goldberry, parents of Legs and Verge, the sisters I'd camped with in the apple orchard after Unaka Mountain all the way back in Tennessee. Taking pity on poor, starving Pony, they gave me an orange, a Clif bar and some jerky to fuel my last 10 miles into Rockfish Gap.

Even so, my head throbbed and my stomach growled with hunger through that long afternoon. I could hear the alien hiss of traffic for an hour before I finally staggered up a few rocky steps into the gap. My feet felt like they'd been beaten with cement-filled rubber hoses all day and I was high with exhaustion. I called Stanimal's hostel down in Waynesboro; they'd pick me up in about 15 minutes.

"You look like you could use some magic," said a burly young guy who approached as I sat there, head hung. "Come over here to my car."

Loopily wondering if he might be a serial killer—or a proselytizer—and which would be worse—I followed him anyway. If he'd proffered a possum he'd scraped off the highway I might have eaten it at that point. Instead, he opened a back door and pulled out two broad, flat cardboard boxes. Pizza.

"You know, I came up here to do magic this afternoon, but you're the first hiker I've seen," he said. "So take as much as you want."

Magic, magic, *magic*. I mumbled thank you and began pushing a slice into my face, chomping and swallowing with slow deliberation, the way a desert tortoise scarfs down lettuce. If this guy was a killer, the pizza was poisoned and I would soon be stuffed into a 55-gallon barrel, I thought, it wasn't such a bad way to go. Not after that day.

But after four pieces, I was still standing. They guy stuffed four more slices into a plastic bag and handed it to me. He asked my name. We fist bumped. He drove off. I wandered down to the bright-yellow King's Gourmet Popcorn truck, where I was supposed to wait for the shuttle, and drank a Dr. Pepper in a single, long slug. It all seemed a little unreal. I'd come so far, but now I was getting off. I'd made good friends, and walked away from them all.

"You look beat. Are you a thru-hiker?" the woman in the popcorn truck asked.

I had walked 39.33 percent of the Appalachian Trail, but that wasn't enough. I was going off into exile in the World, but I'd be right back here in late June.

"I didn't know I was when I started," I said, "but yeah, I am."

"Then," she said, "you get one of these."

She handed me a green rubber wristband reading, *APPALACHIAN TRAIL — GEORGIA TO MAINE.*

FIFTEEN: OUT OF THE BARDO, INTO THE BEARS

June 2016: Waynesboro to Manassas Gap Shelter

The Tibetan Buddhism word "bardo" describes an intermediate or liminal state between lives in the endless cycle of death and rebirth known as samsara. I don't believe in reincarnation or any other kind of life after death, but the next five weeks of my life were a kind of limbo between two episodes of life on the Appalachian Trail.

I'd walked nearly 40 percent of the trail over two months (including a mini-bardo in March and April) then plunged fully back into the World for a series of rewarding events—a visit from my stepson, a Memorial Day presentation, and a reunion with Bonnyman family members in the mountains of North Carolina just 20 miles from the trail, as the crow flies.

But when I wasn't traveling or otherwise occupied, I was infected with trail longing. Summing up my wife's description of me in that state, I was completely lost in the world of the trail and for her, it was sort of like having a large, distracted pig lying around the house.

I enthusiastically recommend taking a break from the trail here and there for those who can. I met many exhausted hikers who returned from a few days or a week in the city, at the beach, at a wedding, or just at home with family, completely refreshed and excited. But if I did it again, I wouldn't take a break much longer than that; a week max.

But being home did give me time to hover over maps, scheme out transportation to get back to the trail, and most important, do my own personal shakedown. By the time I returned, it would be late June, so I could leave my cold-weather gear behind, saving a few pounds. I switched out a technical t-shirt for one made of Merino wool—thanks for the advice, Patches!—and packed a pair of tough, lightweight Arc'teryx shorts. I also followed Lava's lead and bought a long-handled titanium spork, having grown tired of sticky knuckles. Between those and other changes, I was able to shed about five pounds of base weight.

Most important, I reverently replaced the Hoka One One Mafate Speed trail shoes that had carried me 861 miles with the Altra Olympus 2.0. The Hokas had simply become too narrow—or rather, my feet had become too wide—causing serious pain in the ball of my right foot and a mild case of sesamoiditis. Altras have an extremely wide, "foot-shape" toe box, and the Olympus sported as much cushioning as Hokas, which I needed because of an old heel injury.

It took a bit of finagling, but I finally worked out an efficient transportation plan: Following the reunion, I would drop my cousin Helen, aka Margarita, and her sister Claire, who was going to hike with her until early August, when they had to head off to Rice University, on the trail near Buena Vista, Va. (mile 806.4). Then I'd return my car in Charlottesville and catch a shuttle to Rockfish Gap (mile 861.3), where I would restart my hike.

*

By the time Stanimal, owner of the excellent Stanimal's 328 Hostel & Shuttle Service in Waynesboro, Va., dropped me off at the gap, it was nearly 7 p.m.

"You sure you don't want to just stay tonight? I can bring you up tomorrow," he said.

"No," I said. "I really need to start hiking."

Despite the relatively late hour, the air was sweetly warm and a little humid as I walked up Little Calf Mountain, crossing into Shenandoah National Park after just a mile. By the time I reached the summit the sun was gone. My fancy Arc'teryx shorts had proved no more breathable than a Pampers and I felt like I'd been dunked in gasoline.

But as I rambled along through the swiftly fading light, the woods turned into something out of a Disney fantasia, with fireflies blinking languidly in the shadows and owls calling to each other in the branches above. Twice I crossed Skyline Drive, the paved road that runs adjacent to the trail for more than a hundred miles through the park. But the going over rocky, muddy trail was difficult, especially after my headlamp conked out; I hadn't thought to check the batteries while in the bardo.

It was 9:30 and cavernously dark when I got to Calf Mountain Shelter (mile 869). There was just enough room to roll out my pad next to a wall (my favorite shelter position anyway), and I tried to eat a makeshift dinner of bars, cheese sticks and water without making too much noise.

Sometime long after midnight, I woke with a screaming start when 200 pounds of human deadweight smashed down onto one of my legs. A guy on the upper level needed to pee, and hadn't looked where he was leaping.

"My bad," he said.

I hate that non-responsibility-taking expression, almost as much as I hate it when servers say "No problem" in response to thank you. I guess that makes me old.

By 5 a.m., everybody else was annoyed with him too, as he was making an enormous racket at the picnic table. Another guy shrieked like a banshee when a creepy, globular, Shelob-sized spider—one of many living in the rafters—crawled out of his pack and onto his hand.

All that gave me an early start for a pleasant day of walking through lush greenery and warm, humid air. I pitched my tent at Loft Mountain Campground and hitched a ride with a ranger down to the Loft Mountain Wayside—the first of several such restaurant/stores throughout the park—to eat dinner and try one of those famous Shenandoah blackberry milkshakes. Dinner was so-so, but I still wake up with tears in my eyes remembering the shakes.

As I'd feared, five weeks in the bardo hadn't been good for my trail legs, and after 19 miles and 3,700 feet of climbing my feet felt like pounded cubesteak. I slathered half a dozen patches of stinging red chafe with Vagisil (don't laugh; it's *the* miracle cure for chafe), then finally nodded off.

Birds roused me early and I was on the trail at 6:40 the next morning. Twenty minutes into the day, I rounded a corner to find a large black bear slumped in the middle of the trail. He—by the size, I guessed it was a male—leaped up and barreled about 20 yards up the trail before stopping to take a look at the irritating critter that had disturbed his reverie. When I slowly pulled my phone out for a photo, he turned and ran again. I'd glimpsed a bear near Lambert Meadows Shelter, but this was the first time I'd gotten a good, long look. Too bad he wouldn't stand still long enough for me to catch a photo.

I reached the South River Picnic Ground, where I'd heard one could stealth camp, at mid-afternoon. But it didn't look promising, and after dunking myself, clothes and all, in the forceful stream of a water pump, I felt refreshed enough to keep moving. Thunderstorms never materialized, and to my surprise, I kept walking until I reached Bearfence Mountain Hut (as shelters are called in Shenandoah) after a nearly 28-mile day.

I'd exchanged only scattered words with humans since leaving Rockfish, and was glad for the company of Lazy Eagle, a chatty kid who had hiked with my cousin Margarita, a hospital chaplain named Pacemaker, and quiet, serious Honey Badger, who had just finished a hitch in the Marine Corps. We also got a visit from a friendly Appalachian Trail Conservancy ridgerunner, the first I'd seen since the Smokys, an older woman whose name I failed to record.

Chafe city! I wrote about the following day. *I sweat out my clothes, then walk and rub salt into my wounds all day long. I changed clothes at Skyland (Resort and Restaurant, mile 931.7), but it only helped until I got wet again, and now everything is soaked.*

But at least the day featured another blackberry milkshake, this one at Big Meadows Wayside. I changed clothes and hung out with Honey Badger and a few other hikers before rolling on. I did my best to force myself to take hills at a slower pace, hoping it would, as I wrote, *reduce swamp-ass to some degree.*

An hour later, driven half-mad by the oppressive, overcast heat, endless green tunnel and the brutal stinging of chafe, I tore off my shirt and shorts and walked the last four miles wearing nothing but a ragged, 10-year-old pair of Brooks Runderwear—"tighty blackies" that had, over many years of use, faded to a sickly brown hue. I tugged the Arc'teryx shorts back on just before I reached Byrd's Nest #3 Hut (so far as I know, there is no #1 or #2).

A spectacular sunset, viewed from a nearby tumble of giant rocks, along with a visual symphony of fireflies and a roomy shelter—just Honey Badger, Lazy Eagle and me—made up for a long, uncomfortable day. And I was just a day and a half away from a nero at my cousin Margot's luxurious horse property in Upperville, Va.

Life is just good, I wrote before falling asleep.

*

I'm embarrassed to admit it, but I cannot seem to shake my brain's persistent, involuntary competitiveness on the trail. If I see someone in front of me, I feel compelled to try to pass; if I sense someone coming up behind, I'll instinctively turn up the jets. If a guy passes me, my idiot brain immediately starts explaining why, y'know, I'm still tougher than he is—*He probably hasn't walked 15 miles already; he's 20 years younger; etc., etc.* (Curiously, if a woman passes me—and many have—my brain is suddenly all sweet and supportive: *Right on, sister!*)

I'm not proud of that, but I have heard other seemingly well-adjusted hikers—mostly male, but at least one female—admit to the same sort of silly egomania in their own heads. But about a mile beyond Pass Mountain Hut, where I'd stopped for water the next morning, I actually met a guy who owned up to it.

I was surprised (and annoyed) when I heard footsteps rapidly approaching behind me. I turned to see a tall, middle-aged guy in a floppy hat.

"I'm just going to jump in front of you," he said.

I let him—what else was I going to do? After giving him a little air, I started walking again at my usual pace. It didn't take long for him to realize I was gaining on him, and he soon stepped aside. But then he velcro'd on to me and we began talking. He was a vocalist with the San Francisco Opera who was, he admitted, going through a mid-life crisis. He'd lost his apartment and just decided to live on the trail for the next several months. He went by Raiden, an homage to a character from the video game *Mortal Kombat*.

"You're the first person I've passed who I couldn't put in the rear-view mirror," he said.

Despite my initial irritation, the hours and miles flew by as we talked and talked and talked … and *talked* … about everything, including the inherent idiocy of being a competitive male. I got out front of him after stopping for lunch at Elkwallow Wayside (blackberry milkshake No. 3), but Raiden reminded me that I actually liked hiking with other people. (I would meet him again during a section hike in 2019, and we enjoyed each other's company just as much.)

I hit Gravel Springs Hut early, giving me a chance to "do laundry" — i.e. rinse my salt-stiffened, chafe-inducing clothes — before a good crew showed up for a lively evening, including Raiden, Honey Badger and The Grocer, an old Australian guy hauling an absurd amount of food — and an admitted snorer. I pitched my tent up the hill.

Headlamp beams slicing across the walls of my tent stirred me out of sleep sometime after midnight. I put my glasses on and peeked out. A half dozen hikers were out of their tents, slashing flashlight beams around the woods, and somewhere below me I could hear lumbering steps in the dark. Taking the opportunity to relieve myself, I, too, scanned the woods. Two tiny, shining yellow-orange disks reflected back at me. Deer eyes, I recalled, reflected green.

While there is a certain amount of "bearanoia" on the trail, I, like most hikers I've met, am absolutely thrilled by the prospect of seeing bears. True, in Shenandoah and other places where bears have become habituated to humans, they can cause problems. But in reality, they just aren't that dangerous.

While in town somewhere in Virginia, I looked up bear-caused human fatalities. Since the year 2000, there have been 44 fatal bear attacks in North America. Of those, 26 were caused by grizzlies, which live nowhere near the Appalachian Trail. Of the 18 caused by black bears, just four took place anywhere near the AT (in Tennessee, New Jersey and Pennsylvania). Given that some 11 million people visited Great Smoky and Shenandoah national parks *alone* in 2015, it's fair to say that your chances of being killed by a bear along the AT are vanishingly small—something on the order of 1 in 60 million in any given year. That doesn't mean you shouldn't take precautions and avoid doing stupid things, but it does mean bearanoia is completely unwarranted.

Most hikers love bear sightings, and I was thrilled to encounter bears No. 3 and 4 the following day, a couple miles past Jim & Molly Denton Shelter. Juveniles, they were poking around a downed tree trunk perhaps 15 yards off trail. I stopped the instant I saw them, not wanting to appear threatening in any way.

I'm not a big photo taker; my goal is at least one a day, but sometimes I don't even manage that. I should have gotten a shot or two of these very laid-back subjects, but I didn't want to put them on the spot, so to speak. They never seemed the least bit perturbed, even when I started moving again. All I had to do was raise my iPhone … damn.

I did, however, get some nice photos of the well-fed copperhead snake coiled up next to the footpath to the privy at Manassas Gap Shelter that evening, so I guess that's something. I also got to meet Cake, another young hiker who had walked with my cousin Margarita further south on the trail.

SIXTEEN: ACROSS THE MASON-DIXON LINE

June-July 2016: Ashby Gap to Ensign Cowell Shelter

After a pleasant morning walk that included a couple of pastoral miles through Sky Meadows State Park, my cousin Margot picked me up at Ashby Gap (mile 989.1) and drove me to her 50-acre horse farm near Upperville, Va.

Fifteen minutes later, I was in a whole new world. The house built by her partner, Jim, was big, beautiful and clean, surrounded by forest and swales of green pasture. The farm had a pleasant, rustic feel, and Margot, a former Grand Prix competitor in dressage, spent much of her time working with and caring for her tall, German warm-blood mare, Leila, who has a pleasant, almost doglike disposition.

After I showered and tossed my filthy clothes into the washer, Margot drove me into town for a small resupply. The grocery store catered to, shall I say, the rather more upscale clientele who gravitated to this fox-hunting, mansion-dwelling corner of Virginia. There was nary a ramen packet or box of Pop-Tarts in sight.

You might be thinking, "Good! Who eats *ramen* noodles—the very definition of plastic, industrial 'food'—or Pop-Tarts, which are little more than a super-efficient delivery system for the galaxy's most fanatically processed white flour and sugar, the heroin of the snack-food world?"

Well, I do, for one, but only when on trail—and I'm not proud of it. But I'm not the only one who errs on the side of convenience over nutrition on a long-distance hike. A typical eating day goes something like this for me:

Shoot up in the morning with a Pop-Tart or some peanut-butter crackers

"Day" eating—bars (I'm partial to Clif and Kind bars); salted almonds or other nuts; dried fruit—prunes, cherries, apples, peaches; jerky; tuna packets; tortillas with cheese or peanut butter; afternoon sugar hits—gummi bears, Oreos, peanut M&Ms, Snickers, Milky Way, Sourpatch Kids, Skittles, Goldfish crackers, and so on; apples and oranges when I can.

Dinner—Idahoan brand instant mashed potatoes; ramen noodles (I love these especially because they are salty, they put fluids in your system, and because it's super easy to clean up after cooking); Knorr Pasta Sides; or, when I don't want to mess with the stove, I'll make "dinner" out of any of the above.

If you think that sounds terrible, well … you're right. But it's easy and it's calories. And when possible, I do go for produce. After a hiker named Monarch gave me an avocado in Pennsylvania, I made a point of buying one every time I went to town. More than anything, thru-hikers I talk to crave fresh fruit and vegetables.

Like any thru-hiker, I tried to make up calories whenever I hit town. But I also made a point to eat as much fresh food and fiber as possible, to give my system a chance.

At Margot's that night we ate burgers and mounds of fresh salad. Then the three of us sat on the porch sipping margaritas and watching hundreds of lightning bugs in their nightly, spiraling dance from the ground into the highest branches of a sprawling oak tree….

What a place. I needed this. I often forget that it's 'so nice for feet,' I wrote, quoting Smeagol/Gollum, *to take a nero.*

And then, less than 24 hours after I'd gotten off the trail, I was waving to my cousin and walking back to my life in the woods.

*

Sending boxes to yourself is an old thru-hiking tradition. It's kind of fun to anticipate and open a box, but hiking the Colorado Trail I developed a preference for buying supplies in town.

First, two of the four boxes I had sent to me on the CT didn't arrive in time, despite plenty of lead-time. And when I was able to pick up a box, I sometimes discovered that I was sick and tired of all the food I'd packed a few weeks earlier. I go through phases on trail, and my favorite meal one week might repulse me the next. To boot, the cost of sending boxes tends to eliminate arguments from economy. But most important, I realized I wanted to be a good ambassador and support businesses in hiker-friendly trail towns.

But because I'd bought too much before leaving home in June, I did send myself one box, to the ATC's famous Bears Den Hostel (mile 1002.6), a historic stone structure managed by the Potomac Appalachian Trail Club in northern Virginia (for my money, the single best maintaining club out there). Arriving at the hostel at noon, I ruefully recalled another reason I'm not hot on boxes: no staff would be available to retrieve my box until 5 p.m.

I pondered leaving it, but anticipating the box, I had done only a mini-resupply in Upperville. My impatience demon protested mightily, but I did the smart thing and decided to kick back for a few hours, then hike on into the evening. The day was sunny and warm, so I rinsed my salt-crusted clothes and lazed around in ragged Runderwear. When it got too hot, I flopped on a couch inside and picked up a book about bears, enjoying two $1 Cokes purchased on the honor system. Eventually, I began to doze.

At around 4 p.m., I stirred awake. A young, happy-looking hiker drifted in through the door, followed by a bearded middle-aged guy wearing work boots, jeans and a serious expression.

"Hey, Pony!" the hiker said, rushing over. "You remember me? I'm Scavenger. We met in Damascus."

I'd first met him outside The Place, a $7 bunkroom operated by a Methodist church in Damascus that had too many rules for my crew's tastes. Later, he showed up at Crazy Larry's. He was tall and delicate looking, with a tumble of curly blond hair, a feathery beard, blue eyes and long lashes, extremely open and friendly.

I righted myself on the couch while Scavenger made his goodbyes to the man.

"I'm going to come back when I'm finished," he said. "I mean it."

They exchanged a long, sturdy embrace, then the guy went out, climbed in an old pickup and drove away. There had to be a story here, I knew. This kid should have been hundreds of miles ahead of me by then. Turns out that Scavenger had gotten injured and spent the last month working at the Stony Brook Organic Farm in Hillsboro, W.Va., run by a religious group known as the Twelve Tribes. The sect is well regarded among hikers for its cheap or free lodging, its Yellow Deli restaurant in Rutland, Vt. and the nearby farm.

"It was such an amazing experience," the kid told me. "They're all about love."

Having talked to Twelve Tribes members in my hometown, Boulder, Colo., I had a different view. The sect eschews the Christian label, arguing that Christianity is "the whore of Babylon," yet still awaits the return of Jesus. They practice a brand of fundamentalism based on the Mosaic laws of the Hebrew Bible (aka the Old Testament) and preach that the messiah will not come until the "true church" is restored, as described in Acts 2:32-37, which states in part that, "no one claimed any of his possessions for himself, but everyone shared everything he had."

The group, founded by Elbert "Gene" Spriggs, aka Yoneq, who claims a direct line of communication with God, grew out of the 1960s Jesus Movement and is now widely viewed as a cult. Critics cite its alleged authoritarianism, anti-Semitism, and misogyny, as well as child labor and child-abuse practices. I'd certainly picked up on the misogyny in my experience with the group and saw how they preyed on the lonely and vulnerable. Some hikers told me their experiences with the tribe were fantastic, no proselytizing, no weirdness, but I didn't want to put even a nickel in Spriggs' pocket.

I finally got my box a little after 5 and, as expected, groaned at the contents—*more* tuna? But calories are calories, and I dutifully stuffed it all in my bag. Antsy after the long delay, I made a snap decision to follow a different blue blaze than the one on which I'd come, skipping a couple hundred yards of the AT. I'd just casually set fire to my purism, but if anything, it felt strangely liberating.

Bears Den lies about halfway through the reputedly brutal Roller Coaster, described by Awol as "13.5 miles of tightly packed ascents and descents." There are even warning signs at the beginning (upon which one witty hiker had drawn a mark and the words, "Must be at least this tall to ride."). Lava, who had come through here already—he wrapped up his hike at Harpers Ferry on May 27 to attend a wedding and move with Heather to Colorado—texted me that it was "no big deal," and I agreed; at any rate, the Roller Coaster didn't seem any more difficult than the rest of the trail so far. What's more, it provided a happy milestone to celebrate: the Virginia-West Virginia border. I was intrigued, but never seriously considered taking the so-called "four-state challenge," covering the 44 miles from the Virginia border to Pennsylvania in one day.

Thru-hikers often talk about catching the "Virginia blues," mental and physical doldrums that hit somewhere on the 540 miles between Tennessee to West Virginia (nearly a quarter of the trail). True, I'd had a break, but I never came close to getting the blues, despite a couple of brutal days. I adored Virginia—on my last day I saw a beautiful, finger-thin smooth greensnake (*Opheodrys vernalis*), several deer and, as dusk approached, an errant possum—and it would be my favorite part of the trail until New Hampshire and Maine.

I didn't roll into the ATC's Blackburn Trail Center until 8:15, but that was early enough for me to receive a bowl of Neapolitan ice cream and a soda from caretakers Trailboss and Sandi. Despite the fact that Independence Day was still two days away, we got to watch four or five distant fireworks displays through a gap in the hills. The lightning bugs added a local touch on the dewy lawn below.

Before noon the next day I tumbled into the historic town of Harpers

Ferry (mile 1,023.1), home of the ATC and the "spiritual halfway point" of the Appalachian Trail.

The 12.5 to Harpers were relatively flat, but often rocky — not so nice for feet, I wrote in my journal. *Another preview of PA?*

A hiker's judgment of any given town or hostel is dependent on a host of variables, and should be taken with a grain of salt. But considering how large it looms in AT lore, Harpers Ferry was a real disappointment to me. It is a beautiful town, situated on a forested hill at the confluence of the mighty Potomoc and Shenandoah rivers, and steeped in history. It was here that abolitionist John Brown raided the armory on Oct. 16, 1859 with 21 men, including a freed slave and a renegade slave, portending the bloody civil war to come.

Spiritual halfway point it may be, but Harpers Ferry is not much of a hikers' town. The cheapest hostel charges $33 for a bunk, while the outfitter and general store is the size of a small-town barbershop, and surprisingly expensive (I paid $23 to replace my pole tips, though at least the guy behind the counter was nice). The restaurant where I ate lunch was fine, but unexceptional, though I did attract the attention of a nice tourist who wanted a photo with a real— and, I might add, filthy—thru-hiker. Even the staff at the Appalachian Trail Conservancy headquarters struck me as rather cranky.

I spent only a couple of hours in town, then headed for the bridge across the Potomac, where I was stopped by a Harpers Ferry National Historic Park ranger making a presentation to a group of tourists who clearly saw me as some form of migratory wildlife.

"Do you mind if they take pictures?"

Halfway across the bridge, a young guy trotted up behind me and called out. He was just out of the Marines and full of questions about thru-hiking.

"What's the *one* piece of advice you'd give to someone who wants to hike the trail?"

I thought for a moment. "*Always* put everything in its proper place in your pack, no matter what, so you know where to find it." He seemed underwhelmed by that bit of (trust me, excellent) advice, but continued to pepper me with questions as I walked.

"You can do it," I said. "If you made it through boot camp and a hitch in the Marines, trust me, you can do this."

Once across the bridge I turned, gave him a fist bump and stepped into Maryland, sixth state on the NOBO AT. The next three miles, walking alongside the historic Chesapeake & Ohio towpath, are without question the easiest on the Appalachian Trail, and despite walking 23 miles, that was the easiest single day I would have on the trail.

After a hot, muggy, 1,000-foot climb I followed the ridge another few miles to Gathland State Park, where I filled up with water, having read in Awol that the water source at Crampton Gap Shelter (mile 1,034.1) sometimes runs dry at midsummer.

The Fourth of July dawned misty and muggy and stayed that way. I turned my ankle hard, for about the 20th time in my first 1,000 miles (thanks to my sturdy Bonnyman sinews, it caused only a few moments of sharp pain, but nothing worse). Pennsylvania gets all the bad press, but it seems to me the troublesome rocks actually start cropping up in Maryland.

How much worse can PA really be? I worried in my journal. *The Arc'teryx shorts are a disaster. Murderous chafe.*

Next chance I got, I was sending the shorts home, along with (my secret shame) the laptop I'd lugged with me, in case my agent needed me to work on my manuscript or I snagged a quick freelance assignment, and another three pounds worth of stuff.

While walking through Washington Monument State Park I passed by a young female hiker wearing unusually beefy looking leg braces. Intending to ask her about her apparatus, I slowed down. But she was already surrounded by several people and looked busy, so I changed my mind. I found out after finishing my hike that she was Stacey Kozel, aka Ironwill, who was using high-tech "exoskeleton" braces to walk the trail ... with paralyzed legs.

"So I'm able to walk because I'm actually balanced. It takes a lot of core strength, and my braces lock my knees when I'm standing. So when I stand I just have to balance with my upper body," she told ESPN.com. "But it doesn't matter out here. You're a hiker. You're part of the family."

One more time I wish I'd listened to my gut and turned aside from my forward progress for just a few moments.

Much to my dismay, in 2017 Kozel's inspiring story fell apart after she earned substantial media coverage for purportedly hiking the 2,650-mile Pacific Crest Trail during one of the most challenging years ever, due to record snowpack in the Sierras, roaring river crossings, wildfires and more.

After a long-standing, well-known trail angel quietly asked on social media if any other 2017 PCT hikers had seen Kozel—who stands out with her leg braces and highly unusual gait—it became sadly apparent that not a single hiker had seen her anywhere that wasn't at a trailhead.

In addition, nobody at the PCT's most famous, and all but mandatory, resupply points, such as Kennedy Meadows, reported seeing her, and eagle-eyed hikers noted that her "finish photo" contained anachronisms (it turned out to be faked). When she altered her finish date to compensate for some of those problems, she only exacerbated doubts, since hikers do not forget their start or finish dates, and her new start date would have required her to average nearly 31 miles per day, every day, across Oregon and Washington—when she herself has publicly stated, and video evidence confirms, that she is very slow, traveling 1 mph over level ground. Talk about long days.

Soon, the AT community began examining her 2016 "hike" and it became clear that her documentation was similarly sketchy: nobody had seen her on the trail (except at or near well-trafficked trailheads), walked with her, or camped with her, a virtual impossibility. To boot, looking back on media coverage and video, it was apparent that she could not have finished the trail in the time she claimed, and probably not at all. And while she clearly has a disability, hiker-sleuths unearthed three separate stories she'd given media about the cause of her paralysis.

It's too bad. Kozel would be inspiring simply doing sections of the trail, but in her exaggerations, she lost all respect and credibility. Worse, she doubled down on her insistence that she did as she claimed, against all evidence, and began complaining about attacks on her "integrity."

A few people defended her and criticized those who began asking questions and uncovering evidence, but there can be no excuse for misleading people like this, especially when it appears that she gained monetarily from the ruse and potentially put other disabled people in danger by giving them false hope that they, too, might be able to hike these big, dangerous, difficult trails. Indeed, excusing Kozel's fabrications because she is disabled is every bit as prejudiced as mocking or ignoring the disabled, since it singles her out for "different" treatment.

At Annapolis Rocks, the (extremely low) high point of Maryland, I committed my second sin against purity, cutting back to the trail on a different blue blaze than the one on which I'd come in. I ate lunch on a mist-covered cliff with Smeagol, a charming young French woman. By the time I reached Ensign Cowall Shelter it was raining and I decided to call it in after just under 21 miles. A half dozen other hikers breezed by and continued on into the rain.

All these guys talking about their 30-mile days made me feel like an idiot for stopping, I wrote. *Oh well, at least I'm dry.*

It wasn't raining when I crossed the Mason-Dixon line into Pennsylvania the next day, but I wasn't dry.

This humidity is a fucking killer. When it's high 80s and humid you're never dry, I wrote. *I've got chafe in places I'd never imagined—hips, armpits, thighs? Stopped at a spring to wash my salty, slimy self from head to toe.*

Later, I ran into The Dude, one of my favorite people I'd met on the trail down south, but the meeting felt disconnected and unsatisfying.

Maybe I've got the PA blues instead of VA blues, I wrote that night.

But my Pennsylvania purgatory was just beginning.

SEVENTEEN:
PENNS(HELL)VANIA

July 2016: Ensign Cowell Shelter to Port Clinton, Pa.

Here is a piece of advice for anyone considering an Appalachian Trail thru-hike: If at all possible, avoid hiking the mid-Atlantic states—Maryland through Connecticut; some people say West Virginia through Massachusetts—in high summer.

Northern Virginia was plenty hot in late June and early July, but starting at Front Royal, Va., the trail dips below 2,000 feet in elevation for the next 600 miles, half of it below 1,000 feet. So not only are you walking through the frying pan of the AT, but *Ixodes scapularis*—the primary vector for Lyme disease in the eastern United States—flourishes in warm weather at elevations below 2,000 feet.

Despite getting out of camp at 6:15 a.m. and reaching my destination at 2:30 p.m. with minimal climbing, my first full day in Pennsylvania was tough. Amid temperatures bumping up against 90 and a dew point above 70 ("Very humid, quite uncomfortable," per the U.S. Occupational Health and Safety

Administration), my sweat glands went into overdrive. But in the airless confines of the green tunnel, nothing could evaporate. Soon, my clothes were soaked and my skin was coated with a slick, suffocating membrane of sweat. My hips, upper legs and armpits were raw with chafe.

But there were compensations along the way. I passed the actual 2016 midway point (more than 70 miles beyond the "spiritual" halfway point in Harpers Ferry) and, shortly thereafter, the 1,100-mile mark.

All downhill from here, right? I wrote later.

Fortunately, my stopping point offered multiple therapies to soothe my raw body after the day's scalding. First, I reveled in the sting of soap and cool water at the historic Ironmaster's Mansion Hostel in Pine Grove Furnace State Park. After starting a load of laundry, I wandered over to the Pine Grove General Store, home of the "half-gallon challenge"— hikers are encouraged to buy and consume an entire carton of ice cream. Seeing no particular benefit—a stomachache seems to be the most common reward—I declined to participate, instead ordering a grilled cheese and fries, downing two quarts of Gatorade, and mowing through a Snickers and an ice-cream bar.

Then, defying the advice of nannies and mothers the world over, I immediately walked a half-mile and plunged into the clear, cool, ferrous waters of Fuller Lake. Walking back to the hostel, I stopped by the store, where I talked to a super-fit 62-year-old hiker from Denver named Weather or Knot, who was not happy with the AT.

"I'm totally unimpressed," he said irritably. "All you're doing is walking through trees all the time. It's not like Colorado, where every time you look up the view is spectacular."

He was right, of course. Compared to the Rockies or Sierra, the Appalachians do not offer nearly the bounty of sheer, jaw-dropping natural beauty.

The ABCs of the trail: adventure, challenge, beauty, I wrote later in my journal. *I'm looking for all three, and it's true there is less B on the AT than the CT. But that just makes me more eager to celebrate every little change, border, or milestone. The next shelter, a 100-mile mark, a state line, a town, a railroad, a view, wildlife—I appreciate them all on the AT.*

When I got back to the hostel, I saw I wasn't the only one who had suffered in the heat. The Dude, who had straggled in with Alasdair from England, looked like he'd been dropped in a pot of boiling water; his skin was a bright, angry red wherever it had been in contact with his salt-soaked clothing. I tossed him my tube of Vagisil, which he applied liberally to good effect (though he told me later it was still one of his worst nights on the entire trail).

That night we had spectacular views of Mars, Jupiter and Saturn, enhanced by the dance of lightning bugs around the foliage and across the lawn.

Pancakes, orange juice and coffee at the hostel propelled me out the door by 7 a.m. and I was thrilled that I could maintain a speedy pace over relatively level—and not particularly rocky—ground. Maybe Pennsylvania would turn out to be like the Roller Coaster, its reputation for difficulty overblown.

For much of the day I leapfrogged Dragonhead, a young engineer who had been working in Denver but had grown up in this corner of Pennsylvania. I loved walking through cornfields the last two miles into Boiling Springs, a pretty little town that isn't very hospitable to hikers. Besides a camping area on the edge of town, there was no affordable lodging, and lunch with Dragonhead was pretty pricey at the Boiling Springs Tavern, which gave off a kind of wood-paneled, Rat Pack, or perhaps Mafia, vibe.

I'm sad to say that the staff at the Appalachian Trail Conservancy office in town didn't seem any happier about their jobs than the people in Harpers Ferry; it's a great organization, but based on my brief experience, it doesn't seem to be the greatest place to work—or maybe it was just the heat. Following their repeated warnings not to camp in the narrow corridor of AT right-of-way leaving town, I decided to put in a 27-mile day and find a motel in Carlisle.

Walking in late afternoon through mildly undulating hay fields, dells and pastures was extremely pleasant, despite the oppressive heat and the continual appearance of chafe in truly novel regions of my body. As usual when I went into town — one reason I'm not big on zeroes — I spent too much on food and lodging in Carlisle. But I rose the next morning for my 60th day of walking feeling rested, my chafe calmed by women's "intimate anti-itch" cream, and chortling over all those bogeyman stories about rocks. So far, other than the brutal heat and humidity, Pennsylvania was turning out to be breeze.

*

After six more miles of pleasant pasture walking, the next day presented a couple of short, but stout, uphill slogs. This time, the mercury percolated past 90 and the dew point was even higher. Thankfully, by mid-afternoon thunderclouds had begun to gather and as I walked a long ridge atop Cove Mountain, rain began to fall, dropping the temperature by 15 degrees.

But by the time I stood on Hawk Rock (mile 1144.6) the storm clouds were loudly announcing the coming apocalypse and the wail of an emergency claxon was sounding from tiny Duncannon, 700 feet below. Despite hiking only 15 miles, my feet were battered from the 115 miles I'd done over the previous five days. But I hustled down that mountain, fretting over what to do if a twister should actually appear.

Duncannon, with its many desultory buildings and boarded-up windows, is a sad reminder of the Rust Belt's former glory days. But it's home to a rather famous stop on the AT, the Doyle Hotel, which is just as run-down as the rest of town, maybe a little more. The Doyle is the kind of place that forces you to ponder the history behind all those stains on your mattress, and where you wouldn't be the least bit surprised to see Tom the junkie priest from *Drugstore Cowboy* hovering expectantly in your doorway. The high ceiling above the shower on the second floor hung down in moldering shreds that looked a little too much like skin sloughing off a rotting corpse.

On the other hand, Vicky and Pat, the owners, run a pretty good kitchen and make a very fine cup of New England clam chowder, indeed. As the rain slashed down outside and the claxon continued to howl—Vicky explained it was for a car accident, not a tornado—I ate heartily and drank an excellent brown ale.

I met a couple of interesting hikers, including an older guy walking with his black Labrador retriever Olive, aka Olive's Human. He was driving his own vehicle a few days up the trail, hiking back, then hitching back to his truck to drive to the next segment, mixing in SOBO and NOBO days. I also talked to Refill, happy-go-lucky young German who, like several other of his countrymen I'd met, had decided to walk the AT after seeing a documentary on German TV, and who had walked the Shennies at night along Skyline Drive to avoid the heat.

I was jawing with Vicky and finishing a truly decadent piece of chocolate cake when I looked down to see what was tickling my left knee. It was a tiny tick, no bigger than a sesame seed. I yield to almost all living things and will save spiders and worms, but I have no patience for dog-tormenting fleas or ticks. I pinched it between my thumb and forefinger and dropped it into the dregs of my beer.

"That's better than you deserve, you little fucker," I said.

At least it wasn't embedded. And though small, I observed that it was larger than the poppy-seed-sized juveniles most likely to carry dreaded Lyme disease.

"You tell yourself what you have to, honey," Vicky said, eyeing me over half-moon glasses on the tip of her nose.

Crossing the long bridge across the Susquehanna River early the next morning, I walked atop the concrete barrier between the roaring traffic and the "trail" to avoid the myriad fluttering webs woven by spiders during the night.

Spiders, I like. Ticks, no.

*

By the time I pitched my tent near a spring after just 17.4 miles that afternoon, I knew that dreaded "Rocksylvania" was not mere hyperbole, as I'd hoped. There was still some decent tread, but where there wasn't, the trail was a craggle of shattered boulders and smaller, knife-edged rocks.

It made for slow going and battered feet. Still, I couldn't fathom why I felt so wracked after such a relatively short day.

A strange day, worst on the AT so far, I wrote that evening (worse than Cinco de Freezo?). *I sweated like crazy all day, muggy, mix of clouds and sun. Maybe I got heat prostration? But my veins were full all day and I know I was drinking enough. This afternoon was a serious-ass slog and my whole body is just too bloody HOT.*

It was only 3 p.m. by the time I'd made camp and found water. But I didn't have the energy to eat and declined to move even when two SOBOs told me there was magic less than a mile down the hill at the next road. Flopping back on my Z Lite pad, I fell asleep for several hours until two hikers, King of the Freaks and Toastybuns (she had fallen into a campfire) came around after dark offering weed and some rather potent moonshine. I declined the weed, but told myself the booze would "burn out" whatever was ailing me. We talked *Lord of the Rings* and laughed, but soon I had to return to sleep.

I woke at my usual time with the birds the next morning, but forced myself to stay down, hoping more sleep would put a stake through the murderous ache thumping through my head. The night had been miserable, a maniacal oscillation between extreme heat and shivers, accompanied by constant sweating that literally left my sleeping bag sodden.

Maybe I'm just overall weak and vulnerable to sickness because I'm not eating enough? I scrawled in my journal, the last entry I would make for several days. *It better not be Lymes* (sic).

Those next days were a nightmare blur as I dragged myself a few miles—looking back, my longest day was 11, the shortest around 6—to a shelter or someplace where I could toss up the tent and collapse. Now, besides the constant thrumming in my head and fever, with its whiplash swings between teeth-chattering chills and brain-poaching heat, my joints creaked with jagged pain every time I moved. I had zero appetite.

Evidently I did not accept the obvious until several thru-hikers, including Dragonhead, and Pennsylvania day hikers convinced me that I should see a doctor. If it was Lyme disease, letting it go could permanently jeopardize my health. And so I got a ride from a local guy (Eric?) to a Subway restaurant where I called a number for a shuttle.

A nice older woman named Joyce drove me to Port Clinton (mile 1,217.2), where I dumped my pack near the hiker pavilion sponsored by St. John's Church, pulled out my sleeping bag—despite a high of 95 degrees and a dew point above 70, I was shivering—and slumped once more into an uneasy sleep.

Had I been smart, I would have had Joyce drive me straight to a doctor, but the stubborn part of me was still hoping this would pass. The next day, feeling worse than ever, I got a shuttle to a doc-in-a-box about 15 minutes away. I called ahead, but when I arrived, the nurse looked at my temperature—103.5 F—and said I needed to go to an emergency room. The shuttle guy drove me to Reading and dropped me off at St. Joseph Medical Center.

After an hour's wait, a nurse brought me to an open bay, where I would lie for the next five hours. She took blood and vitals, covered me with a blanket, and left. When Dr. Deborah Chun finally came around, she told me my white blood-cell count and platelets were low, indicating infection. Given my symptoms, and the fact that I'd come off the trail, she diagnosed and "presumptively" treated me for Lyme disease with a three-week course of doxycycline.

(Studies have found that the oft-cited calling card of Lyme disease, a "bullseye" shaped rash around the bite, is in fact present in only 40-70 percent of cases. Dr. Chun found a mark under my waistband that may have been a sign of this "erythema migrans," but it definitely wasn't a bullseye.)

Feeling only a tad better, I staggered out into the early evening sunlight and called Joyce again. Her husband Lance picked me up after about an hour and hauled me back to West Hamburg, where I got a hotel room instead of pitching a tent at the hiker pavilion five miles up the road.

Between three shuttle rides and the hotel, that cursed tick had already cost me $400, plus whatever the ER visit would end up costing, and put me through the most miserable stretch of my hike so far. I had hit rock bottom. When I called Jody, she said it was time to come home.

But I wasn't about to let the joys of Pennsylvania—the heat, the humidity, the chafe, the endless, airless green tunnel and monotonous miles of brutal rocks and bloody *ticks*—defeat me.

(In August 2020, I went back and hiked the 38 miles I "sick-blazed" during my bout with Lyme disease in Pennsylvania.)

EIGHTEEN: ROCKY II: GRANITIC BOOGALOO

July 2016: Port Clinton to Delaware Water Gap, Pa.

Springing for a room at the Microtel in Hamburg, Pa. was a smart, if expensive, move on my part after my ordeal with Lyme disease. I ate heartily for the first time in many days, watched a great movie I'd never seen before (*Goodfellas*) and slept. A lot.

I even ordered another new pair of Altra Olympus 2.0 trail shoes. While I loved the shoes, the rocks of Pennsylvania had eaten the first pair for lunch, splitting out both sides after only 350 miles. And while I have my issues with Amazon, the fact that the shoes would arrive just 20 hours later testifies to the astonishing convenience of our online world, whatever its downsides.

Accumulating evidence from hikers and shelter logbooks, I would soon realize that Pennsylvania kills not only shoes and boots, but also many hiker dreams. So many people get sick, suffer serious injuries among the rocks, lose their mojo or simply get bored somewhere along those 229 miles of trail.

I slept until 9:30 a.m., feeling better already after the first two doses of antibiotics and a handful of Ibuprofen. After repacking, I walked across the road for a resupply, then waited in the lobby until mid-afternoon until the shoes arrived. I caught a hitch back to the pavilion in Port Clinton.

"But the doctor says it's OK, and I'm on antibiotics," I explained to Jody, who (understandably) thought I was being stubborn—nay, stupid—to continue. "I'm going to gather a day or two of evidence, see how it goes. If I still feel crappy, then I'll quit."

And while I felt better, I was all too aware how exhausted I felt after only minimal activity. But the company that night at the pavilion gave me back a little pep. I ordered a pizza with a smell-the-roses young Bayou hiker named Ninja Turtle; Toastybuns had yellow-blazed to Port Clinton; Olive and Olive's Human showed up; and I met Rumblejunk, a correspondent for the *Sounds of the Trail* podcast—who, despite my nifty Lyme horror story, was not moved to put a microphone in front of my face.

That night I tried to moderate the argument running through my mind: *Going to be hot and humid again tomorrow. I should be taking it easy. There's no rush,* I wrote. *Except I hate sitting around! I really want to do a 16-20 day tomorrow.*

By morning, I still felt a little feverish, but impatience had won the debate during the night. I packed up, gave Olive a pat, and headed north.

*

On the advice of Dr. Chun, who said further exposure could result in reinfection, I had resolved to put up with a little discomfort in an effort to ward off ticks. I tucked the cuffs of my zip-off Columbia pants into a pair of calf-high REI socks, donned a loose, long-sleeve Columbia shirt and doused myself with DEET. I also had sprayed my clothes with permethrin from the hiker box at the pavilion the night before.

But maybe a half-mile into the steep, 700-foot climb out of Port Clinton, I couldn't bear all that responsibility and heat. I dumped my pack on the ground and ripped off of all that clothing as if I were a man aflame. Re-outfitting myself in my good ol' Brooks Sherpa running shorts and a short-sleeve shirt, I made a miraculous conversion to DEET-ism, placing all my faith in the miracles of modern chemistry. Still hot, but no longer on fire, I continued up the hill.

*

In Pennsylvania the basic pattern of the AT is as follows: Steep climb to a ridge, long ridgewalk in a northeasterly direction, almost always on rocks, steep descent to the next road or river, repeat. That day alternated stretches of decent tread—if I could see dirt, I was thrilled—with big, chunky, gnarly rocks.

In early afternoon, I gave myself a break and walked two-tenths of a mile down Hawk Mountain Road to Eckville Shelter, located behind a caretaker's house and featuring a solar shower. Cloudy skies meant I was in for a gasping, Navy-style session behind the curtain, but I scrubbed every crevice of my body vigorously with Dr. Bronner's, muttering triumphantly at any ticks I might have picked up.

An 800-foot climb brought me to the Pinnacle (mile 1226.7) and Pulpit Rock (mile 1224.5)—*Clambering over everything from refrigerator-sized boulders to basketball-sized blocks for mile after mile*, I wrote. But at least those spots offered long, lovely views of the Lehigh Valley, including of the virginal rain curtains trailing down from sky to the west.

For my first day back on trail, and considering all the rocks, I was pleased at my progress. After slipping and sliding two-tenths of a mile downhill to fill up at Dan's Spring, I finally looked at Guthook's and was thrilled to see I was just 1.5 miles from the Allentown Hiking Club Shelter—a half hour more!

Five minutes later, I was completely drenched after the sky's cup ranneth over. I spent the next mile splashing and grumbling. Then, as if I were in a ridiculous cartoon, the torrent stopped a minute before I reached the shelter, which was already crowded and draped with wet gear. I snagged one of the narrow, shelf-like upper bunks and set about making dinner and preparing for the next day.

I am, I confess, an unregenerate "pack exploder"—once I've got my pad out, whether in a tent or shelter, I can't seem to help but haul out virtually everything in my pack. I am downright ritualistic when it comes to placing items back where they belong—as thru-hiker and ATC ridgerunner Miss

America says, "You should be able to find anything you need in total darkness"—but I view every day as a new opportunity to achieve Packing Perfection®, that elusive state of hiking nirvana in which everything comes out of the pack *precisely* in the order needed. For this reason, and no other, I can't see myself ever using a hammock—I love sleeping in them, but there's no place to safely explode!

My fellow travelers that night included chatty Chef Ducky from Indiana and her friend Monarch, a woman of few words from Utah, and Tapeworm, a quiet, good-looking younger guy. Later, those on the floor scooched and made enough room for a soaked SOBO couple that burst around the corner in a hail of noise. Bonnie and Clyde immediately turned on music and began the lengthy project of rolling cigarettes on clumsy, hand-cranked machine that had to weigh two pounds, at least.

There was something off about the pair from the get-go. I heard Bonnie tell someone she was a former medical student who had recently spent time in a mental hospital. And when Clyde couldn't find his cell phone, he began muttering immediately and audibly that someone in the shelter had stolen it.

"We're thru hiking SOBO," Bonnie announced. "We started at Killington, Vermont. We're from up there so we don't need to do the Whites and Maine."

Clyde complained bitterly about the misery of the "boardwalks in New Jersey" and railed against the exposure and difficulty of the Knife Edge (mile 1246.4), blasting an unnamed "they" for forcing hikers to traverse a rock formation so insane you could easily fall to your death.

"They're gonna get sued someday," he proclaimed, cigarette embers flying from his emphatic hand.

It was one of just two times on the AT that I was uncomfortable with people I met.

"I wasn't too thrilled about that crazy couple," Monarch said a couple days later. She thought they might be on meth, and I agreed.

At the bottom of the hill the next morning I saw a hand-written note from someone who had found a cell phone on the trail: *Call your number and I'll get it back to you!* But Bonnie and Clyde were headed SOBO and I doubt they ever saw it.

*

I've traversed another feature called the "the knife edge," on the way to the summit of one of Colorado's more challenging 14,000-foot mountains, Capitol Peak. It's extremely exposed but not that difficult if you know what you're doing. I couldn't imagine Pennsylvania's version was anywhere near as exposed, and I was right. It was a rocky ridge that required the use of hands here and there, a little slippery in the rain, but it seemed no more dangerous than many other places on the trail.

I spent much of the day walking with Old Spice, a speedy, 51-year-old Pennsylvania guy who was hiking the trail with his son, Axe. His son was (for reasons I can't recall) off trail that day, so Old Spice was slackpacking. Our conversation made the time and miles pass swiftly. But once again, the skies burst asunder 1.5 miles from the nearest shelter, unleashing battering deluge. It poured for a solid half hour, but by the time we reached Outerbridge Shelter, the clouds had moved on and the sun was out as if it had all been a dream.

Reclining in the shelter was a group of six battered-looking but cheery young people on a SOBO section hike. When I found out that two of the girls had horrific blisters, I rummaged for my trusty roll of Leukotape and played trail doctor. I could not believe what I saw when one girl put her feet in my lap: the aqua-painted nails on two middle toes of one foot had been pushed up by pearls of white blister, giving them the appearance of googly Gollum eyes. After lancing them with a clean needle to reduce the pain and pressure, I taped her up. Then I cleaned and taped ragged, bloody blisters on the other girl's feet.

"Your trail name should be Doc," said the girl with blue-eyed toes.

In a most welcome impersonation of typical Rocky Mountain summer weather, the rain had yielded to a warm, breezy, surprisingly dry afternoon. Despite our soaking, Old Spice and I were thoroughly dry by the time we hit the bridge across the Lehigh River. His cousin arrived to pick him up 15 minutes later and they gave me a ride to beautiful downtown Palmerton.

Palmerton was long notable to hikers for two things: the Sunny Rest nudist resort on the edge of town (I didn't go, but The Dude later told me he'd enjoyed it) and the Jail House Hostel, a bank of unused jail cells in the basement of a government building. After the jailhouse closed following the 2015 season, the enterprising owner of the excellent Bert's Steakhouse & Restaurant rigged up a shower off the alley, set out a bunch of cots in a cinder-block garage and, voila!, a low-key, cheap hostel was born.

During a short after-dinner walk—I did mention I can't sit still, didn't I?—in the park across the street, I was baffled to see dozens of people, young and old, wandering around at dusk staring resolutely at their smart-phone screens. Finally, while dabbling my feet in a small stream where two earthier boys were fishing, I asked their mother what was going on.

"Oh, that's Pokémon GO," she said. "I can't believe you haven't heard of it."

This cultural wave—a virtual geocaching game in which you seek out and collect Pokemon characters and items—crested in a few faddish weeks in July, then crashed and receded just as quickly. I learned later that the whole thing was (surprise) just another method of collecting data on unsuspecting humans, which was later sold to the highest bidder. Thankfully, I never saw anyone playing on the AT.

Tapeworm also took a $10 bunk out behind Bert's, joining me and a kid who was waiting to be picked up the next morning. The kid (I neglected to write down his name) was abandoning the AT for good after contracting a gruesome-looking case of cellulitis on one leg following a spider bite.

"I was going to just get off for a week or two, until I got better," he said. "But then I started thinking. I'm not having that much fun, so what else could I be doing with my time?"

PA DESTROYS DREAMS, I wrote that night.

Still, every time I truthfully answered a local's query, "How are you enjoying Pennsylvania?" by declaring their state the armpit of the AT so far, most cheerily agreed and seemed to take it as a compliment on their "toughness." Fair enough. But tough is one thing, and miserable is something else entirely. The trail had been plenty tough all along but there were rewards. Pennsylvania's many physical miseries were, for me, compounded by the mental drudgery of an endless green tunnel suffocating under astounding heat and humidity, which only occasionally coughed up a view or glimpse of wildlife.

Having said all that, the next morning turned out to be a highlight. Tapeworm and I rose early and quickly caught a hitch from an old local guy who took us all the way up to the trail. I reveled in the rocky scramble from Lehigh Gap up to the Palmerton Zinc Pile Superfund site, which is, according to some geeks at WhiteBlaze.net, the 32nd steepest half mile on the trail. This was my kind of hiking.

Just like shootin' womp rats in Beggars' Canyon back home, I wrote in my journal.

And, thanks to the ongoing mitigation of the environmental contamination atop the ridge, the next four miles are a lovely stroll along a grassy hillside. I sang out loud and stopped every few minutes to eat ripe blackberries and raspberries like a bear, not caring even a little whether they might be loaded with toxic chemicals from the EPA site just up the hill.

Views! Berries! Open air! No rocks! I wrote.

But then, after a few miles of this pleasant ambling, you come to a gravel road used by vehicles working on the Superfund site. Following the road would be a blue blaze, so in good conscience, you follow the white blazes into the woods, and you are soon back to the grind, painstakingly picking through a jumble of granite blocks and rocks for several miles. It appears to be perfectly flat in Awol, but only because the scale of the elevations can't pick up the constant hopping up and down from rock to rock, boulder to boulder, crag to crag. It's not just tiring and tough on your feet, but also mentally exhausting—lose focus for one second and you might well sprain an ankle, bust a wrist or knock yourself silly.

Halfway through the obstacle course, I caught a tantalizing glimpse of the Superfund service road through the trees. All I'd have to do was scramble 50 yards down, then walk it out on a smooth gravel track ... ahhhh. But no. I'd blown my purism several times over, but never just because it was a pain in the ass. So I turned away from temptation, and several miles later, feet throbbing, tears springing to my eyes, crossed the utility road for the last time.

It irritated me because it showed that, in theory, the trail could have been routed along the flanks of all those Pennsylvania ridges, rather than sadistically forcing hikers to navigate all the endless, brutal, rock-strewn miles that geological history has scattered like broken glass across the top. It's almost as if they (not that there is really a "they") said, "We're going to make this mofo as hard as we can possibly make it, no matter what."

But, as if in reward for my refusal to blue-blaze, shortly after I saw bears No. 5 and 6 on that rocky ridge. I heard a cub yowl, then turned to see it tumble out of a tree and join mama. I got a nice view before they barreled off the south side of the ridge, but once again, no photo.

After another long, hot, mind-numbing march through the green tunnel, I decided to hike a full mile down into Wind Gap on the promise of a good meal. But here was a town that didn't seem to cater to, or particularly appreciate, hikers. I ate some greasy high-priced food at a sports bar, where the server squinched her face in disgust each time she approached and plucked up the cash I laid upon the bar as if it were used toilet paper; she probably went back and put it in the microwave.

Tired and cranky, I considered knocking on a door to ask if I could pitch a tent in one of the big yards along the road. But fearing I'd be greeted with a shotgun, I instead hiked a mile uphill back to the trail. Two full sideways miles for a crummy, expensive supper.

After mounting the 500-foot climb to the next ridge, I found a flat spot off in the woods and pitched my tent. As I was cooking dinner, Monarch came rolling by, planning to hike into darkness to complete her first 30-mile day. She wanted to get within 10 miles of Delaware Water Gap—the end of PA!—where she planned to take a nero.

I feel sad, hot, tired and lonely, I wrote. *Pennsylvania sucks. So glad it's almost over.*

In a reflection of the exhaustion the Keystone State had wreaked upon my body and soul, from the time I left Duncannon until the day I crossed into New Jersey, I took a grand total of four photos, averaging just one every two days.

Fortunately, I was only 14 miles from the end of Penns(hell)vania myself. I pushed hard through more dastardly rocks and a very long, hot downhill slog, arriving at the Presbyterian Church of the Mountain Hostel—the oldest continuous hostel on the AT—just after noon the next day. Monarch was there. Tapeworm arrived later, as did a yellow-blazing Chef Ducky.

An old guy hanging around the hostel offered resupply rides for tips, and on the way back, I had him drop me at a barbecue place up the road. My thrill at putting Pennsylvania in the rearview mirror was tempered somewhat by a strange phone call with my mother in Colorado and a nasty email connected to a business relationship I'd severed before I'd even set foot on the AT. My mom claimed her 2004 Honda Pilot had been stolen in broad daylight in downtown Boulder, Colorado, an exceedingly unlikely proposition that would of course turn out not to be true when police towed it eight days later. This was the first clear indication to me that she might be experiencing the early stages of dementia, and I vowed to look into it once I'd finished my hike.

I also spent 45 minutes on the phone with Laura Richards, a former Scotland Yard investigator and co-producer of a new documentary who wanted to talk to me about my work on the JonBenet Ramsey murder case as a journalist. I wasn't in the two-part movie, and haven't seen it myself, but it was widely panned as exploitative, and the producers later were sued by the person they chose to more or less finger for the murder based on irresponsible speculation.

Still, my spirits were high. I enjoyed a peach ice-cream cone from the parlor across the street with Monarch and Chef Ducky, and Monarch later gave me some cheese sticks, Cutie oranges and an avocado she couldn't fit in her food bag. For the remainder of my hike, I would carry an avocado whenever possible.

And once more, the trail schooled me in the folly of judgment. Upon first meeting Monarch I had made up a story in my head—standoffish, snooty, East Coast city type. Talking to her, I saw that she was reserved, but no snob, and we had a great conversation. Far from the person I'd conjured in my imagination, she was a veteran of the Iraq and Afghanistan wars who had been widowed at 23 when her spouse committed suicide.

My judgment of Monarch was—surprise!—wrong, I wrote. *When will I ever learn?*

*

At 6:20 the next morning, I crossed the Delaware River.

The best thing about Pennsylvania, I wrote, *is that it makes* New Jersey *feel like the Promised Land. Free at last! Free at last! Thank you trail gods, I'm free at last!*

Not that I believe in trail gods.

NINETEEN: JERSEY JOYS

July 2016: Delaware Water Gap to Fingerboard Shelter, N.Y.

I crossed beneath the rumble of traffic on I-80, remembering the time I'd driven the highway more than three decades earlier. My girlfriend, best friend and I were in my two-toned green '73 Ford F150 pickup, on our way from Colorado to New York.

The long, gentle climb to the flat summit of Kittatinny Mountain was refreshingly open, compared to the suffocating woods of the state-that-shall-not-be-named. Five miles into my day, I spied the largest bear I'd seen, sitting on his haunches perhaps 30 yards off trail. Violating a well-known rule of bear encounters, I just couldn't take my eyes off him as I continued up the trail. Plenty of time to take a photo, but once again I didn't, not wanting to stop and unduly alarm this large beast. In fact, my overall photo production was slipping every day—I took only six photos in all of New Jersey, none of myself.

In his AT thru-hiking memoir, David "Awol" Miller frets that he hadn't seen any bears by Standing Indian Mountain (mile 87.8), where he met two SOBOs who never saw a single one in more than 2,100 miles. He sees his first near the 300-mile mark: "A small bear is running away from me. But the time I get my camera, the bear is out of sight. ... that may be the only bear I see." As soon as he puts his camera away, two more appear, the first of many more.

"I'll catch the next one," I told myself.

Alas, No. 7 would turn out to be the last of my bruin encounters (though in later section hikes I've added several more to my tally). I was happy to have seen seven bears, though wish I'd seen more; Awol saw 21; some 2016 hikers saw 30 or 40.

Although there were rocks aplenty on the trail, walking in New Jersey was a joy. There were sprawling ponds, shimmering meadows, and generous views from nearly every ridgetop. I began to see a heartening number of frogs, toads and snakes, as well as many deer.

Ten miles into that pleasant day I came upon the Appalachian Mountain Club's Mohican Outdoor Center, which I'd managed not to notice in Awol. After downing two quarts of Gatorade, eating some snacks and charging my phone at the visitor center, I resisted my usual forward-motion obsession and detoured a half a mile to the swimming beach on Catfish Pond, where I spent the next hour lazing in the cool, clear water and drying in the hot sun. I resolved that day to swim at every available opportunity for the rest of my hike.

As I'd heard from several trail-hardened SOBOs, New Jersey was hardly less rocky than the previous state—ditto for most of the final 900 miles of the trail—and my feet were throbbing by the time I reached Brink Road Shelter (mile 1317.8) after a 25-mile day. But New Jersey was just the right balm to soothe wounds inflicted by that bitter purgatory behind me. Who knew the "armpit of America" was so lovely?

"Well, we *are* the Garden State, after all," a friend remarked when I expressed my newfound admiration for her native state.

*

My Jersey high tailed off somewhat on the second day, as the trail traversed rocks through a green tunnel, causing a certain amount of Pennsylvania PTSD. Still, occasional views to enticing lakes far below helped break the monotony. I was feeling worn out, having rather foolishly averaged more than 20 miles a day since starting treatment for Lyme disease. And though I'd dismissed warnings that the antibiotics would make me sun-sensitive, every bit of exposed skin now sizzled uncomfortably. My spirit was burning out, as well.

Maybe I'll leave NH-ME for next season, I wrote. *But I'm committing to VT!*

On the spur of the moment, I stopped and called a '15 thru-hiker who had posted a handwritten sign at the foot of Kittatinny advertising her "home hostel" in Port Jervis, N.Y. Mosey, a retired postal worker, picked me up at the headquarters for High Point State Park just before it started to rain.

For the next 15 hours, it was like having a personal assistant as she shuttled me to a fantastic local burger joint (mind-blowing strawberry shake) and we talked trail. Back at her place, I took a much-needed shower and did laundry while she rescued four sodden young hikers from the downpour. We all stayed in the same room and watched the ridiculous movie *Jaws 2* before I fell asleep.

And though it was not promised, Mosey had pancakes, bacon, coffee and fresh orange juice ready for me when I rose at 6 a.m. Thanks to her hospitality, I felt refreshed and ready to run all the way to Katahdin when she dropped me off just before 7 a.m. After passing beneath the 220-foot spire of the High Point State Park veterans' monument, the trail takes a 90-degree turn and tickles the New York border for the next 30 miles or so.

For the first time in weeks I wasn't boiling over, as temperatures peaked in the mid-70s. The dewpoint had tumbled to a mere 50 degrees ("very comfortable," according to the U.S. Occupational Health and Safety Administration) and a sweet little 10 mph breeze blew throughout the day. Eleven miles in I was feeling no pain, singing to myself as I strolled merrily along.

The trail pops out of the woods for a 0.7-mile roadwalk before turning straight south into the Wallkill Wildlife Refuge. As I meandered along Oil City Road, Mudpuppy rolled up behind me. Tall, laid-back, with a mop of curly brown hair, we'd met all the way back at Partnership Shelter. We walked together until I stopped to buy a tomato at an honor-system farm stand. But soon I saw him coming back down the road.

"We're not on the trail," he said.

I pulled out my phone to look at Guthook, which has the advantage of showing you precisely where you are in relation to the trail (courtesy of GPS that works even in airplane mode). Sure enough, we were nearly a mile away from where the trail turned into the preserve—how had I not noticed all those missing blazes?

"Dammit," I muttered.

But at least I was in good company. After three more right angles and two miles through in the preserve, the trail emerged onto Lake Wallkill Road—just three-quarters of a mile from where Mudpuppy had turned around. Plus, I hit the first magic I'd seen since southern Virginia just before the road, a cooler full of soda left by a former thru-hiker named Pigpen, who requested only that hikers leave a note in his logbook. This was mine:

There once was a hiker's good friend,
Who went by the name of Pigpen.
Soda pop he'd provide,
And those who imbibed,
Thought they'd died and gone to hea-VEN.

The crazy couple Bonnie and Clyde had raved about the terrible, hot hassle of New Jersey's boardwalks. But I found the mile-long elevated walkway over the marshlands between the Pochuck River and Wayawanda Creek both beautiful and fun, a truly new experience on the trail. After a pleasant walk through a pasture full of cattle, I turned left on NJ 94 and walked one-tenth of a mile to Heaven Hill Farm, beloved among hot hikers for its ice cream and fruit.

I was already packing a fat, ripe tomato from the farmstand, and had an avocado in my bag. Now I added grapes and a nectarine to my personal produce section. I also downed a Dr. Pepper and snapped up a bit of candy for the road.

Checking my phone—I kept it in airplane mode almost of the time, checking for messages when I could get wifi—I saw a text from Mosey: She had found my solar phone charger still plugged in to the wall. In an incredibly angelic gesture, she offered to drive it out to me the following day if we could agree on someplace to meet.

Feeling energized, I crossed the highway and began the 900-foot climb up the side of Wayawanda Mountain, aka the "Stairway to Heaven," the 74th steepest half-mile of the AT. The view from the Pinwheels Vista blew my mind: That 220-foot tower I'd passed in the morning was now a barely visible splinter at the absolute limit of the horizon.

It's hard to believe I can walk that far, I wrote later, and I would walk another three-and-a-half miles to Wayawanda Shelter (mile 1361.9). In a welcome change from my usual convenience-first diet, my dinner that night consisted entirely of real food, raised in dirt: fresh tomato, avocado, grapes and nectarines.

Mudpuppy showed up a little later and declared his intention to hike 26.4 miles the next day to Fingerboard Shelter. Naturally, I took that as a challenge to do the same. Having promised to meet Mosey at 11 a.m. at a hot-dog stand on NY 17A, I left the shelter at 6:20 a.m.

But the going was surprisingly tough and slow, especially after I crossed into New York (mile 1365.4). Rolling through miles and miles of forest, the trail constantly crosses short, very steep, sometimes mildly technical, ribs of granite—including the famous Lemon Squeezer, which I managed to eke through without removing my pack—all of which slowed my pace considerably.

"Despite the unimposing profile," Awol writes in a note marked with a (!), "rocks, abrupt ups & downs make this section challenging."

The grouchy old man at the hot-dog stand wouldn't let me sit at his picnic table unless I bought something, so I ate chips and drank a Coke while waiting for Mosey. She showed up right on time, and then, out of the goodness of her heart agreed to drive me down to the tiny burg of Green Lake. It was an expensive place to resupply, but I had inexplicably neglected to shop while staying with her and my food bag was on the light side. I tipped her $20 before waving goodbye again.

New Jersey and New York, which I'd heard were somewhat inhospitable, were turning out to be a magic kingdom. Exhausted after battling the terrain, I was deeply grateful to find Chief Two-Sticks and Paddy-O, each of whom had set up on remote roads, offering Gatorade, soda, Oreos, candy and even Yuengling beer.

More worrisome than food was the fact that New York was experiencing an extreme drought, and many of its seasonal springs, brooks and streams were turning out to be dry, as were a few sources listed by Awol as reliable. But trail angels were on top of the problem, and I hardly crossed a road where someone had not set out jugs of water, though occasionally they were empty by the time I got there.

When I left Paddy-O at 3:30, he predicted I'd reach Fingerboard Shelter (7.6 miles away; mile 1387.7) at 7:30. I doubted it would take me that long. Four hours of hiking what I later described as *Tough $#!@@! stuff, not even 2 mph!* later, I ruefully had to admit that Paddy-O knew this terrain better than I did.

There was one, last 700-foot EoDMoFo after I entered New York's Harriman State Park. Near the top, I ran into some guys handing out Yuengling beer. Among the other takers were thru-hikers BASA (an acronym for Big Ass Stone Arrows, a name he received on the PCT), a retired firefighter from the Bay Area, and Achilles, a young college cross-country runner from North Carolina—an odd couple who had walked together since meeting near the beginning of the trail—and a cheerful Japanese couple with enviably small packs and minimal English skills.

Although it was hot, the long, steep hillsides in the park in Harriman were open and beautiful. Late-day filtered sunlight sprinkled through a canopy of widely-spaced trees, dappling acres of silky grass. It looked like something out of a long-lost Maxfield Parrish print.

Built in 1928, Fingerboard is the oldest shelter on the trail, and it shows. But despite its lumpy construction, sagging roof, crumbling mortar and healthy population of globular, Shelob-sized spiders, the place had an undeniable charm. BASA and Achilles rolled in not long after I did and pitched tents, as did the Japanese couple. Mudpuppy never did show up, though I would see him again. All this meant I had the funky old stone shelter to myself.

No idea what I'm doing tomorrow, but after 52 miles in two days over tough terrain, I need to back off. Legs are hammered and my hands, nose, arms and top of my head are sizzling with doxycycline-induced photosensitivity, I wrote. *Do like the Eagles, dumb-ass—take it easy!*

TWENTY: HOT AND BOTHERED

July 2016: Fingerboard Shelter to Ralph Peak Hiker Cabin

I was surprised to find that BASA, Achilles and the Japanese couple already breaking camp by the time I got up at 5:30. They were long gone by the time I got going at 6:10, and it was already hot.

After walking for about 15 minutes, I came upon BASA and Achilles at a road leading down to Lake Tiorati. They headed on, but I decided to walk three-tenths of a mile down to the beach area. When I got there, I found it fenced off and locked up.

Refusing to waste my sideways investment, I walked to the end of the fence, shrugged off my pack, took off my shoes and socks and waded in. Well outside the artificially sandy bottom of the designated swimming area, I sank ankle-deep into oozy mud. I dived out and otter-rolled a few times, hoping to remove at least some of the sweat from my shirt and shorts, but it wasn't very satisfying, or fun. At least my clothes were cool for the next mile or two.

The walk to Bear Mountain, like so much of the trail in New Jersey and

New York, dipped and rose frequently between granite-ribbed ridgetops. With temperatures ticking toward 90, I was sweating like a horse. I'd left the lake with 2.5 liters of water, but drank it all before reaching the steep stone steps up Bear Mountain.

I always carried a tall, liter-size bottle in a side pocket of my pack, where I could easily reach it. When expecting a long walk to the next water source, I also filled up the bladder in my pack to 1.5 or 1.75 liters, securing the pinch-valved tube to my pack strap for easy access.

(Embarrassing aside: Throughout my hike, I made the mistake of setting my loaded pack on the pinch valve, causing water to drain out of the bladder all over a shelter, tent or hostel floor. You'd think, like forgetting my poles, this would be a rookie screw-up, but I continued to do it until well into Massachusetts, where someone showed me that the valve has a locking mechanism.)

Usually I treated water with Aqua Mira drops, an excellent, virtually tasteless system that requires only a five-minute pit stop, followed by a 15-minute wait to allow the chemicals to do the job. I also carried a Sawyer Mini filter, which could be screwed right onto the liter-bottle, but like so many other hikers, I lost the use of it after the O-ring fell out without my noticing. Against the advice of many, I sometimes drank unfiltered, untreated water from springs, and streams when atop a mountain or high ridge.

Near the summit of Bear Mountain, I came upon a pride of hikers panting like savannah lions around the oasis of two overpriced vending machines. Heedless of the price gouging, I glugged two quarts of PowerAde and greedily filled my face with the blessedly salty contents of two stubby canisters of Pringle's potato chips.

Though exhausted and half-delirious with heat, I forced myself to walk up the stairwell to the Bear Mountain observation tower. I'd had my doubts, but sure enough, on this clear, dry July day, I could actually see the distant skyline of New York City some 40 miles away.

Feeling a tad woozy, I tramped as fast as I could down the other side of the mountain, drinking in occasional glimpses of dark blue Hessian Lake 1,100 feet below. On the way down, I passed a gaggle of teenagers clustered on a hairpin turn of the trail.

"Don't go down there!" one kid said. "There's a hornet's nest in that dead tree trunk."

I have some kindness in my heart for virtually every living thing, except for fleas and ticks. Also, though my wife used to tease me about my efforts to save "your beloved 'hor-nays'" when I balked at putting out a yellow-jacket trap, I'm not a big fan. I edged cautiously down the trail, close enough to see the broken trunk sizzling with a cloud of hyperactive hornets.

Unfortunately, there was really nowhere else to go on the steep hillside, unless one wanted to bushwhack through brush and weeds that were probably teeming with something even worse, say, ticks. In a moment of bravery— or perhaps stupidity—I decided to make a run for it. The tread was smooth enough, and if I didn't fall and break my face, I might get through the gauntlet unstung. Thankfully, my gambit paid off. The kids up the hill shouted after me—"Dude, you are *crazy!*" and "No way I'm doing that!"

When I finally staggered out of the woods at the bottom, I was disappointed to find the lakeshore bristling with signs prohibiting all swimming. But I was able to pour water from a drinking fountain over my head, after which I cameled up, filled my bottle and bladder, and continued on, somewhat refreshed. Alas, the two bandanas I had tied over my head weren't doing much to shield my head from the relentless sun.

Then, as I approached the pedestrian tunnel under US 9, I heard the unmistakable summer sound of children shrieking and splashing. Around the next corner I saw a vast, wedge-shaped pool glistening with sapphire water and more than a hundred revelers, mostly kids. This was magic of a different sort, and I wasn't about to miss it. I got in line to pay the $4 fee.

"Hikers get in free," said the girl at the cash register. "You're a hiker, right?"

I was too hot to bother showering before stripping down to boxer-briefs. Ignoring a few disapproving looks, I plunged into the bracingly cold waters of Bear Mountain Pool. After lolling there like an overfed seal for 10 minutes, I got out to lie on the hot deck, then repeated the process. Twice. I leisurely ate an ice-cream bar from another overpriced vending machine before reluctantly scraping back into my salt-encrusted clothes and headed up the trail.

When reading about the AT before you've hiked it, it's difficult to envision what it's really like. My vision of the Pennsylvania rocks was completely off, and so was my impression of the famous "zoo walk" at the foot of Bear Mountain, at 124 feet the lowest elevation on the trail. The Trailside Museum, as it's called, houses animals native to the area that cannot be released to the wild due to injury or disability. The place had a desultory feel to it; the poor deer, foxes, bears, raptors and other critters barely moved in the oppressive heat. Still, they appeared well cared-for, and were probably just reacting to the extreme heat.

After crossing the Hudson River on the Bear Mountain Bridge (its walkway studded with signs for suicide-prevention hotlines; apparently it's a hotspot for jumpers), I began climbing the flanks of Anthony's Nose, the 71st steepest half-mile on the AT. Sweating profusely, I already missed that cool jewel of a pool.

I kept walking until I reached US 9, where a number of hikers had gathered at picnic tables outside the Appalachian Market. I ordered and ate half of an enormous quesadilla, drank two bottles of Gatorade, and hung out with Five Fingers, the quiet hiker wearing minimalist Bedrock sandals I'd met way back in Virginia. He talked me into stopping at Graymoor Spiritual Life Center, a Franciscan monastery just a mile's walk away, where hikers could pitch tents on an unused ballfield free of charge. There were portable toilets, a small pavilion with electrical outlets to charge a phone, even a solar shower.

It was a fine night. I talked with Five Fingers and got to know BASA and Achilles better. That dynamic duo, three decades apart in age, were putting up even more miles than I had with my crew in Virginia, and even more impressively: They'd given themselves a challenge to walk 300 miles in 12 days—25 miles a day, every day—then gone out and done it.

There also was an older hiker who I learned was from my hometown, Boulder, Colorado. When he said I looked familiar, I explained that I'd worked for the local paper, and my photo had appeared weekly with my column for more than 20 years.

"Sometimes people recognize me from that," I said.

When he asked my name, I told him.

"You're not Clay Evans," he said.

I assured him I was.

"You don't look like your photo in the paper."

"Yeah, well, that's a pretty old picture." Ten years old, in fact, and since then, I'd started hiking and lost considerable weight. I pointed out how curious it would be for someone who *wasn't* me to claim my identity on the Appalachian Trail. What would be the point? He agreed.

Alan Carpenter, 69, didn't go in for trail names. Already a veteran of a PCT thru-hike, he was now was nearly two-thirds the way through the AT. He typically hiked 20 miles a day, and almost never took zeroes, which, I thought, was pretty darned impressive, given his age. We've remained friends over the years, getting together when I'm in Boulder. Since we met, he's done three cross-country bike tours (San Diego to Jacksonville; Anacortes, Washington to Bar Harbor, Maine; and the entire Pacific Coast) and, at the time of this writing, was completing the Continental Divide Trail, which will make him a Triple Crowner at age 73!

Although we never really formed a proper trail family, BASA, Achilles, Alan and I would see each other off and on over the next several weeks, and I enjoyed the continuity. The trail was telling me once again that maybe I wasn't quite the lone wolf I told myself I was.

That night, my body felt totally thrashed. I had just hiked 22 miles in extremely hot, dry conditions, and become semi-dehydrated on the way up Bear Mountain. I'd walked more than 90 miles in the past four days.

This would be a good time to take a zero, I wrote in my journal.

But of course, I didn't.

*

The next day was even hotter, with a high temperature of 95 in nearby Peekskill. Rambling through a suffocating tunnel of forest, the trail ambled through an endless series of small, steep climbs and descents, the kind of hiking I find most taxing.

But major props to the state of New York, which has an excellent, well-managed system of state parks. It was a full mile downhill on a rocky blue blaze to Canopus Lake in Clarence Fahnestock State Park, but I would have gone even further in my desperation to dunk my baking brain in cool water. Speedy BASA and Achilles were already there, and Alan showed up not long after.

I ate lunch, a burger and fries, a few snacks and, grudgingly, an overpriced Adidas cap made of technical fabric. Still photosensitive from the antibiotics, the sun had been drilling a hole in the top of my head through two bandanas.

After buying three quart bottles of Gatorade—my tolerance was rising—I strolled down to the sandy beach. Dumping my pack in the shade, I headed for the water with Achilles. Barefoot, we found ourselves yelping and sprinting the last few yards across the sizzling sand. But then I stood in the cool, clear, chest-high water in shirt and shorts, a strand of weed dangling from my new cap. I felt like a contented moose.

I stripped off to boxer-briefs and tried to lie in the shade for a while, but I'm just not a nap taker. After dipping myself once more, fully clothed, I retraced my steps along the shore, and climbed back up the hill to the AT. Looking down on the lake from a rocky perch at mile 1423.4, I was already streaming with sweat. Swimming is great, but it doesn't last.

RPH Shelter (mile 1428.7) is actually a small cabin, formerly known as Ralph's Peak Hiker's Cabin. I couldn't help but refer to it as RPG (Rocket-Propelled Grenade) Shelter. It's famous for being just two-tenths of a mile from New York's Taconic State Parkway, which means you can order take-out from several local restaurants. Achilles and BASA had set up their tents on the broad lawn where several other hikers lay about in hammocks. Although the interior of the building was stifling, I opted for a bunk and crossed my fingers that it would cool down after nightfall. I opened every window in the place, then called a Chinese place whose menu I'd plucked from a stack on a table.

Only two other hikers decided to brave the airless heat of the cabin. One was Skeeter (not her real trail name; you'll see why soon), who hailed from a Nordic country and expressed deep and genuine gratitude when I'd offered her my leftover Chinese. The other was a young guy with a big red beard who put in earplugs, rolled over, and never said a word.

Skeeter was in mourning. Her visa was about to run out, and the next day she was going to board an Amtrak train at the official Appalachian Trail RR Station. After staying a couple days with a friend in the city, she would fly back across the Atlantic. She was eager to talk, long after hiker midnight.

"I'm really going to miss the trail," she said as we lay in the dark, our heads just a foot apart. "Where I'm from, we have nothing like this. Even in the country, you can barely go five kilometers without houses or roads or towns. I wish I had time to keep going, but I'm going to come back and finish."

On the other hand, she said, she would *not* miss the mosquitoes that had been plaguing her. While she was eating Chinese leftovers, I'd noticed myriad scabs on her limbs and long, thin trickles of blood from too much scratching.

"Mosquitoes are attracted to people who have been drinking and who have a certain blood type," Skeeter said in her sing-song, but grammatically precise, English from the shadows behind my head. "Also, people who haven't had sex."

"Who have *not* had sex?" I asked, never having heard this theory before.

"Yes. That's why they like me, I think," Skeeter said thoughtfully. "I've been really, really horny. … You know?"

"Uh, yeah," I said, my attention now sharp.

"I think it's hormonal," she cheerily speculated. "Like, when you don't have sex, your body just keeps producing hormones that attract the mosquitoes."

Lying there so close, I could literally hear her every breath. With summer insects screaming in the high trees, I pondered the situation. She was cute. It seemed unlikely that this smart, fun, attractive 20-something woman was coming on to a grungy, skinny, unshaven guy more than twice her age. It's just her refreshingly frank Nordic attitude about sex, I told myself. On the other hand, maybe she was feeling so grateful for the gift of food…?

Sex on the trail. It happens. When he joined our family in Virginia, Eazy-E had just ended a month-long relationship with Bambi, widely reputed to be the most attractive woman on the AT in 2016 (personally I would nominate Kaleidoscope, the young Ecuadorian-American hiker, though when I really think about it, *everybody* I met on the trail was mighty beautiful by simple virtue of being out there and helping to create the experience for everyone else).

But considering the general lack of energy after hiking all day, and quandaries concerning hygiene, I'm guessing sex mostly happens in town.

Which doesn't mean that hikers don't think about it. There were days when that's virtually *all* I thought about. As Eazy-E so colorfully put it, "All these dudes out here are up to their eyeballs in baby-batter." Taking care of your own business, so to speak, isn't exactly something you can do in a shelter—unless you have it all to yourself; anyone who pulled that kind of stunt would be strung-up as bear-bait and sprayed with bacon grease right-quick. But tents are private and the woods are vast....

I surveyed a handful of women (including my wife) about whether Skeeter had been hitting on me when she presented her mosquito/sex theory, and the verdict was unanimous: Telling a man, no matter how pungent, haggard or old he may be, that you are horny is a come-on. My own baby-batter levels were peaking that night, and I confess that had I not been married, I would have been happy to help Skeeter with her little mosquito problem....

"Well," I finally said, feeling a tad pouty about missing out, "mosquitoes don't seem to bother me much."

"Oh, OK," Skeeter said after a pregnant pause. "I guess that's a good thing...."

TWENTY-ONE: COOLING IT IN CONNECTICUT

July 2016: RPH Shelter to Salisbury, Connecticut

I n his memoir, "Awol on the Appalachian Trail," David Miller remarks that the trail through much of New Jersey and New York doesn't get the respect it deserves—it can be tough going. But all that changes north of RPG Shelter, he writes: "The trail is much less difficult than it had been in the southern part of the state. There is less rock on the footpath and more packed dirt and grass. The trail rolls over small hills and cuts through pastureland."

On the whole, I found Awol (who has since passed the AT-guide torch to Tinman) to be a wealth of impressively accurate information about the Appalachian Trail, in both the memoir and his widely used guidebook. Yet I ran into a surprising number of hikers, mostly younger, who casually tossed off the accusation, "Awol *lies!*"

While there are a few minor inaccuracies in the guidebook, most should be attributed not to Miller, but changes that occur between the time he publishes the guide and peak hiking season. The book usually arrives in January, which means Miller has had to assemble information on every hostel, restaurant, outfitter, water source, shelter, mileage change and so much more no later than October or November, at the outside.

His pampered critics whine about a puny percentage of misinformation (personally, I didn't encounter any mistakes) and seem to assume it's deliberate, or that he's "lazy." They know nothing about the exigencies of publishing or the amount of time it must take to gather such granular details, year after year. These are no doubt the same hikers one hears bitching about the mysterious "they" who have placed an inconvenient rock or hill or puddle before their delicate tootsies.

So, if Awol said things got better after RPG, I believed him. And thank goodness. Generally, my glutes, calves and quads make uphill my best gear, but the accumulation of miles was now making every climb a chore. This was the kind of long-term wear-and-tear that AT veterans warn about, to which I had smugly considered myself immune. But just as I should have been backing off the miles and taking the occasional zero, I stupidly entered myself in a competition with speedy Achilles and BASA, who were blissfully unaware that it was taking place.

The terrain did get much less arduous after RPG. What's more, that day offered lots of varied scenery and curiosities and what PUDs there were weren't too severe. Continuing to honor my get-wet vow (Gollum was right: "Stream and pool is wet and cool, so nice for feet") I stopped for a pleasant early afternoon swim in the cool waters of Nuclear Lake (mile 1442.1).

The unsettling name stems from the fact that in 1972, a chemical explosion at a nearby nuclear-research lab spewed an unknown amount of weapons-grade plutonium into the lake and nearby woods. An intense cleanup and monitoring effort ensued, and in 1986 the Associated Press reported that, "Tests of soil and vegetation in 1984 showed that radiation was no higher than normal background levels."

I spoke to several hikers who gave the lake a wide berth, based on that history. Radioactive or not, the waters of Nuclear Lake soothed my overheated body and rinsed away corrosive salt. I was charmed by the laid-back little bluegills that nibbled at my feet and hands. None of the fish had three eyes or anything weird, and given that I still had to use my headlamp that night—no handy glow—I figured I was in the clear.

At County Road 20 near Pawling, trail angel Sidetrack provided a much-needed dose of magic, including Gatorade (what makes that stuff so much easier to drink than water, anyway?), fresh water, chips, candy and more. A couple of miles later I crossed a boardwalk through a lovely marsh full of croaking frogs and rolled passed the Appalachian Trail Amtrak stop, where I said a silent "adjø" to my alternate-timeline trail girlfriend, Skeeter. After meandering through a cattle pasture, I stopped at the Native Landscapes and Garden Center, where I bought a Klondike bar, some juice, a pear and a fuel canister.

That night at Wiley Shelter (mile 1454.0) I scribbled down an alphabetical list of things people hope to find on the AT:

A – adventure

B – beauty, beasts

C – challenge, compassion

D – divinity

E – equanimity, excitement

F – fun, fitness, family, friends

G – glory, goals, God

H – happiness, health, humanity

I – introspection

J – joy

K – knowledge, Katahdin

L – love

M – mastery, mindfulness

N – nature

O – optimism

P – peace

Q – quiet

R – romance

S – survival, spirit, sex, strength, stamina

T – tenacity, toughness

U – understanding

V – valor, victory

W – wonder, wildlife

X – exhilaration, experience (give me a break; everyone cheats with X)

Y – youth, YOLO

Z – zest, zoology

I thought it was a pretty good list, though I suspect it only scratches the surface.

*

On Day 76 of my Appalachian Trail thru-hike, I quite suddenly began to hate my beard. I hadn't liked it much in the early days, when it was pokey and irritating, but once it filled out I'd grown rather fond of it. Now, in the relentless heat of the mid-Atlantic states, I was constantly raking away at the sweat trickling through that tangle of hair, and by the end of New York, I began giving serious thought to shaving it off.

Eight miles into the day I passed a sign welcoming me into Connecticut, "Gateway to New England." Nine states down, five to go. I'd come more than 600 miles in 29 days since returning to the trail in June, with no zeroes. After crossing the Ten Mile River on the Ned Anderson Memorial Bridge, I found a spot for an early-morning swim in the Housatonic River, which the trail follows well into Massachusetts.

Although mosquitoes had not found my undersexed, booze-free, type-O+ blood particularly appealing, on this day I learned that deer flies did, as did swarms of tiny, fanatical black gnats who wanted nothing more than to suck the nectar from my eyeballs. Thankfully, I'd risked an ounce of weight on a bug-net for my head; it made me sweat even more, but it did keep the worst of the insect menace from my eyes, ears and neck.

I caught a quick hitch into the pleasantly pastoral town of Kent. After asking an older SOBO section hiker named Jim if I could share his table at The Villager Restaurant, I wolfed down an enormous breakfast-burrito platter, orange juice, a biscuit and several cups of well-creamed coffee. Following the feast, I resupplied at the IGA grocery store, thrilled about my upcoming dinner of avocado, tomato, cheese and bagels.

After scoring another quick ride back to the trail—to my great relief, hitching on the AT proved far easier than it had on the Colorado Trail—I trudged through blazing afternoon heat to Calebs Peak. Descending St. Johns Ledges, I was happy to be a NOBO: it's rocky, blocky, technical, and … the 41st steepest half-mile on the AT.

The next four-and-a-half miles, walking a dirt road alongside the Housatonic, are among the easiest on the entire AT, comparable to the stroll along the Chesapeake & Ohio Canal in Maryland. After about a mile, I came upon Al and Sandy, local angels who had put out an incredible spread.

"Where are all the hikers? We've hardly seen anybody today," Al said.

I hadn't either, which meant I could eat my fill, no questions asked. Beer, soda, Gatorade, juice, watermelon, oranges, candy, cookies. And they had parked their white pickup just a few yards from a swimming hole, just across the river from a knot of families seeking relief from the 95-degree heat. I ate and drank, then wandered down to the water, where I swirled and lazed for 15 minutes before returning to eat some more while reclining in a camp chair.

After about an hour, a trio of SOBO slackpackers arrived, faces shiny with sweat after jogging the last several miles of trail: a 30-something married couple, Optimist and Purple Mist, and their companion, 18-year-old Sunflower, whom I'd met down south.

"We heard there was magic," Purple Mist said, settling into a camp chair. "And we didn't want to miss it."

The trio had joined up earlier on the trail, then later split. When "the Mists" heard via the miracle of texting that Sunflower was feeling discouraged and ready to quit, they invited her to walk with them again. Sunflower's mother shuttled her north and they'd been together ever since, slackpacking as much as they could, just one more unique, HYOH trail family.

I enjoyed listening to Purple Mist, a physical therapist, opine on the subject of feces.

"You can touch your own poop, no problem," she said. "You just can't touch anyone else's poop. Not if you don't want to get sick."

Pretty good advice, I'd say, and not hard to follow!

I hung out until Al and Sandy started to pack up, nearly two hours after I arrived. At their invitation, I stowed a beer, a couple of Gatorades, chips and candy for the road. Walking north along the Housatonic, I saw two blue-black crows hassling a bald eagle and a pair of spotted fawns fleeing into the wood behind their mother. I openly cursed the insects that forced me to remain inside the stuffy confines of my bug-net.

After a few miles, I came upon a group of young hikers taking a "safety meeting" at the bottom of the steep, one-mile climb up to the Silver Hill Campsite (mile 1477.0), where I planned to stop for the night. I declined Goodtalk's generous invitation to participate in the festivities and ground out my EoDMoFo.

There was already a family at the site, which had a privy, a water pump, picnic tables and an open shelter for cooking. The OSHA committee arrived a bit later in good spirits, as did yet another family of weekenders, with their big, happy, slobbery pit-bull mix, Mojo. I worried about the dog when he went baying off down the hill, but he soon returned of his own accord.

Though not always the most careful reader of Awol, I had noticed his remark that the water pump at the campsite could be tricky ("May take many pumps to get water flowing") so I'd filled up down below. After watching others flail briefly at the handle before giving up, I decided to give it a try. I yanked that thing up and down as hard and as fast as I could for a minute or more and was on the verge of quitting when suddenly, cold, clear water blasted out of the pipe.

"Hey!" I shouted, continuing to pump. "If you need water, hustle up. We'll have to take turns filling up and pumping ... hurry!"

You'd have thought I struck gold. People ran to the spigot with pots, bottles and bladders. Eventually someone took over the pumping, so I could top off my own supply. I felt like a minor hero (in truth, I was just stubborn) and a festive mood prevailed for the rest of the evening. I enjoyed talking to an earnest Czech woman with John Lennon spectacles named Vera (for the moment; it seemed to change frequently), whom I would see many more times, as well as Goodtalk.

That night, just as I was drifting off to sleep, I heard a loud snuffling sound and a sturdy snout poked the top of my head through my tent. Bolting upright and tumbling to the opposite wall, I jerked my sleeping bag around me, heart racing, fearing that I was receiving some sort of comeuppance for refusing to freak out about bears.

"Gahhh!" I shouted. "Git!"

Then someone shouted, "Hey, Mojo! Come on, boy! Leave it!"

My fear evaporated instantly. Laughing, I unzipped the tent, whereupon the big lug shoved his huge, grinning, slobbery head into my face.

"Dang, buddy! Don't scare me like that," I said, rubbing his ears.

That night I had bearanoid dreams for the first time on the AT. I can't imagine why.

*

I was out at 6:15 the next morning, aiming for 22 miles and more than 4,000 feet of climbing. Only after 12 solid miles of PUDs did the trail relent with another smooth glide alongside the Housatonic. I soon picked a spot, dumped my pack, and paddled out to the middle of the slow-moving, foam-flecked current just downstream from a small hydro-power plant.

Just after the plant, I crossed the "iron bridge" near Falls Village (mile 1492.1) and immediately saw that the swimming was much better here. I followed a short side trail down to a low, chuckling cascade, where I left my pack on a flat, sedimentary rock shelf, took off my shoes and socks, and fell into a cool green whirlpool.

After about 20 minutes, with the sky threatening rain, I saddled up. It was time to face today's EoDMoFo, a 1,000-foot climb to Mount Prospect. But two-tenths of a mile on, I came across an even *better* place to swim, where scads of teenagers were cavorting and splashing in deep pools below a high, tumbling waterfall. Ignoring the coming storm, I took my third swim break in less than two miles. Gollum surely would have approved.

The rain began falling not long after I left the falls. But it was gentle and cool, absolutely perfect for regulating my body temperature as I chugged three miles to the summit. My brief, long-ago experience with Connecticut had left the impression that it was an extremely flat state, fairly urban, but with cornfields. But given that I was on the Appalachian Trail, I should not have been surprised to find that there were plenty of hills, some of them quite steep.

I considered hiking past Salisbury, but my feet were sore and my legs were tired when I hit Undermountain Road. Pulling out Awol, I saw that there was a home hostel run by an older Italian-American woman named Maria McCabe (her second husband was Irish) half a mile down the road. In a snap decision, I turned off the trail.

Maria loves thru-hikers and has opened her home to them for years, though now she's getting older and worries that she won't be able to keep it up for much longer (as of 2019, she was still going). She greeted me at the door, told me to take off my shoes and leave my pack on a covered porch, then showed me upstairs to a small, mothball-scented room. After I showered, Maria drove me into town, where I ate an enormous meatball sandwich at Mizza's Pizza while doing my laundry next door. When I'd finished, Maria picked me up. It was like having my own personal grandma for the night.

Back at the house, I made a snap decision. Locking myself in the bathroom, I snipped and scraped every strand of hair from my cheeks and chin before I could change my mind. When I was finished, the naked visage in the mirror looked gaunt, immature and frankly ridiculous. In an instant, I regretted my hasty butchery.

Nobody's going to believe I'm a thru-hiker now, I wrote in my journal. *Oh well. At least I'll be cooler.*

TWENTY-TWO: FAIRIES, HORNETS AND PCBS

July 2016: Salisbury to Mount Wilcox North Lean-to

I didn't take a zero in Salisbury, but I did cut myself a bit of slack with a leisurely start and a 13.4-mile nero upon leaving Maria's. After making myself eggs and coffee, per Maria's instructions ("I don't like to get up that early"), I walked to a small grocery store to resupply. After packing up and saying goodbye to Hotrod and Slowpoke, 55-year-old twins from Florida, and their 20-something hiking partner, Rock City (as in, Detroit) I walked back up the road and hit the trail about 10 a.m.

Heading north from Salisbury, the AT climbs 1,500 feet to the summit of Bear Mountain—I have zero memory of the stone observation tower on top—before dropping down the precipitous, rocky north side (60th steepest half mile on the AT). Somewhere on the ascent, I chatted briefly with a fast-moving SOBO hiker about all the unexpectedly intense PUDs.

"I hate to tell you, but it's kind of tough where you're headed," she said.

"You mean like, New Hampshire?"

"No, I mean just ahead," she said. "But hey, at least you're coming up on some excellent swimming holes."

She was right on both counts.

After the steep descent, the trail continued on a gentler downhill course, following Sages Ravine across the Massachusetts line (mile 1505.8), where dappled sun reached down through a thick canopy to an extended series of small cascades and pools full of clear water, tinted faintly green, like an old-fashioned Coke bottle.

I wandered along until I found a deep, rock-walled jug where rays of sun coruscated invitingly down through the water. I dumped my pack on a rocky platform, stripped down and teetered on a small ledge before jumping in.

I came up spluttering. It was by far the coldest water I'd entered since faraway Watauga Lake in April. I once dived into a fast-running, icy, stream of glacial-melt waters in Glacier National Park because I could not bear *not* to swim in water so perfectly, purely blue. This water was gorgeous in a different way, so despite the cold, I dived and paddled and jumped in a couple more times before emerging, covered with goosebumps. As hot as it was, I didn't stop shivering until I'd been walking for about 10 minutes.

After the trail crosses into Massachusetts, it ascends nearly 1,000 feet to Mount Race, which offers spectacular views from ledges along the ridgeline. After a short descent, the march from Race Brook Falls to 2,602-foot Mount Everett incorporates the 38th steepest half-mile on the trail. It's a crank—beleaguered hikers refer to it as "Everest" in shelter logbooks—but I felt strong and made good time to the summit.

Two songs alternated in my head for much of the day: "Sons of God," a gospel hymn we used to sing in Catechism (aka CCD)—"Sons of God, hear His Holy word/Gather around the table of the Lord/Eat His body, drink His blood/And we'll sing a song of love/Allelu, allelu, allelu, allelu-u-u-u-u-ia" and the English-language South African folk song, "Marching to Pretoria." I do not understand my brain.

The descent from Everett wasn't as steep, and when I emerged into the graveled parking area at Guilder Pond Picnic Area, I was thrilled to find two coolers full of Gatorade and several more filled with cold, potable water. No people around.

Ahhhh, thank you, angels! I wrote.

Just four-tenths of a mile down stony, sloping tread brought me to The Hemlocks Lean-to (as shelters are called in that part of the world), which was well kept and featured an upper level sleeping platform. It was empty. I shucked my pack, tossed out my bedroll, put on my flip-flops, then walked another one-tenth (!?) of a mile to check out Glen Brook Lean-to; these two shelters are closest in proximity than any others on the AT. There, resting and chatting on the trail was a gaggle of perhaps 15 teenage girls with big packs, waiting for the rest of their group. Fifteen girls tittering in the woods is a charming sound, like a fairy convention. Not that I believe in fairies.

"Are you a thru-hiker, sir?" one asked.

"Here's a good rule of thumb, girls: if you can smell someone from this far away, you don't have to call him sir," I said.

Glen Brook turned out to be older, mustier and decidedly creepier than The Hemlocks, surrounded by barren ground and witchy, bony trees. And yellow signs warned of bear activity in the area. The Hemlocks it would be, I decided.

Back at the homestead, I enjoyed a dinner of couscous, avocado and yogurt. Then, feeling almost effervescently happy, I grabbed my valuables, left my pack (something most AT hikers will do on occasion, despite the slight risk of theft) and flip-flopped back up the hill to see what Guilder Pond had to offer in the way of an EoDS—end-of-the-day-swim.

After rambling down a blue-blazed path through the woods for a half-mile or so, I followed a short side trail to a wide, granite shelf that sloped down to the breeze-feathered surface of the pond. The westering sun was piercingly white in a sapphire sky and the air felt like warm velvet. I could hear a hound baying in the woods far across the pond, but seeing no one and feeling in high spirits, I stripped off all my clothes and slipped naked into the cool water. I breaststroked 50 yards out and rolled onto my back to laze in the sun like a contented otter.

Back on shore, I sprawled naked to dry out while sipping one of the Gatorades

I'd scored at the parking area. I rinsed my shorts and shirt in the water, then pulled them back on just as I heard the jingle of dog tags and a smiling little Shiba Inu appeared from the woods, followed by a friendly houndish dog, a border collie, and a man. Walking back to the lean-to, I stepped aside to allow a gaggle of chatty, giggly fairies to continue on their way down to the water.

Back at the shelter, three section-hiking SOBOs, two young women and a Frenchman named Jerome, had arrived. Remembering the alarming signs down at the neighboring shelter, I was concerned when Roobar and Rootabaga plopped their food bags on the ground right outside their tent, right in front of the shelter.

"You sure you don't want to hang those bags?" I finally asked when it became clear that the women intended to leave them there overnight.

"You don't think it's OK?"

"Well, there were bear warning signs all over the place at that shelter just down the trail, so...."

They asked Jerome if he would mind babysitting the food bags in the upper level where he had settled in, which seemed like an acceptable solution to me. I had the whole bottom floor to myself. I was not worried about bears, and the end of the day had cheered me considerably. A couple days earlier, I had seriously contemplated bailing out on my hike.

I woke up this morning feeling stupid about deciding to quit, and this was such a great day, I wrote before falling asleep. *Remember: Never make a decision at the end of a hard day and your feet feel like they've been smacked with police baton for the last eight hours.*

I also wrote: *Zeroes (and true neros) are important for physical and mental relief. Why do I forget that?*

*

I was on the trail at 6:05 the next morning, which first took me on a long, fairly gradual descent back down to the Housatonic Valley and US 7, which leads to Sheffield and Great Barrington.

I thought I might go for a swim but right before I reached the river encountered an alarming sign: "WARNING: HOUSATONIC FISH AND

WATERFOWL CONTAMINATED WITH PCBs. DO NOT EAT." Pregnant women were advised to keep their distance. It didn't say "NO SWIMMING," but then, it didn't have to. I wasn't actually worried, despite having swum several times downstream; PCBs are dangerous, but my level of exposure had been minimal. But I did find it odd that this was the first time I'd seen the warning.

I passed a plaque commemorating Shays Rebellion—a 1786-87 uprising led by a Revolutionary War veteran against civil and economic injustices, which influenced the writing of the U.S. Constitution—before starting the 1,000-foot climb up East Mountain. I have always prided myself on a well-developed natural sense of direction, but somehow, I got turned around on top and actually walked a quarter of a mile back down the way I'd come up before realizing my mistake. After getting back on track, I heard a pair of hikers grumbling in the trees above me that they'd done the same thing; must be some sort of distorted gravitational vortex on that particular summit....

In the afternoon I took a dip in the south end of Benedict Pond. That happened to be the mucky end, so it wasn't very satisfying. I arrived at Mount Wilcox South Lean-to (mile 1532.3) at 2:30 and decided to call it a day after 19.7 miles, pleased to have the shelter to myself. I got water, made dinner, cleaned up and lay down on an upper bunk.

My preferred hiking schedule is to start early, hike hard with few, or no, short stops. If possible, I like to hit my 20 miles by mid-afternoon, which gives me the option of calling it a day and kicking back for the next 15 or 16 hours before cranking it up again, or continuing on for a longer day. But I do like to get to camp early and aggressively rest as many hours as I can. Back in Virginia, Eazy-E had at first found my system odd, but later decided it worked for him, too.

I was reading in my bunk when I heard the tramp of feet and loud conversation approaching around 5:30 p.m. First to appear around the corner, to my dismay, was Bad News, the woman who'd hollered at me about my bear-bag setup all the way back in Hot Springs, N.C. She was followed by a squint-eyed, silent guy with a shaved head and a big red beard, and a few minutes later, an exhausted-looking woman sagging beneath an enormous pack.

From the moment this crew rolled in, they were violating nearly every commonly accepted rule of shelter etiquette. The guy (I neglected to write down his name) immediately cranked up loud music. He and Bad News began smoking cigarettes and weed at the picnic table in front of the shelter, where the smoke instantly found its way to my nostrils. Soon, the dude started watching a loud action-movie video in his hammock, which he'd strung up just to the right of the shelter. I tried to endure the intrusion for several hours.

Then, remembering Five Fingers at the noisy shelter in Virginia, I made a snap decision. I packed up, put on my headlamp and saddled up. After all, Mount Wilcox North Lean-to was a mere 1.8 miles away.

"We're not disturbing you, are we?" Bad News asked as I turned to leave. I couldn't tell if she was being a wiseass or was really that obtuse. I was just glad she didn't recognize me.

"Just decided to move on," I muttered, echoing Five Fingers. It was just the second, and thankfully, last, time on the trail when I didn't feel comfortable with my shelter mates (the others were the troubled couple Bonnie and Clyde in Pennsylvania).

*

I didn't sleep well, no doubt because I had worked up a sweat so late. In the morning, I was back on the trail at 5:45 a.m., ambling through a dim, cool forest. I knew I was in for a day of PUDs that would add up to 2,000 or 3,000 feet, depending on how far I decided to go.

At mid-morning, as I strolled along a flat stretch through widely scattered trees, I suddenly felt the brutal, searing pain of hornet stings on my wrist and thighs. Adrenaline surging, I let loose a yowl and started running, slapping wildly at my head and body. Fleeing madly, I tripped over a protruding stone, and though I didn't fall, I yanked hard on my right hamstring in a desperate attempt to stay upright. I literally never saw the nest or even any hornets, but when I stopped running, I tallied at least five stings.

"Assholes!" I shouted, shaking my fist back toward the silent forest.

Less than a half hour later, still feeling grumpy, I emerged into a brief, narrow clearing to see five wild turkeys before they slipped away into the underbrush.

The trail is fickle, I wrote that night. *She giveth, and she taketh away. She delights, and she stings.*

TWENTY-THREE: MY WHITE WHALE

July 2016: Mount Wilcox North Lean-to
to Bennington, Vermont

A few miles after leaving the shelter, I dropped steeply (in fact, the 66th steepest half-mile of the AT; yes, I'm obsessed with this steepness thing) to Jerusalem Road (mile 1540.1), where there was a sign advertising trail magic just a hundred yards down the road. I walked down to find a small cabinet and refrigerator stocked with soda, water, hard-boiled eggs, Pop-Tarts, chips and other treats, all available for a very reasonable price on the honor system.

I paid for (and swiftly inhaled) cookies, chips and a Coke, then bought Pop-Tarts and another Coke for the road before heading back up the hill. Just as I got to the trail, I stopped to talk to two young hikers, Frodo (who looked a good deal like actor Elijah Wood, who played that character in Peter Jackson's *Lord of the Rings* movies) and Tank.

"Are you going to Upper Goose Pond Cabin?" Tank asked.

"I'm not sure where I'm headed today," I said. Especially after going an additional 1.8 miles the night before, stopping at the cabin (operated by the Appalachian Mountain Club) would mean just a 14-mile day.

"You should go," Frodo said. "I hear it's the best shelter experience on the whole AT."

"Sounds cool, but I'm thinking of going a little farther," I said.

I trundled down through a pasture while they went down the road to the magic cabinet. After the fairly steep, 1,000-foot ascent of Baldy Mountain, followed by a few miles of mild but annoying ups-and-downs, I stopped at the junction for the blue blaze to Upper Goose Pond.

"Half a mile?" I said with a snort, eyeing the sign. "I'm supposed to walk *half a mile* to check out this allegedly wondrous cabin?"

Although I hadn't driven myself especially hard since leaving Maria's place, I was still feeling pretty worn out. The ache of the hornet stings had faded, but they were now beginning to itch. My feet throbbed and I found myself thinking of how Frodo and Sam managed that last, desperate leg of their journey into the heart of blasted, craggy Mordor in Tolkien's story, going only as far as they could manage each day to get the job done. Lost in an internal debate about my next move, I was startled to hear someone call my name—my *real* name. It was Alan, the older kick-ass hiker from Boulder whom I'd met at the monastery campground in New York.

"Are you going to the cabin?" he asked.

"Man, I don't know," I said with exasperation, not wanting to admit to Alan that I was bushed after just 14 miles. "But walking half a mile just to check it out seems kind of dumb."

"I agree," he said. "Anyway, I'm going on."

When my idiot man-brain didn't flare instantly with a need to compete, I took it as a signal from my poor body to take a chance.

"Well, shoot," I said. "I guess I'll go have a look and at least go for a swim."

"See you up the trail, then," Alan said, and strode off.

About three-tenths of a mile up the trail to Upper Goose Pond Cabin, I ran into Bonnie, who with her husband Rob was the AMC Berkshire Chapter's caretaker for the week. The two-story red cabin, originally built in the early 20th century, was bought by the National Park Service in 1984 and is now managed by the club exclusively for the use of AT thru-hikers and section hikers.

If I decided to stay, Bonnie said, I could just go in and claim a bunk. I could fill up from jugs of water on the porch, collected daily by caretakers and hiker-volunteers who canoe over to a spring on the far side of the pond. And in the morning, she said, there would be pancakes and coffee. She sensed my hesitation and possibly, my exhaustion.

"You should stay," she said. "I think you'll like it."

"How's the swimming?"

"Absolutely the best. Cool, clear water," she said. "You can even fish if you want."

Five minutes later, I mounted the porch stairs, where Rob greeted me. Flipping through the logbook, I realized that while some hikers just did a bit of near-shore dabbling in a canoe or kids' swim ring, more amphibious types (including Olive Oil, whom I'd run into several times) were bold enough to swim to a tiny, tree-covered island several hundred yards offshore. That sold me. I humped my pack upstairs, claimed a bunk, donned flip-flops and walked down the short, steep hill to the water.

The water was indeed beautifully clear and pleasantly cool. Diving off the smaller of two docks, I alternated between breaststroke, backstroke and freestyle (aka crawl), making slow progress toward the island, which was farther out than it appeared from the cabin. Once ashore, I poked around and chatted with a family that had docked their small motored skiff so their two girls and dog could explore. I declined their kind offer of a ride back, eager to loll about in those comforting green waters.

While cooking on the porch that night, I was surprised to see that my food bag was on the light side, since I'd just resupplied in Salisbury (after years of long-distance hiking, this remains tricky for me; I always seem to have way too much, or not enough...). While eating dinner, I struck up a conversation with a friendly woman and her 11-year-old son from Springfield, Massachusetts, who were nearing the end of a 100-mile section hike. Ellen and Merlin (the boy's trail name, taken from a popular young-adult book series by T.A. Barron, a friend of mine) lived most of the year in the dry deserts of Senegal, where his father taught school.

"It's hard hiking the trail," Merlin said, "but I love being in the trees and so near water all the time."

I felt a tad sheepish eating a Knorr Pasta Side and tortillas with Jif while Ellen and Merlin whipped up a considerably healthier dinner from things that actually grew in dirt—dried fruit, nuts, some kind of hummus.

I also talked to a young hiker from Florida named Bearbait, who happened to be in the photo I took of the lake and island. When she arrived, she'd been wearing thick wool socks and Chaco sandals. I'd meet her again, and years later, I'd interview her for a story about hiking in sandals.

By dark, the bunkroom was full. There are few things as comforting to me as a hiker than the sound of rain falling on a rooftop, and I drowsed away into sleep with the fresh scent of wet leaves in my nose, very pleased I'd decided to stop.

The next morning, I woke with the birds and had to force myself to wait a couple hours for breakfast; I'm glad I did. The pancakes were vast and spongy, and in my case, gloriously sopped with butter and syrup. The coffee, whether due to my good spirits or some ineffable magic of the cabin, was literally the best I've ever had in my four-decade caffeine career; I've been chasing that flavor ever since, without success. To cap off my magical stay, Ellen and Merlin gave me organic dried mangoes, crackers and other real food before I headed out at 7:15.

"Think of us when you climb Katahdin!" Merlin said from the porch as I headed out.

Two roads diverged in a green wood at mile 1548.1 of the Appalachian Trail, and I—I took the one I sorely needed at that moment. Upper Goose Pond Cabin remains among my top five favorite stops on the trail.

*

I didn't have to do a huge amount of climbing that day, but it was something of a letdown after that dreamy interlude. The trail was mostly green tunnel, alternating between pace-killing roots and rocks, and smoother, duff-covered tread.

Stopping for a snack at October Mountain Lean-to, I came upon an exhausted-looking Achilles, the young cross-country runner from North Carolina. He had no clue who this clean-shaven stranger was until I asked about BASA, the 50-something Bay Area firefighter he'd hiked with from their first week on trail in Georgia.

"Pony?" he said, looking startled. "Man, you look totally different without a beard and long hair."

Turns out that after more than 1,500 miles, this speedy odd couple had recently split up when Achilles decided to go into town with Goodtalk; BASA continued on. Achilles was hurting after having bashed out a 29-mile day in an effort to catch up to his old partner.

I hiked on and, no surprise, Achilles soon caught up to me. We walked together into Dalton, Mass., where we ate an OK lunch at Jacob's Pub. We then walked over to the Cumberland Farms convenience store where I did a small, expensive, resupply, and ran into Alan. Alan and I decided to split a motel room at the Shamrock Village Inn, but Achilles decided to head on.

Eating at the pub had given me an unsurprising case of "town belly"— gas, semi-constipation, diarrhea, all the fun GI symptoms combined—and I did not sleep well. Feeling grouchy and unrefreshed, I rose early and headed out into a cool, cloudy morning.

I can taste that Dandelion Wine-*type melancholy in the air*, I wrote later, referring to Ray Bradbury's classic novel of a boy's summer in 1928. *It's that inevitable day when you know summer must end, after all.*

*

I somehow got off track at the beginning of the 1,000-foot climb up Crystal Mountain, (my third such goof in recent weeks, suggesting mental fatigue), but was able to bushwhack my way back to the trail through dry, open woods. At MA 8, I hiked down to a Dunkin' Donuts, where I inhaled two glazed and two chocolate-frosted like a crazed addict while slurping down an uninspiring cup of what I call "melted brown crayon coffee" to shake off my fuzziness. Thus fueled, I began the 2,500-climb up Mount Greylock, at 3,491 feet the highest summit since northern Virginia.

The mountain is famous because of its association with Herman Melville. The great 19th-century author wrote part of his greatest novel, *Moby Dick*, from his home at Arrowhead, where his view of the mountain reminded him of the humped back of a sperm whale. He dedicated his next (and now all but forgotten) novel, *Pierre*, to "Greylock's Most Excellent Majesty ... my own... sovereign lord and king." Preach it, Hermie!

The first 1,000 feet up was fairly steep, then the trail leveled out to a false summit near Mark Noepel Lean-to before steepening again near the top. As I walked, the surrounding forest transformed from one of sleepy deciduous monarchs to a pitch-scented thicket of conifers, reminding me of Colorado and Tennessee's Clingman's Dome, the far-away high-point of the AT. I was thrilled to find a vast treasure trove of magic about a mile below the summit, where I plopped onto the grass to devour homemade brownies and cookies, chips and a banana and slurp down a Coke. I'd been cranked on sugar from start to finish that day.

By the time I reached the top in early afternoon, the skies were gray and the air hovered between warm and cool. The curious looking Veterans War Memorial Tower, with its globular head, built in 1932, was surrounded by scaffolding for a renovation to improve safety, and had been closed to the public since 2013. I meandered briefly through the lodge, bought some Gatorade (more sugar!), then went outside to eat. I asked an impeccably dressed Boston woman—I believe she belonged to that species they call "Brahmin"—and her two grown sons if I could share their picnic table. She said yes, then gave me a chicken sandwich and peppered me with questions about hiking the trail.

One of her sons turned out to be an attorney in Los Angeles who had worked previously in New York publishing. We talked for a long time about the business, my latest book project and both the rising respectability and pitfalls of self-publishing. He gave me his email, in case I had further questions.

It had begun to rain lightly by the time I started down the mountain, and I tried to hustle, knowing that a big storm was on the way. The three-mile descent to Wilbur Clearing Lean-to (mile 1589.2) included the 59th steepest half-mile on the AT, and I was annoyed that the shelter was an unacceptable *three-tenths of a mile*—the horror—off trail.

When I arrived at the shelter, I knew I'd met the lone woman huddled in her sleeping bag in the corner, but couldn't place her. Eventually she introduced herself: She'd been with my occasional nemesis Bad News and the squint-eyed dude who had driven me out of Mount Wilcox South Shelter with too much smoke and loud music. The rain was beginning to come down harder, and it would only get worse, but if those two were on their way, I knew I'd be hiking on to find a tenting spot.

"No, I got ditched," Jenny said sadly when I gingerly asked about her partners.

She had traveled all the way from Illinois to join the guy, whom she'd been dating, for a section hike, but he had found her inconvenient and abandoned her. Bad News was kinder, Jenny said, but had also ditched her. She'd gotten here through a combination of yellow-blazing and hiking.

"I was so excited to be doing this," she said. "Now I just feel stupid."

"Don't," I said. "Not everybody is going to hike at the same pace, especially if someone is just starting out. But if you invite someone to hike with you, then ditch them, sorry, but you're just a jerk." Jenny didn't disagree.

She didn't remember me until I described how rude her erstwhile companions had been.

"Oh, God, I wondered what happened," she said. "Bad News told me you were uptight."

Unlike her former companions, Jenny was very nice. She had spent her career working with large mammals at American zoos and African nature parks. She planned to hike the trail for a few more days before heading back home.

Alan showed up later, as did Bearbait, the lively blond sandal hiker I'd met at Upper Goose Pond. She wasn't the only hiker I'd met who'd dispensed with shoes up north.

"I just got sick of blisters and super sweaty feet," she said, peeling off her fascinatingly grungy socks to reveal toes completely blackened with trail filth.

"Don't you stub your toes?"

"Not too much, but I've definitely jammed my heel against a few rocks. You just have to be careful about where you step."

At the time, I wasn't sure sandals were for me. Now, years later, having backpacked some 500 miles in minimalist Xero Z Trail sandals, I'm a convert.

As predicted, the rain really cut loose that night, and it was still pouring when I woke at 5 a.m. Groggily hoping it would stop, I forced myself to lie back down. Somewhat surprisingly, I fell back asleep. I woke again at 6:30 when Alan began stirring. It was still coming down.

I've never seriously considered taking a zero in a shelter; even during my Lyme disease nightmare in Pennsylvania I always made at least a few miles. Not wanting to start now, I steeled myself for a soggy day. I set out at 7:30 wearing rain gear, the first time I'd done that since southern Virginia. I was soaked almost immediately, which meant I needed to maintain a good pace to stay warm.

After the steep, slippery descent from Mount Prospect to the northern foot of Greylock (since you asked, the 12th steepest mile on the AT), the trail almost immediately leaped into a 1,500-foot ascent to a lush, unnamed ridge, where the tread had turned to ankle-deep mud soup. Somewhere in there I crossed into Vermont; 11 states down, three to go, though I got no pleasure out of the milestone in that moment. Beginning to fret about hypothermia, I made a snap decision to take a break at Seth Warner Shelter (mile 1599.1).

The shelter was loaded with bedraggled hikers. Some were temporarily huddled out of the rain, hoping for a break, while others had given up entirely on this nasty day and lay sleeping or reading in their sleeping bags. Nemo, the loquacious guy I'd met in Georgia, who loved to pack luxury items like bottles of wine and expensive chocolate, was there. Shivering, I ate my last two Clif bars, essentially the end of my food. But I still could not bear the thought of hanging out in a shelter all day and, feeling little better than when I had arrived, I headed on.

The trail on the way up to Consultation Peak was either muddy or a sloshing with icy rain water, take your pick. It was also vexingly rocky and rooty, and my feet were really feeling it. Just before hitting mile 1,600, I took a wrong turn downhill. I caught my mistake soon enough, and as I hiked back up in search of the trail, I ran into Nemo and another guy, who had taken the same wrong turn. The three of us quickly found our way back, then they blazed off at a vigorous pace, leaving me once again alone and cold in the woods of Vermont.

As I had more than once back in Virginia, I found myself thinking of the haunting Ray Bradbury story, "The Long Rain," about three Earthmen trying to find their way back to safety after their airship crashes in the endless, rainy jungles of Venus (now known, of course, to be a brutal desert). The tale begins, "The rain continued. It was a hard rain, a perpetual rain, a sweating and steaming rain; it was a mizzle, a downpour, a fountain, a whipping at the eyes, an undertow at the ankles; it was a rain to drown all rains and the memory of rains. It came by the pound and the ton, it hacked at the jungle and cut the trees like scissors and shaved the grass and tunneled the soil and molted the bushes. It shrank men's hands into the hands of wrinkled apes; it rained a solid glassy rain, and it never stopped." The men go mad.

Although I usually refrained from distracting myself from my hiking experience, this was a bad, brutal day and I needed distraction. To take my mind off the misery, I plugged in my headphones and was deeply grateful for the digital ministrations of Scott Brick and Isaac Asimov, narrator and author, respectively, of the 1973 novel *The Gods Themselves*, which held up better than I'd expected after all those years.

Awol describes the final descent to VT 9 as especially rocky and steep, and it is; the 31st steepest half-mile of the trail, in fact. But blessed trail maintainers had turned it into a pleasant, stony staircase in the 13 years since; it's still tough on the knees and quads, but not as treacherous as Awol reported. The rain was falling somewhat less cruelly by the time I sloshed out of the trees, imagining that I looked like a white, wrinkled cadaver drawn from a river.

To my amazement, the very first car that passed my upturned thumb skidded onto the shoulder and gave me a ride down into Bennington, Vermont. Oddly, the driver insisted on showing me around town for about 30 minutes before dropping me off at the Catamount Motel, which, though not exactly cheap, was the best deal available in this college town.

I missed the camaraderie of a true hiker hostel, of which there were few between Virginia and Vermont, but I was indescribably grateful to be out of that freezing rain. After taking a long, hot shower to warm up (the rain had scrubbed me clean already), I walked back up to Main Street in a light sprinkle. I wandered along until I came to the Bennington Pizza House, where I ate salad and a large plate of spaghetti and overdosed on Dr. Pepper. After eating a strawberry ice cream cone across the street, I walked back to the motel.

I was fed and warm, wrapped up like a burrito in the starchy bedding so characteristic of cheap motels. I had not, so far as I could tell, been driven mad by the rain, but my still-wrinkled feet throbbed in complaint and suddenly, I couldn't bear the thought of taking another step on the Appalachian Trail. Back in Connecticut I had promised to "commit to Vermont," and now here I was, 10 miles over the line.

For more than 1,600 miles, I'd been mad Captain Ahab, recklessly pursuing my own white whale, no matter the cost. And now I felt like I was swirling down into the maelstrom, exhausted, battered, lonely and lost....

The rest of Vermont, New Hampshire and Maine would still be there next season.

I was done.

TWENTY-FOUR: VERMONT BLUES

August 2016: Bennington to Killington

I woke up with a queasy feeling gnawing at my brain, as if I'd murdered someone or slept with my best friend's girlfriend. Oh, yeah: Last night I *quit* the Appalachian Trail.

But now, in the dim morning light, I knew I'd never forgive myself if I bailed. I'd cringe every time I glanced in the mirror: *Pussy! Loser! Crybaby!* The trail had taught me time and again not to make momentous decisions at the end of a hard day; why couldn't I remember?

But while wandering the trail of my dreams, my brain—the same twisted organ that fixated on ridiculous songs and refused to be kind to the body that hauled it around by taking a few zeroes here and there—had come up with a plan I *could* live with: I'd pack up that morning, head back to the trail, and start walking north to see if I could rekindle my enthusiasm. If that didn't happen within a few days, say, where the AT turned east from the Long Trail—America's oldest long-distance trail, contiguous with the AT for some 87 miles—then I'd take a real break. I'd rest up, maybe even go home, then come back and flip-flop up to Katahdin to change the scenery and my attitude, and finish my mad pursuit of Moby Dick as a SOBO.

*

The sky was cloudy and I felt the prickle of a few tiny raindrops on my cheeks as I walked east on Main Street, but thankfully the deluge had passed. I bought enough food for five days at Henry's Market, weighing down my pack more than I would have liked. Then I put my thumb out and in 10 minutes I had a ride—from the *same* guy who'd given me a lift in. By the time I hit the trail, it was late, after 10 a.m.

Another reason I decided to continue was the somewhat unlikely chance that I might catch up with Patches, who had been traveling with Yosamite (cq—that's newspaper-speak for "correct spelling") and Doc. I'd seen his name in shelter logbooks in northern Massachusetts and I had been gaining on him; now he might be no more than two days ahead. We'd been texting and he explained that he and his new crew had (wisely) adopted a less-maniacal pace for New England, backing off the crazy miles so they could enjoy more time in town. (Lava had gotten off at Harpers Ferry, as he'd planned, and moved to Colorado with Heather; none of us had any idea where Eazy-E might be.)

I also hoped I might see BASA or Achilles again, since we'd been in the same general neighborhood. But they always moved fast, and I suspected by now they'd put me permanently in the rear-view mirror. And maybe I'd run into 69-year-old Alan, who did 20s like clockwork, since we were at the same shelter just two nights before and he wasn't big on staying in town.

Intellectually, I accepted the wisdom of AT veterans who said, "Nobody ever regrets spending *too much* time on the trail." But as Patches had said, "Pony, you're the most restless hiker I've ever seen," and foolish as it is, I too often chide myself for not going far or fast enough. So, off I went, feet still thrumming and legs churning at less than optimum.

*

The climb from VT 9 to an unnamed summit and powerline (mile 1612.7) was fairly steep, gaining some 1,300 feet in a couple of miles. Hikers often rue the conditions in "Vermud," especially in early summer, when the trail can be a continuous soggy sump. Despite the previous day's soaking rain, my sense was that the state was experiencing a drought like the rest of the northeast, but the first 20 miles or so were definitely sloppy.

For the most part the ridgewalk and climb to Glastonbury Mountain was enclosed in a green tunnel. The fire tower at the summit offered a 360-degree view of endless blue-green spruce tops and rippling mountains, but lingering gray clouds obscured the summits of Greylock to the south, and Mount Stratton to the north.

I arrived at Story Spring Shelter in late afternoon, and pondered calling it a day after 19 miles and a solid 3,000 feet of climbing. But the weather was pleasant, neither too hot nor especially humid, with no rain predicted for that night, so I decided to roll on a couple more miles and pitch my tent. I ended up stopping at a campsite at the foot of Stratton Mountain.

I feel lost, I wrote in my journal, *and tired.*

In hindsight, I can't say if it was true, or a perception colored by my weariness and declining enthusiasm, but the following day offered more of the same and Vermont seemed hardly distinguishable from northern Massachusetts, even though it reminded me of the coniferous, stony heights of Tennessee and Virginia.

The climb up Stratton Mountain was much the same as ascending Glastonbury, only longer and steeper, four miles and about 1,800 feet. The perspective from the fire tower was essentially the same, but on this day the views were unobstructed by clouds and the beauty of the vast, green ocean that is Vermont finally registered. The land of Ben & Jerry's and Bernie Sanders seemed from here to be an almost uninterrupted carpet of forest.

Stratton is famous in AT lore because it's where Benton MacKaye is said to have been when he first had the inspiration for the trail. He formally proposed the idea in his article, "An Appalachian Trail: A Project in Regional Planning," published in the October 1921 issue of *Journal of the American Institute of Architects*.

After slipping several times on the steep descent, I stopped to wash up in

Stratton Pond. The water was pleasantly cool on my face but I didn't swim. Instead I ate peanut butter, tortillas and string cheese, then stretched out in the sun for a luxurious half hour.

The trail was relatively flat after Stratton, but the tread was still sloppy in places and cluttered with slippery roots and rocks. Given how dry the summer had been, I felt sorry for hikers who had to come through here in a wet year.

I stopped for a couple of minutes at VT 11 to ponder my next move. Vermont frankly wasn't doing anything to renew my psych, and I actually considered bailing out to Manchester Center, which would have left 538.4 miles of hiking for my SOBO leg. I finally decided that my goal should be to hike at least another 38.4 miles, so I'd have no more than 500 to finish up.

I was smart (and tired) enough to pull up at Bromley Shelter (mile 1652.7) after just a 19-mile day. Three Long Trail hikers came in behind me and pitched tents.

I had spoken to a hiker somewhere in Massachusetts who declared Vermont his favorite state on the Appalachian Trail. I understood, after hundreds of miles through Maryland, Pennsylvania, New Jersey, New York, Connecticut and Massachusetts, why it was so appealing to so many. The trail was identifiably "northern," rolling through vast evergreen forests and, just as in the South, going up and over summit after summit. The air was a little cooler and the smells wilder. But to me it seemed much like the lower elevations of the Colorado Rockies, minus the spectacular grandeur above timberline.

VT's not doing it, I wrote that night. *Time to make a bail-out plan.*

Jody was thrilled when I told her I was coming home ... until I told her that it was just a break, after which I would fly up to Maine and finish my hike. I would hike beyond the 500-miles-to-Katahdin mark (mile 1689.1, near the foot of Killington Peak) and give myself a much-needed break.

I remember Baltimore Jack saying that tortoises are more likely to succeed on the AT than jackrabbits—speedy hikers (or "big-dick" hikers, in the parlance of Mathrage, who provided such excellent magic at the foot of the Roan Highlands) are not only at higher risk of injury, but also of wearing down mentally after too many miles in too few days. I wasn't hurt, but I was psychologically trashed. It annoyed me to admit it, but I knew if I had just given my body a break—remember, I'd taken *no zeroes*—I would have fared better. But I felt confident that a couple weeks off and the prospect of starting back in Maine—which would definitely *not* be like Massachusetts—would give me the renewed vigor for a strong finish.

The AT hikers I admire the most—people like The Dude, Olive Oil, Two-Pack, Terrible Lizard, Trekkeroni and many others—are those who make steady progress, taking time to rest and care for themselves so they don't burn out. That is a more elegant, a more artful, Appalachian Trail thru-hike, if you ask me, than the way I'd done it. I'd been a jackrabbit, starting and stopping, allowing my ego to override common sense when I should have taken a break. Now here I was in Vermont, drained and even a little depressed.

Not as graceful as hikers who pace themselves, I wrote that night, *but I will finish.*

In fact, simply making my plan gave me a spark, at least mentally. Such tricks weren't enough to fully reinvigorate my exhausted muscles, but knowing I had just 48 miles to cover in three days was more than enough for me to push on.

I enjoyed walking along the open, grassy lanes leading to the top of Bromley Mountain (NOBO mile 1653.7; SOBO 536.4). I chose not to ride the lift down to the base of the ski area, where many hikers go to pig out at a resort restaurant, partly in fear that I would never make it back up the hill.

From Mad Tom Notch, the trail climbs to Styles Peak, then dips up and down along a ridge to Peru Peak. After dropping fairly steeply for about a mile, the trail levels out for several miles before reaching a short, steep, but fun scramble up granite slabs to just below the summit of Baker Peak.

The morning's climbing wasn't brutal, but the tread continued to be less than ideal—mud, rocks, roots—and the temperature was in the mid-70s, with little breeze. I swam briefly in Griffith Lake on the north side of Peru, but decided I wasn't up for the chilly waters of the Big Branch River just six miles further up the trail.

The trail leveled out quite a bit after that, and, feeling good, I bypassed the fee-tenting area at Little Rock Pond and managed one more semi-EoDMoFo to an unnamed summit before finding a stealth spot just off the White Rocks Trail (mile 1674.7). That meant I only had to average 16-mile days to reach US 4.

I sort of like having a deadline, I wrote that night. *Still an old journalist, I guess.*

Though I felt better having made my decision, I was now just "making miles." I took almost no photos in Vermont and my journal entries were cursory. Consequently, my memories of that part of the trail are vaguer than for anywhere else along the way.

I'll be more mindful when I get to Maine, I promised in my journal.

*

Bear Mountain was my 1,000-foot BoDMoFo the next day, which dawned clear and even warmer than the day before. About eight miles in the trail offered a panoramic view that included the Rutland airport. After a fairly steep and rocky descent, I crossed the suspension bridge over the Mill River at Clarendon Gorge.

I followed a path down to the water, where I dumped my pack on a stony perch. I slipped into one of the many pools and stony buckets of cool, clear, greenish-yellow water, fully clothed, with the sun beaming overhead.

Feeling refreshed, I crossed VT 103 (mile 1683.1) and immediately ran into the buzzsaw of a steep, rocky ascent (68th steepest half mile on the AT) past Clarendon Shelter. Following a brief descent, there was another climb that, if anything, seemed steeper to the summit of Beacon Hill (but as it was less than half a mile long, I can't say for sure). Just a few miles later, I stopped to photograph a small, carved wooden sign reading, "KATAHDIN 500 MILES."

And then I was in for a genuine, Southern-style (but with worse tread) EoDMoFo, some 2,500 feet and seven miles up Vermont's second-highest summit, Killington Peak. This was my last real crank before I bailed out, and I didn't want to leave half the climb until the next morning. By the time I arrived at Cooper Lodge Shelter (mile 1694.5), I had hiked less than 20 miles, but it was the biggest climbing day—around 4,500 feet—I'd had in a long while, and I was bushed.

Fortunately, I made it in time to walk two-tenths of a mile to the (overpriced) ski lodge, so I didn't have to mess with dinner. Then, in a snap decision, instead of going back to the shelter I decided not just to stealth camp, but cowboy camp. The weather was gorgeous, clear, warm, with barely a breeze, and I wanted to make the most of my last night outdoors.

I don't like having to admit that I'm getting off, I wrote that night. *But it's going to be good.*

As it turned out, the night got cooler than I expected at nearly 4,000 feet. I woke a couple of times, thinking I'd heard the rustling of one of the mountain's allegedly ravenous porcupines, but all I saw was stars and the silhouette of evergreens against a blue-black, moonless sky.

I woke early and after a fast, fairly easy 15 miles and a 2,000-foot descent to my exit ramp, I was on vacation from the AT. I put my thumb out at 2 p.m. and in 15 minutes, I was on my way home.

I never did catch Patches, BASA, Achilles or Alan. But when I flipped up to Maine in late August, I knew I stood a good chance of running into all of them again.

Months later, BASA would say something about Vermont that rang in my ears as I headed home: "We all know about the unofficial halfway point, the official halfway point, and the historical halfway point. I often told Achilles the most important halfway point that no one talks about is the mental halfway point of the trail that I figured was around 1600 or 1700 miles."

TWENTY-FIVE:
THEY CALL ME FLIPPER

August 2016: Millinocket, Maine to Abol Bridge

I chose to take a third break from the trail for several reasons.

Because of my own impatience, mindless sense of competition (if only, at times, with myself) and foolish refusal to listen to my body, I didn't take a single zero while hiking from Georgia to mid-Vermont, and the cumulative toll on my body left me feeling wiped out at the end of every day. A night's sleep, as always, made a huge difference, but after 1,700 miles, its curative benefits were greatly diminished.

Also, I was anxious to get home and take care of some family issues that had cropped up concerning my mother's health and welfare. These were things I simply could not accomplish on my phone from a hostel. It also would give me a chance to do a small amount of freelance work so I didn't feel like a total bum.

Mentally, I needed a break, and I knew that flipping up to Maine would break me out of the Vermont Blues (that's unfair to Vermont; they were a hangover effect of many long, hot weeks going all the way back to Pennsylvania). My brain thrives on variety, and I knew the radical change in scenery would spark my enthusiasm. I might even catch a taste of New England's fabled autumn palette.

Finally, I was just so *hot* (except for those days when I was wet and cold). My core felt like a glowing orange heating element and even my stomach burned. Perhaps it was Lyme hangover.

So, I went home to South Carolina, where the average daily high temperature in August is over 90 degrees and the humidity was as bad as in Pennsylvania. But I got to wallow in the warm-but-refreshing waters of the Atlantic any time I wanted, blessed relief.

Jody thought it was more than extravagant to come home for just a couple of weeks and was hoping I was just done. She wasn't wrong. But, like an inexperienced marathoner, I had merely failed to pace myself properly, burning up mental and physical reserves I was going to need for the final leg of my journey. Hiker Dan "Wingfoot" Bruce, author of *The Thru-Hiker's Handbook* (the most popular AT guidebook before Awol came along), famously declared that NOBOs who get through Vermont have completed 80 percent of the miles, but a full 50 percent of the *effort* still lies ahead of them in New Hampshire and Maine.

I am an adamant believer in HYOH (Hike Your Own Hike) and I resist phony hierarchies or adamant claims that one way is better than the other. But I have come to see those who properly pace themselves on a sustained thru-hike (a short break or two notwithstanding) are the most admirable of AT hikers. Such hikes, to me, are like elegant, finely threaded tapestries, where I would describe mine as more of a patchwork quilt.

*

Cooled off, chilled out, and pumped up, I flew to Bangor, Maine in late August. I was far more nervous than when I'd started the trail back in March, fretting about transportation logistics. But in the end, my flight touched down on time and I took a $5 taxi ride to the bus station with plenty of time to spare before the Cyr Bus Line ferried me north. I spent time talking to an older flip-flopper, Marmot, until the bus arrived.

Riding an hour north as the sun set over a wall of dark conifers, I felt as if I were in a Stephen King novel set in the mid-1950s. I waited with Marmot and a couple of other hikers for just 10 minutes at a gas station in Medway before the shuttle from the Appalachian Trail Lodge in Millinocket arrived, piloted by a somewhat prickly woman named Mighty Mouse.

Arriving at the lodge, I got my first look at hikers who had finished the trail. They struck me as battle-hardened, wise and in many cases, a bit dazed. Five or six or seven months and then, quite suddenly, their grand adventure was over. Meanwhile, I still had the two most challenging states to go.

The lodge's SOBO special includes the shuttle, a night's stay, and breakfast the next morning at the Appalachian Trail Café. That night I ate spaghetti at the Scootic Inn with a young hiker named Foodie. I slept fitfully and rose at 5 a.m. to catch breakfast before the shuttle departed at 6:30 for Baxter State Park.

Much to my dismay, I couldn't find one of my sturdy old Mountain Hardwear rock gaiters, which had been with me on every mountain I'd climbed for more than 10 years. I frantically searched until just before the shuttle left, to no avail.

The ride to the park was beautiful, rolling through thick, shadowy forests past long, dark lakes. Deposited at the Katahdin Stream Campground, five of us walked into the ranger station to obtain our permits to climb the mountain on this day, Aug. 25, 2016. There was a good deal of anxiety and confusion about camping rules.

Baxter is an unusual entity. Created in 1931 on 6,000 acres of land donated by former Maine Gov. Percival P. Baxter, it has grown to more than 200,000 acres. The park is funded entirely through a trust created by Baxter and private donations, but overseen by a panel of three public officials.

In recent years, park officials have complained that AT hikers, whether thru- or section, consume an inordinate amount of staff time and frequently violate rules that prohibit alcohol, parties of more than 12, camping in non-designated areas, and others. I will just note that AT hikers make up just 3 percent of the park's annual users.

The record-setting 2015 AT thru-hike by ultra-athlete Scott Jurek brought the issue to public attention. Rangers issued summonses to Jurek for uncorking a bottle of champagne at Baxter Peak, littering and having too many people in his party. Media were issued tickets for not having proper permits. Jurek, a truly decent guy who wasn't out to break the rules, paid a $500 fine and bore the brunt of public criticism.

In response, the park began requiring AT hikers to obtain a free permit before climbing Katahdin in 2016 (in 2017, they limited the number of permits to 3,145). The park maintains a shelter and campsite exclusively for AT hikers, The Birches, where a limited number of hikers may stay.

But frankly, the rules are not all that clear, and several hikers worried out loud that if they take too long to climb and descend the mountain, they'd have no place to stay.

"Don't worry," the ranger quietly told Marmot, "we'll work something out."

He wasn't quite so friendly with me, but I must take some of the blame. After he scoffed when I said I planned to climb Katahdin, descend, and hike 10 miles out of the park, my ego took the reins.

"You can't do that," he said. "No way."

"Eh, I'm not too worried. I grew up in Colorado and I've climbed much harder peaks in the Rockies," I said.

"Well, you're in for a rude awakening. I've seen hundreds of people from Colorado come off this mountain and tell me it's the hardest thing they've ever done," the ranger huffed. "I'm telling you right now, you aren't going to be able to do it. And if you camp illegally in the park, you'll get a $1,000 fine."

I left the ranger station at 7:45 a.m., burdened only with a light-blue daypack, since the park prefers that hikers leave full packs below. I exulted in every second of the next five hours as I climbed up, then down, this spectacular mountain. Katahdin may be 9,000 feet lower than the highest peaks in the Rockies and Sierras, but it is every bit as majestic, beautiful and fun as any I've ever climbed in North America.

After a brief warmup on gentle, duffy tread, the Hunt Trail/AT crossed a bridge over clear, cold Katahdin Stream and headed steeply uphill into dense coniferous forest. The weather was beautiful, clear and cool, but I was soon sweating profusely as I made my way up deeply rutted, root-choked, rocky tread.

Perhaps a mile up this first steep ridge the trees fall away, leaving hikers to scramble the next couple of miles over, around and through enormous boulders, and pull themselves up some steeper faces using rebar handholds and steps. The ridge includes the 2nd steepest mile segment on all the AT—gaining an astonishing 1,640 feet—as well as the 21st steepest 1/2-mile segment.

It's Class 3+, rocky with a ton of scrambling up the ridges, I wrote later. *Super fun and mountain goaty, slow going but breathtaking. Favorite climb on the trail so far.*

I leaped joyously up the ridge, feeling right at home, and reached the flat, stony "tableland," where I could see Baxter Peak (terminus of the AT, though not actually the high point on the mountain, which lies further east). Although fairly flat for the first half-mile or more, the going across the tableland was rocky and required careful foot placement.

Walking rapidly up the last hundred yards to the iconic Katahdin sign, I could see there were perhaps a dozen other hikers on top. I reached out and touched the sign at 10:10 a.m., then turned slowly to take in the spectacular views of virtually unspoiled forests, mountains and lakes spreading in every direction. Katahdin, which means "The Greatest Mountain" in the Penobscot Indian language (which is why I refuse to call it "Mount Katahdin," which means, "Mount Greatest Mountain"), rises above all that wild land like a proud but benevolent emperor.

I turned my attention to these hikers, many of whom had just completed a 2,200-mile odyssey. I was almost giddy to find that Legs and Verge, the sisters whom I'd camped with in the old apple orchard way down in Tennessee, whose parents I'd met in Virginia, were among them, as were their sometime hiking companions, Sweets and Jingle.

Legs took my summit photo. I chose not to mount the sign, as most hikers do, having always felt uneasy about that triumphal pose; surely kneeling before it would be more appropriate. I also was keenly aware that unlike these happy-sad thru-hikers, I still had another 500 miles to go.

Sweets told me it was almost impossible to describe what she was feeling.

Relief, exuberance, mourning and probably a half dozen other potent impulses, juked with adrenaline and endorphins. Something like that.

"But I don't think I can describe it," she said. "You have to experience it."

I realized at that moment that in flip-flopping, I might never experience it. The Colorado Trail trickles out into southeast Denver, for NOBOs, and Durango, for SOBOs; the Continental Divide Trail starts and ends on flats in the middle of nowhere, ditto for the Pacific Crest Trail. The AT ends on a literal high, the most spectacular point in all its 2,189.1 miles. I felt giddy, as I always do on summits, but I knew that I would never really experience the emotions of my erstwhile NOBO compatriots.

I stayed on top for only 20 minutes or so before starting down. About halfway across the tablelands, I saw a familiar figure approaching.

"Looks like someone needs a haircut and a shave," I shouted.

"Pony!" Patches shouted back, and we rushed toward each other for a hug. He eyed me and laughed. "Man, you look so weird without your beard and long hair. You're all clean-cut!"

He also pointed out my perfectly—and, it must be said, accidentally—color-coordinated outfit, from my light-teal headband to the blue technical t-shirt I'd scored in Palmerton, Pa. for just $15, and even the light-blue daypack I'd borrowed. Even my socks were aqua-hued.

And, in a move I would soon regret, I decided to be "economical" and return to the trail wearing a pair of aqua Hokas that had been languishing in my closet rather than buy another pair of Altras, with their ultra-wide toebox.

But he was right. My clean cheeks and banker-length hair left me feeling like a poseur, a doofus, a day hiker. But there were plenty of miles ahead to fix that.

It's tempting to think of our meeting as miraculous or ordained (*not* that I believe in miracles or ordination), but we had semi-orchestrated it ourselves. I had told him I'd be on the mountain Aug. 25, barring a missed or late flight, and he was close enough that he could time his own ascent for that beautiful, late-summer day. He was planning to slackpack Big K with his brother-in-law and then, he'd be done. I assumed he was the first of our Virginia crew to finish, but later we learned that Eazy-E had beaten us all to the punch, on Aug. 16.

We laughed and swapped stories and ate Jolly Rancher hard candies (on which I'd gotten Patches hooked) for 15 minutes before he rolled on toward triumph and I headed down the mountain with 14 miles to go before I slept. If anything, the trip down involved as much hand-work and care as the ascent—a fall here could put an ignominious end to my hike. But I arrived back at the campground at 1:15.

Including stops, it had taken me five-and-a-half hours. Ambling through the campground I saw Legs, Verge, Sweets and Jingle eating at a picnic shelter. I got water from the stream then sat down to eat and chat. Spying Sweets' filthy Dirty Girl gaiters, I got an idea.

"So, I guess you won't be needing those gaiters now...." I began.

Explaining that I'd lost one of mine, I asked if she'd be willing to sell hers to me for the rest of my journey. Sweets had bought them for $20, put 2,189 miles on 'em, and now was willing to part with them for the low, low price of just $5. Deal. (It was purely coincidence that the pale turquoise of my new accessories perfectly matched the rest of my outfit that day, I swear; I couldn't care less about fashion in any sense.)

I made a point to say an extravagant "hi" to the skeptical ranger when I hoisted my pack for the flat, 10-mile stroll along the Penobscot River to the park boundary. I walked awhile with park trail steward Long John, who answered my questions about the natural and human history of the area and told me some good spots to stealth camp once I was out of the park.

I reached Abol Bridge in late afternoon. The sun was now hidden behind a layer of dull clouds, and the air was hot and muggy, promising rain. Walking into the Northern Restaurant I had my sixth reunion of the day, this one truly remarkable: Focus, whom I'd met the year before on the Colorado Trail (she was NOBO on the CDT), was just a day away from finishing the AT and completing her Triple Crown. In flipping, I'd sacrificed the experience of finishing at Katahdin, but it would turn out to have a distinct upside: Over the next month, I ran into almost all the hikers I'd met along the trail, whom I otherwise would never have seen again.

The restaurant was expensive, but I was famished. I ate a burger, salad and clam chowder. I believe that the Samuel Adams Oktoberfest ale to be the single finest beer, in the moment, of my life. The server was no doubt trying to boost her tip when she urged me to buy a 16-ouncer, but I was glad I did (and it had no effect on me, intoxication wise).

I crossed the bridge and pitched my tent in a small glade near the river and collapsed in a heap. I probably wouldn't have admitted it to the Doubting Ranger, but I felt thoroughly thrashed, having jumped back on the trail with a 20-mile, 4,200-foot day.

My feet definitely took a beating on K. Butt chafe. Def. a long day to start, I wrote before falling asleep. *I had to get out to avoid Baxter hassles. I won't be doing this every day, promise. Slow down. Take more pictures. Take more breaks.*

I woke around midnight to the lonely sound of rain pattering on my tent.

TWENTY-SIX:
THE HUNDRED MILE
WILDERNESS

August 2016: Abol Bridge to East Branch Lean-to

In *A Walk in the Woods*, Bill Bryson makes Maine's Hundred-Mile Wilderness sound like something from a Grimm's fairy tale, and he bailed out after just 25 miles.

"It was hell … ominous … brooding … unbearable," he writes. His descriptions call to mind *The Wizard of Oz:* "The trees have ugly faces and malign intent … a woods for looming bears, dangling snakes, wolves with laser-red eyes, strange noises, sudden terrors."

Reading that you think, *Holy cow!* But Bryson gets paid to tell a good story (which, in my opinion, he does quite well), and sometimes he exaggerates. To be blunt, his description of the wilderness is 100 percent, industrial-grade, melodramatic baloney, very likely conjured up to rationalize his decision to bail out.

The Hundred-Mile Wilderness is the section of the AT that runs between Abol Bridge and the small town of Monson (NOBO mile 2074.6; SOBO 114.5). It is the most remote part of the trail, connected to the rest of the world (or as thru-hiker and much beloved YouTuber Dixie calls it, the "synthetic" world) only via a couple of logging roads and a hostel that can be accessed only by canoe. But presumably that's exactly what many thru-hikers are after, and it's not like you're walking into the forest of Fangorn (yet another Tolkien reference; sorry); at any rate, I saw no Ents.

Glancing at AWOL's elevations, many hikers are no doubt encouraged by what appear to be long stretches, up to 30 miles, of level land interrupted by just a few puny-looking climbs, compared to New Hampshire, southern Maine and even the South. But it didn't take long for me to grasp that this was anything but a stroll in the park.

*

I rose early after a rainy night beside the Penobscot River. After rolling my sopping-wet tent inside a plastic garbage bag, I hit the trail at 6:40 and just a few miles later, ran into someone I'd been chasing way back in Virginia: Juan Durer, aka Wanderer, a 50-something guy from San Francisco who was sharing his experiences as a correspondent for the trailblazing *Sounds of the Trail* podcast (first to have "correspondents" semi-live-casting their hikes). I had always looked forward to the skillful, comical self-portraits—always strumming his ukulele and typically accompanied by a dancing bear, smiling dog, dancing serpent or some other creature—he'd left in shelter logbooks.

I chatted with Wanderer and another hiker of about our same vintage named Junco for a few minutes, noting that they both displayed what I call the "thousand-yard Katahdin stare." When we parted, the sky was overcast and the air was cool and humid, an unusual combination. My feet were still feeling the effects of Katahdin+10 the day before and while the grade ranged from flat to gently climbing, the tread was a perpetual hopscotch of tricky roots and rocks.

Theory: roots and rocks are hard on feet not just because they poke and prod, I wrote later. *In stepping over and around them, I think your feet also are forced to slam the ground harder than they would on even tread. And that adds up over several thousand steps.*

The AT is indescribably steeper in the north than in the steep South and relatively flatter mid-Atlantic, and the tricky tread considerably magnifies its difficulty. There are breaks here and there, but I'd say 80 or 90 percent of the trail through Maine and New Hampshire is wet, muddy, rooty, rocky, blocky, or slabby, whether it's steep or even. That's not only tough on feet, but also drastically reduces your speed. It's also mentally exhausting.

"I'm so sick of tripping and falling on roots," triple-crowner Focus told me at Abol Bridge. "Pretty much every day I fantasize about the tread on the PCT and CDT. That's one reason the AT is so tough."

But hiking along the rough contours of Rainbow Lake, the trail treated me to long, beautiful views across peaceful waters. After 15 miles I came to Rainbow Stream Lean-to (mile 2159, NOBO; 30.1 SOBO). It's generally considered one of the most uncomfortable shelters on the AT because of its "baseball-bat floor"; why anyone would choose to build a floor with rounded poles instead of flat planks, I can't imagine.

Although the air didn't feel especially hot, the humidity had left me drenched in sweat. So there went *that* justification for flipping up north. But Rainbow Stream obligingly provided an opportunity to desalinate myself.

I plunged fully clothed into a deep bucket of clear green water just upstream from the lean-to. I stripped in the water, then dunked my shorts, shirt and socks and wrung them out until the water dripping back into the stream was no longer cloudy. On a whim, I walked the 50 yards back to the shelter wearing nothing but my shoes.

I pulled on my zipoff Columbia pants and hung my tent and clothes to dry in the pale sunlight that had begun to seep through the clouds. Then I went back to the water to soak my throbbing feet while eating lunch.

Feeling greatly refreshed, I enjoyed the afternoon despite the continuing chunky tread. With just eight miles to go to Wadleigh Stream Lean-to (NOBO 2150.9; SOBO 38.2), where I planned to spend the night, I took it pretty easy. The 900-foot climb up Nesuntabunt Mountain was at times steep, but paid off with a spectacular 16-mile line-of-sight view to Katahdin and the long waters of Nahmakanta Lake below.

Some helpful NOBO had left a note at the shelter suggesting that the feet-mangling roots and rocks would ease up about 10 miles south and urging SOBOs to take advantage of the many swimming opportunities down the trail.

*

My feet still hurt the next morning, and I now questioned the wisdom of trying to save a few bucks by using this pair of Hokas, which had already become an uncomfortable vice on my right forefoot. But the weather was cool and sunny, perfect for walking. I put my head down, hoping to grind out the remaining miles of jumbly tread as fast as I could.

After three miles, I came to the end of Nahmakanta Lake and found an unexpected camping area near a logging road, complete with privy and picnic shelter where, to my astonishment and early-morning joy, I found the most elaborate spread of magic since Grayson Highlands.

Two 2014 thru-hikers, Owl and Mumblemumble (I forgot to record his name), had driven their pickup into the heart of the wilderness on the logging road to provide full-service hiker dining from Friday night through Sunday morning (another demonstration that Bryson's rhetoric is a tad overheated). When I arrived, it was breakfast—hashbrowns, coffee, and Cap'n Crunch, for me—followed by breakfast dessert: Coke, Ding-Dongs, Snickers, potato chips, and, in hopes of pushing all that deadly, delicious stuff out of my system quickly, two apples and some grapes.

"If you see any hikers tell them we'll be here through about 11 Sunday morning," Owl instructed, and I was happy to oblige.

Another six-and-a-half miles down the trail (to me, SOBO is always "down" the trail, NOBO always "up"), I stopped to dip my feet and splash around in Pemadumcook Lake (NOBO mile 2141.2; SOBO 47.7), which offered yet another unimpeded view of lordly Katahdin.

As I sunned myself dry on the rocks, the sound of approaching NOBOs drifted down to the water, including a voice that sounded very familiar. Moving fast, a crew of five or six hikers passed through the trees about 25 yards away and I recognized Olive Oil, whom I'd spent time with in Virginia. They didn't see me, and I didn't call out, but I picked up on their giddy determination—less than 50 miles to go!

After the briefest of climbs to Potaywadjo Spring Lean-to, I descended to find a small, beautiful sandy beach on the shores of Jo-Mary Lake (NOBO mile 2139; SOBO 50.1), where I stripped down for my second swim-and-sunshine session of the day.

Just as I'd read in the Rainbow Stream logbook, the flat, brutal tread soon turned smooth. I was so thrilled that I began shuffle-jogging, to make up time lost dancing with rocks and roots. Just after Jo-Mary Road, I came up behind a young hiker with a rather large pack making her way up the path alongside Cooper Brook. We exchanged pleasantries and I realized she wasn't American.

"Are you French?" I asked. I'm usually pretty good at pegging accents. Usually.

She laughed, white teeth contrasting with her deep tan. She had a kind of elfin beauty, a blond, hiker-trash version of Emma Watson.

"French?" she said. "That is nice you would think that."

In fact, Simba was from Israel. At 22, she was fresh out of the Israel Defense Force and was hiking the Maine sections of the AT after working at a summer camp in Massachusetts. All Jewish, Christian and Druze citizens of Israel, male or female, are required to serve after completing high school, with controversial exceptions for religious scholars. Women are eligible for 90 percent of jobs in the IDF, including combat roles, which should dispel idiotic American notions that they can't hack it or would disrupt unit cohesion; 51 percent of IDF officers are now female.

Having enjoyed my own backpacking experiences in the deserts of Israel, I slowed down to continue the conversation. Simba had hiked the 1,000-kilometer Israel National Trail, from the Lebanon border to the Red Sea, after her hitch was up. I recalled to her the hidden wonders I'd encountered in the remote corners of the Negev Desert—bottomless pools of emerald-clear water, ringed with tiny frogs— the grassy hills around Kenneret (known by

Christians as the Sea of Galilee) in the north, the gorgeous beaches of Eilat, where she lives, and elsewhere.

Eventually, Simba decided to take a break, and despite enjoying her company, I decided to go on. Shortly thereafter I came across a hiker jogging the other direction. It was Redbeard, the silent third occupant of "RPG" Shelter the night Skeeter had apparently propositioned me. He was shirtless, haggard, and said he was going to bash out another 41 miles to Abol Bridge.

"Wow. That's a long day," I said. It was already late afternoon, and even if he could keep a 3-mph pace—a tough proposition amid roots and rocks—he wouldn't get there until sunrise.

"At least it's flat," Redbeard said. I didn't have the heart to tell him about the tread.

I, on the other hand, thought I was home free, and I continued to jog all the way to Cooper Brook Falls Lean-to. Overall, I was pleased with my progress, having averaged about 2.7 miles an hour, despite 10 miles of cluttered trail.

When I arrived, a smart, vivacious Texas hiker named Sourpatch was gearing up to hike another three miles to Crawford Pond with a section hiker she'd started with at Katahdin (I neglected to record his name, a problem I seem to have with male hikers more than female... ahem; anyway, he was recently out of the Marine Corps). Sourpatch asked if I'd passed a young blond hiker with an accent.

"Simba? Yes, she's great," I said enthusiastically. I told Sourpatch the Israeli beauty was probably no more than a half hour behind me.

"If she stops here, will you tell her we're camping at Crawford Pond?" Sourpatch said.

I said I would, but sadly, Simba did not stop by the shelter.

After tossing my sleeping pad and bag out, I went for my third, and least enjoyable, swim of the day. The cascading waters of Cooper Brook were chilly and I kept having to pluck eager leeches from my feet and ankles.

While I was drying off, Goldrush appeared around the corner; I'd last seen him at the Howard Johnson's Express in Daleville, Va. He said he had injured his foot at 501 Shelter in Pennsylvania, not far from where I'd been knocked to my knees by Lyme disease, and was now flipping SOBO.

I slept well that night, despite the persistent scrabblings of shelter mice, who did no more damage than drag a forgotten gummi-bear bag from a side pocket of my pack.

*

I woke before 4 a.m., then forced myself to go back to sleep until 5, when nature called. A thermometer in the shelter read 59 degrees F, and for the first time I slipped on my long-sleeve Merino wool shirt (bought on the advice of Patches). For breakfast I ate Pop-Tarts and drank a Coke I'd carried away from Owl's magic pavilion. High on sugar, I hit the trail just before 6.

Not even five minutes into my day, I was elated when I came upon a huge female moose grazing just a few feet off the trail. She bashed away through the trees before I could get my phone out, but I got a great view of her impressive derriere as she fled. Now I could check *that* Maine experience off my list.

Crawford Pond was covered in a thin mist when I rolled by and it was too chilly for an early-morning dip. I soon came up behind Simba at the beginning of the 750-foot climb up Little Boardman Mountain. This time, I slowed down.

"You are very fast," she said in that oh-so-charming accent.

"Not really fast," I said. "I just like to keep rolling along."

"But you were *running* away from me last time I saw you!"

"Not really running, just sort of shuffling while I had decent tread. And I sure wasn't running away from *you*...."

We walked together for the next half mile or so. She said she felt guilty that she was so slow, and worried that she was holding up Sourpatch.

"She doesn't seem to mind," I said. "You really aren't that slow. But you are carrying a pretty big pack." The thing teetering over her head reminded me of "the beast" portrayed in Cheryl Strayed's *Wild* and the subsequent Reese Witherspoon movie.

Simba laughed.

"Next time I will not bring so much."

A happy, lunk-headed pit bull came barging out to greet me when I reached East Branch Lean-to (NOBO 2121.3; SOBO 67.8). Her name was Medusa and she belonged to a woman named Grub, who looked like she had settled in for a long stay.

I wondered if she might be homeless, but Grub explained that she was hiking to raise awareness of distressed counties along the AT. She had hiked parts of Pennsylvania before flipping up to Maine. But now she had hurt her foot and had slowed to a crawl. She told me she expected to take another *eight* days to reach Monson, an average of less than four miles a day.

"My church group is expecting me a lot sooner than that," she said. "I'm worried that they'll call search-and-rescue. If you see anyone looking for me or signs that I'm missing, will you tell them I'm OK?"

I said I would, though I was a little worried for her myself.

"Do you have enough food for the two of you?" I asked. "I'll be in town day after tomorrow, and I'm happy to share."

"We're fine, thank you," she answered. "And if I run out, the Lord will provide."

I couldn't help thinking of the old joke about the man stuck on his roof as flood waters rise, praying for God to save him. Confident in the power of prayer, he declines help from a man in a canoe, another in a motor boat, and finally, one shouting down from a helicopter.

"No thanks," he tells them all. "I have faith God will save me."

He soon drowns, and when he gets to heaven, he asks God why he didn't reward his faith by saving him.

"I sent you a canoe, a motorboat, and a helicopter," the exasperated Almighty replies. "What more did you expect?"

I later looked up Grub's website, 2000milesforchrist.com. Her last blog post, dated September 6, was blank.

The Lord may or may not provide, I thought as I hiked away, *but in my book, the Hundred Mile Wilderness may not be the best place to put Him to the test.*

(I was relieved when Sourpatch told me several months later that Grub and Medusa made it out of the Hundred Mile Wilderness safely).

TWENTY-SEVEN: FAIR COMPANY

August 2016: Logan Brook Lean-to to Monson, Maine

Much of the Hundred Mile Wilderness is flat, but that doesn't make it easy. There are climbs, including the ladder-like ascent from Logan Brook Lean-to to the summit of Whitecap Mountain, which includes the 25th-steepest half-mile section on the AT.

That day, the temperature barely topped out at 70 and the dew point was only 50 degrees, but I was drenched by the time I was on top. I tugged on a ragged pair of Brooks Runderwear in an effort to stave off an even worse case of swamp-ass.

My expectations that the next three small summits would be easy were soon cruelly dashed. Hay Mountain, West Peak and Gulf Hagas Mountain were not only steep, but brutally rooty and rocky. By day's end, I had tallied up some 4,200 feet of uphill marching.

Stopping by Carl A. Newhall Lean-to (NOBO mile 2110.5; SOBO 78.6), I found Lazy Eagle, the hiker I'd met in Shenandoah National Park who had walked with my cousin Margarita down south, as well as one of four Sunshines I met along the trail.

The descent to the West Branch of the Pleasant River was knotted with rocks and roots and included the 39th steepest half-mile of the trail. To my dismay, it took me 2 hours and 40 minutes to hike just 5.6 miles down to the river, a pace of 2 mph. I was beginning to sense a disconcerting trend.

AT hikers often have to ford multiple rivers and streams in Maine, but in this year of drought, the Pleasant was the only one where I had no choice but to get my feet wet. After removing my socks and insoles, I waded across in my Hokas. On the other side I walked four-tenths of a mile the wrong way looking for a campsite, only to have to return and toss up my tent near the banks of the river.

Will reel off 20 mi. tomorrow, then a short day to resupply in Monson. Four-and-a-half days through the Hundred Mile. Not so bad, I wrote.

It rained steadily for most of the night, but I felt warm, comfortable, and pleasantly alone in the middle of nowhere.

*

A warm, dense fog hung in the air when I began walking at 6:30. I immediately hit the first steep incline of the 1,500-foot climb to Chairback and Columbus mountains.

There followed so many annoying PUDs that each one was given a number rather than a name—Third Mountain, Mount Three-and-a-Half, and Fourth Mountain—but at least the ledges on Barren Mountain offered nice views. For a stretch that was supposed to be "flat," it felt pretty steep to me.

The air was once again muggy, leaving my skin slick and stinging in places from chafe. But once I got above the suffocating fog, a welcome breeze found me atop Chairback. Not far from the summit I was happy to see a ruffed grouse scurrying with her two chicks along the trail.

I was also extremely heartened to see countless toads and frogs, given scientific concerns about the decline of amphibian populations. I have always felt confident in distinguishing their respective genera, *Bufo* and *Rana*, but the trail taught me a new trick to tell from a distance: Frogs fling themselves away from you, far and fast, while toads just sort of flop awkwardly from inch to inch.

The day also provided more of the unexpected pleasure of running into so many NOBOs I'd met further south. I ran into BASA, who never reunited with Achilles after they'd hiked together for more than 1,500 miles. I was sad to learn that Alan, who had been brooding over the coming challenge of the White Mountains when I'd seen him last, had left the trail in Hanover, N.H.

I also talked with Diesel and Coldsnap, a couple I'd met at the Howard Johnson's in Daleville. And, as further proof of my poor prediction skills, I ran into Trekkeroni—the kid with the 65-pound pack and pepperoni duct-taped to his poles— whom I'd last seen in Pearisburg, Virginia and predicted would never make it to Maine.

I stumbled into Wilson Valley Lean-to after more than 10 hours of hiking, which translated to a pace just under 2 mph over some 19.9 miles and 4,500 feet of climbing. Remind me again why the Hundred Mile Wilderness is "easy"....

I shared the shelter that night with 65-year-old Just Charlie, who then owned As Time Goes By, a bookstore-coffee shop in tiny Marion, Alabama. He'd begun section-hiking the AT in 1977 and was finally about to finish the trail nearly 40 years later.

He wasn't thrilled with many of the changes he'd seen over the years. His most interesting observation (quoted at length in a previous chapter) was that over time, trail designers had insistently rerouted the Appalachian Trail from "boring" road walks or pastures to ridgetops.

"That makes sense for weekend hikers, who want to get up into the trees," Just Charlie said. "But it makes the trail more monotonous, and considerably harder, if you are hiking the whole thing or doing long sections."

We talked until late about his store, William Faulkner, the wreck of the Sultana on the Mississippi River following the Civil War, and life as a longhair in the deepest reaches of the old South. At twilight a young couple showed up in a pouring rain and pitched their tent behind the shelter.

*

I felt refreshed when I headed out early the next morning for a 10.4-mile walk that would take me out of the wilderness and into the storied trail town of Monson for a much-needed nero. Despite an endless series of PUDs, I would only have to climb 1,400 feet that day.

The southern end of the wilderness was beautiful, as the trail traipsed across brooks and streams, past ponds and much-photographed Little Wilson Falls. Eager to get to town, I didn't swim, though I did slip and take an impromptu dip in Big Wilson Stream.

As I approached the highway, the peeling hiss of rubber on pavement and the grinding whine of engines grew ever louder. After four days in the remote Maine woods, this pervasive soundtrack to modern life was profoundly disheartening. I hit the road just after 10 a.m., which gave me plenty of time to rest and recuperate before I headed out the next day.

I hitched a ride to Shaw's Hiker Hostel, a historic wayside for AT hikers now owned and operated by Poet and Hippie Chick, who thru-hiked the trail in 2008. They now spend the hiking season at the hostel with their daughter, Baby Chick, and laid-back springer spaniel named Ringo. (Hippie Chick is the daughter of Ole Man and NaviGator, owners of the Appalachian Trail Lodge in Millinocket.)

Poet runs an extensive, and (not surprisingly) somewhat pricey resupply of both food and equipment out of a barn on the property, where he annually battles clever squirrels who manage to find their way in somehow.

"I'm thinking of getting a cat," he said. "Or a gun."

After dumping my heap of filthy clothes next to five other reeking piles awaiting ablution in the washing machine, I wandered into town and bought some pretty gross, greasy pizza slices and Gatorade at the mini-mart. While walking back, I was happy to run into Achilles, who was staying at the Lakeshore House hostel. He explained that he and BASA had parted company because Achilles' wanted to slow down a bit and take more time to chill out. Even so, he was just a day behind his old partner.

Back at Shaw's, I found Applejack, whom I'd met in the Smokys during my first week on the trail, and again in Virginia and Pennsylvania. Toward evening

I was beyond psyched when Sourpatch and Simba tumbled out of the hostel shuttle.

That night I walked back to the Lakeshore and shared a table with a German woman named Spacious and Alpaca, whose shelter logbook entries had been bugging me since at least Pennsylvania. A very nice guy, Alpaca frequently espoused the common trail myth that anyone going "too fast" (i.e. faster than *you*) is robbing themselves of enjoyment and experience. It was the same stop-and-smell-the roses line as the one preached by Slow Man, who gave me my trail name on the Colorado Trail.

Halfway through dinner I said, "So, Alpaca, I have a bone to pick with you...."

A friendly debate ensued, and we both gave some ground. Alpaca made the point that if you go fast, you have to pay more attention to your feet, and therefore you might miss seeing something cool, a bear, an eagle, a side trail to a waterfall.

"Fair enough, but can we admit that *everyone* has to keep their head down if you don't want to break a leg, especially once you get to Pennsylvania?" I countered. "Anyway, I can't tell you the number of times I *didn't* stomp on toads, frogs, salamanders, and snakes because I was watching my feet."

I've had fantastic experiences while hiking 20- or 30-mile days. But I confess that the Appalachian Trail forced me to accept a hard truth the 500-mile CT couldn't teach me: I was able to rack up big miles, day after day, well into New England, but over 2,000 miles, the cumulative strain on my body and mind did indeed imperil my ability to finish. Moving fast doesn't necessarily diminish a long-distance experience, but I now know that at my age, at least, I need to pace myself on a very long hike.

Despite all my fuming at a faceless nemesis along the trail, I liked Alpaca. He was even in the newspaper business, my old career. Once more, the trail made a mockery of my ill-informed judgments.

*

I hadn't signed up for breakfast at Shaw's, but when I went into the kitchen for coffee at 6 a.m., Poet talked me into staying. It was a greasy affair, not at all what I'm used to, but I ate my fill of scrambled eggs, potatoes, and pancakes, while passing on bacon. Simba didn't show up, though Sourpatch did.

Among those sitting across the table from me were Boss and Samsquatch, a young British couple I'd met a million miles away in the South. They had been part of the boisterous bunch my crew had dubbed Chuck-E-Cheese, or sometimes, The Mickey Mouse Club, who had noisily, and good-naturedly, invaded a couple shelters in Virginia.

Boss, a garrulous, dark-haired young woman, was still quite chatty. But Samsquatch, a bookish-looking blond chap with a voice even louder than mine, spoke hardly a word. He looked haunted, like a man freshly arrived from combat.

I've heard it said that by the time most NOBO women reach Maine, they are glowing with strength—both inner and outer—health, and beauty, but most men have the appearance of someone who has just barely survived a death march. Gary "Green Giant" Sizer, former Marine, 2014 AT thru-hiker, and author of the memoir, "Where's the Next Shelter?," famously posted a before-and-after shot that horrified many who saw it; post-trail, he looked ghastly, gaunt and grungy. Based strictly on anecdotal evidence from my miles on the AT, I'm inclined to think women are more natural long-distance hikers than their testosterone-soaked species-mates.

Coming back downstairs after packing up, I noticed Simba sitting at the picnic table outside, arms wrapped around pajama-clad knees, a curl of steam rising from her coffee cup. Dumping my pack on the porch, I sat down next to her.

"No breakfast for you?"

"I don't like American breakfast," she said, yawning. "It's too much, too greasy, too heavy. I'm not used to it."

"I loved eating Israeli-style breakfast when I was there—plain yogurt, cheese, tomatoes, cucumbers, hummus...."

"Yes, it's much better," she said, flashing those lovely white teeth. "You know, after I met you, I told Sourpatch I was sure you had an interesting story."

Encouraging me to tell stories can be a mistake of grave proportions, as it's one of my favorite pastimes. Lava Monster even came up with a hashtag for my tendencies, #ponytales.

"I'm warning you, once you pull the string in my back, you might have to kick me to get me to stop," I said. Simba shrugged. "Don't say I didn't warn you! But first, I need more coffee."

Simba laughed when I returned and took off my shoes.

"Wow. Your stories really *must* be long," she said, laughing.

"Ah, I *knew* you were something interesting," Simba said when I told her I was a writer. Sourpatch had now joined us at the table.

Now uncorked, I talked about my six years working as a cowboy, my newspaper career, and the obsession that had led to my latest book project: finding and recovering my Medal of Honor-winning grandfather's remains from the Pacific battlefield where he fell in 1943.

"You were a *real* cowboy?" Sourpatch said.

"Yup."

"God. I think I love you," she said with a wink.

Simba talked about hiking the Israel National Trail after her army hitch was up.

"In the desert you need to prepare water and to put it somewhere hidden in the places you where you'll stop to sleep," she said. "Or to you have to carry enough water for three days."

After the hike, she worked on an organic farm, then took the job at a Massachusetts summer camp, which inspired her to sample the AT.

"I love being in nature," Simba said. "I want to work in nature."

I know many people won't believe me, but there was nothing tawdry or untoward about the mutual connection Simba and I felt. Sometimes you meet a person you just click with, almost as if you'd known them in some other life (*not* that I believe in other lives), and you want to spend time with them, no matter your difference in age, gender, or any other trivial detail. That's how I felt about Patches and Lava, whose combined ages were less than mine, and who have remained close friends. That such connections are so common and accepted on the trail, where the synthetic world might look askance, remains one of thru-hiking's greatest gifts.

But when I'd risen at 5:30 that morning, my plan was to get going no later than 6:30. At 8:15, I said goodbye to Simba and Sourpatch, and Poet drove me back to the trailhead.

Maybe I should have zeroed, I wrote in my journal that night, feeling empty and alone. *Now maybe I'll never see them again.*

A few days after leaving Shaw's, I was kicking myself for not resisting my stupid forward-motion compulsion and walking with her for a day or two. But I later connected with both Simba and Sourpatch. Simba finished her hike in Stratton and took a job on a farm in Eilat, Israel, hoping to return to the U.S. and hike more long trails. In July 2017, I spent a night with Sourpatch at a hostel in Salida, Colorado, during her hike of the Colorado Trail.

TWENTY-EIGHT: OVER THE RIVER

September 2016: Monson to the Kennebec River

The trail was relatively flat out of Monson, with just a few hundred feet of climbing in the first six miles, followed by a quarter mile downhill to the Piscataquis River (NOBO mile 2067.9; SOBO 121.2), which I was able to "ford" by simply hopping from stone to stone, courtesy of a dry summer. Alas, I slipped and soaked one foot.

That's where I met Two Pack, from the story at the beginning of this book.

*

After the river, the trail rose some 700 feet over the next 11 miles to Moxie Bald Mountain Lean-to. Although not thrilled by my realization that this endless tangle of roots and rocks was *normal* for the trail in Maine, I was making decent time.

While eating a snack at the shelter to fuel the 1,400-foot ascent of Moxie Bald, I talked to an older SOBO named Glacier, who was curious about my ULA Catalyst pack.

"I love it, but I bought it before my first long-distance hike and these days I don't really need this much volume," I said. "Also, it presses right up against my back, so no air gets in there and I'm constantly sweating. But really, it's great." (Only after my hike did I learn that the pack has two aluminum struts that can be adjusted to improve air flow to the back.)

Glacier said he had semi-retired, working construction just three months of the year to fund his hiking habit.

Then, just before I left, another older guy arrived at the shelter with his younger female hiking companion.

"Porcupine?" I said.

"Yeah?" he said with a slight scowl. "Do I know you?"

I was not so memorable as he, it seemed. I'd met him at the Raven's Rest Hostel in Lake City, my final night indoors while hiking the Colorado Trail in 2015. A smart, funny, acerbic New Yorker in his sixties, he'd told the rest of us at the hostel that he was traveling NOBO on the 3,100-mile Continental Divide Trail.

I zeroed the next day in Lake City, but Porcupine hopped a shuttle in the morning with CT SOBO MoonBeam, whom I'd gotten to know a little. I shuttled out with another trail friend, Bigfoot, 24 hours later and was surprised to pass Porcupine that afternoon while descending from the 13,200-foot high point of the CT, considerably south of where I'd last seen him.

"Wait ... I thought you were NOBO on the CDT?" I said.

"Naw, I just said that. I just go where the trail takes me, usually to follow women," he said. "Currently, you could say I'm chasing a moonbeam. But she's too fast for me."

He was harmless, I was sure, but there was something creepy about drifting around various trails to stalk women. Now here he was, possibly doing the same thing.

He didn't remember our previous meetings, but explained that he was hiking with "Danielle" to help her finish the AT. Evidently, I didn't have enough X chromosomes to warrant further interest, but at least he was honest about what he was up to.

The afternoon was mostly cloudy, but oppressively hot as I made the steep climb up Moxie Bald (including the 49th steepest half-mile on the trail). The top was gorgeous, a cap of cold granite fringed by spruce trees stunted and gnarled by fierce northern winds. It was the first summit that really said "Maine" to me.

Not only were there gorgeous, 360-degree views—I could see tiny Monson glittering in the distance—but this was the kind of place Stephen King was always writing about, where the spirits of long-dead original inhabitants might still be watching over the land. Moved by the sense of eerie remoteness, I took about 15 minutes on top to accomplish the most frivolous of tasks: Writing out the words "PET SEMATARY" in stones for the viewing pleasure of the next few hikers who decided to wander that part of the summit.

That night at Bald Mountain Brook Lean-to I carefully placed a bottle of Sam Adams Oktoberfest beer in the stream that rushed down through a mini-canyon not far from the shelter. The only other occupant that night was an older hiker named Don, a former undercover New York state police officer, Marine, long-distance bike tourist, lumberjack, and hotel owner.

We had a long, fascinating conversation about everything, though nothing I recall except his tales about working construction during the summer in Alaska, where it rained so much and so frequently that he simply became inured to getting wet. I was grateful for the company.

As we talked, a frazzled-looking guy with a dog named Charlie rolled around the corner. He didn't stay long, saying he was going to walk down the hill to a stealth-camping site he'd heard about. He had recently mustered out of the military, he said, due to mental-health issues, and was hiking the trail to smooth out the jagged edges of his mind. Right after he left, the skies unleashed a ferocious downpour. Don and I both worried about him, as he didn't seem to know much about hiking or the trail.

The next morning, I passed through the stealth site and asked the one hiker who was awake if she'd seen the man and his dog. She hadn't. I never saw them again.

*

My first day out of Monson I walked 22 miles, which included 2,200 feet of climbing. The next day, I hiked only 18.3 miles (and about 2,300 feet of climbing), but felt beat.

"You should plan on scaling back your miles, not just in the Whites, but also in southern Maine," said BASA, an iron man about my age who had, with Achilles, reeled off 300 miles in 12 days in the mid-Atlantic.

Every AT hiker hears about—and often frets about—the looming challenge of New Hampshire's White Mountains. Now a little more than halfway through Maine, I wondered why this state didn't have a more fearsome reputation, if for no other reason than its persistently tricky tread. Unbeknownst to me, the 155 miles I'd walked since Katahdin were a playground compared to what Maine had to offer in the last 125.

*

I was making good time on relatively decent tread—I could actually see soil!— when I stopped at Pleasant Pond Lean-to to fill up with water. Slick with sweat after humping over Pleasant Pond Mountain (where I ran into Pending, whom I'd met all the way back in Franklin, N.C.) on a muggy, post-rain morning, I gave myself a bandana bath in the small stream before moseying on, feeling much refreshed.

Less than a mile after the shelter, I was happily rolling along when I saw what appeared to be a round gray stone about the size of a volleyball smack in the middle of the trail. As I got closer, my brain didn't immediately register what I was looking at, but it appeared that the "stone" had been pierced by the trunk of a thin, fallen birch tree.

Did you know that insects live in a "faster" version of reality than we do, thanks to the fact that their eyes send updates to their tiny brains more frequently than ours do? They exist in a kind of Matrix-like world where time subjectively goes faster. That's why it's so hard to smack a housefly.

I barely saw the cloud of furious hornets that boiled up out of their fallen nest—not a rock, after all—and by the time the first shriek escaped my throat, nearly tearing my face off, they were stinging their little hearts out. Riding on a rocket-burst of adrenaline, my body flung itself—my conscious brain had *nothing* to do with it—over the teeming hazard and I fled down the trail yelping like a man aflame.

At least 4 zeroed in on me, BAM, and stung me, 2x upper left thigh, 2x right ass cheek, 1x on each wrist, I wrote later. *I literally yelled "shit" and ran as fast as I could, slapping at the stings. Lucky for me the tread was relatively smooth.*

Cursing and sucking on one of the wrist stings, I slowed down and allowed myself to imagine what I'd do if the same thing had happened while I was, say, on a steep, rocky mountainside—such as my recent descent of Pleasant Pond Mountain, the 36th steepest half-mile on the trail. Would my brain instinctively know *not* to run in that situation, or would it be perfectly happy to break its own neck in an effort to flee the danger? I did not care to find out, and for the rest of my hike, I was a confirmed "hornet-noid."

*

The official, Appalachian Trail Conservancy-approved, AT route across the Kennebec River is on a canoe ferry paddled by a contracted employee from May 1 to Oct. 31. The trail, as initially envisioned by Myron Avery, would have traversed the river just below Wyman Lake about 10 miles south of the current crossing. When Ralph Sterling, owner of a hotel in the tiny village of Caratunk, built his Pierce Pond Camps, he began a ferry service, which convinced AT route finders to splash the trail across the river at its current location. Alas, Pierce's service ceased after just a couple of years and the new "ferry" was a couple of rowboats tied up on the bank.

The river, though wide, doesn't seem particularly daunting. But that's not what Gene Espy, who in 1951 became the second person to thru-hike the trail (after Earl Shaffer, aka The Crazy One, pioneered thru hiking in 1948), found when he tried to swim it: "Before I could make a second stroke with my pole, the boat was about 20 yards downstream."

For decades, fording the Kennebec was a tricky affair. Sometimes hikers found inner tubes on which they could paddle across, while others built their own clumsy log rafts, and many simply waded through the torrent, precariously balancing on slippery stones. But unannounced releases of water from a dam upstream can cause a sudden increase in flow, and in 1986, a hiker named Alice Ferrence drowned while making the crossing.

Concerned about liability, the following season the ATC hired local paddler, registered Maine Trail Guide and Wilderness First Responder Steve Longley, aka The Ferryman, to safely propel hikers across the river for the next 20 years. Several others have served as the Charon of the Kennebec since his retirement in 2008; in 2016 it was Greg Caruso, another registered Maine Trail Guide.

I knew the ferry operated from 9 a.m. to 2 p.m. during September. Not wanting to find myself stranded on the northern shore, nor caring to make like AT renegade Warren Doyle and wade across (though as dry as it was, 2016 was probably the year to do it), I forlornly decided not to go into Caratunk or nearby Northern Outdoors, where I could have eaten a hearty lunch.

Greg soon appeared out of the woods. I tossed my pack in his canoe and the two of us paddled across in just a few minutes. It was just after noon on Sept. 1.

TWENTY-NINE:
THE PAIN OF MAINE

September 2016: Harrison's Pierce Pond Camps
to Crocker Campsite

After paddling across the Kennebec, I lounged for a half hour on the southern bank, dabbling my feet in the cool water of Otter Pond Stream while I ate peanut butter and tortillas.

From there, I made somewhat slow progress on the long, gently sloping climb beside Pierce Pond Stream, stopping twice to swim in deep buckets of cold, clear, greenish water. After four miles, I came upon a sign pointing to a battered bridge leading to Harrison's Pierce Pond Camps. I hadn't planned to stop, but now pouting that I'd passed up a chance for a milkshake in Caratunk, I decided to stop in and see if the proprietor might have a Coke or Gatorade.

Tim Harrison did not have anything to sell, but I was immediately drawn to his place. A collection of wood-sided cabins with cockeyed doors and small wood stoves, and a main lodge with creaking, sloping floors, an array of large animal trophies on the wall, and an enticing assortment of dusty books, maps and other curiosities, it reminded me somehow of William Faulkner's famous novella, *The Bear*. It was only 2:30 and I'd planned to go farther, but on the spur of the moment, I decided to stay.

I had a great time talking with Tim, playing with his clever little poodle puppy, Charlie, and lounging in the brisk waters of the stream just below my cabin, where fingerling trout waved like tiny flags in the current. I'd only come 40 miles from Monson, but I was beat.

My feet, especially, were feeling the miles. The Hoka One One Mafate Speed trail runners that I'd started with on Katahdin (only because they were in my closet and I didn't want them to go to waste) had not turned out to be a good choice. My feet, especially my right foot, were wider than they used to be, and it was beginning to look like the condition might be permanent; guess that's what slapping them up and down on rocks and roots and hard earth several million times with 25 pounds of extra weight on your back will do to you.

Now, the side of the ball of my right foot burned with sharp pain most days, squeezed by the toe box of my Hokas, and the tiny sesamoid bones that lie beneath the skin between the ball of the foot and the instep felt like hot little BBs. My poor feet demanded to know why I didn't stick with Altras, with their gloriously roomy toe box.

I hear you, feet, I wrote in my journal. *Gonna have to order some Altras soon.*

That night, I plopped down onto an ancient couch made of stiff leather in the lodge, where I pored over coffee-stained maps and old books until I nearly nodded off. I staggered down the hill to my cabin and fell asleep to the babbling lullaby of Pierce Pond Stream.

Breakfast at Pierce Pond Camps is legendary. Tim gets up early to make coffee, then fixes up a mess of "red, white and blue" pancakes—infused with raspberries, blueberries, and some white fruit—eggs, and sausage. Nobody else stayed in a cabin that night, but a dozen hikers had rolled in from nearby Pierce Pond Lean-to the night before to lay down $12 for the feast.

And then, for dessert, my day started out easy, with 10 miles that are among the top 20 easiest miles on the AT in Maine. Mostly level, the tread is intermittently Maine-ish—roots and rocks—but also offers regular relief on soft, duffy singletrack. The day was partly cloudy and pleasantly cool for walking, so much so that I bypassed an opportunity to get wet at West Carry Pond (NOBO mile 2023.9; SOBO 165.2), flagged in Awol's guide for its excellent swimming. For the first time since I could remember, I was moving faster than 3 mph.

By the time I stopped to eat lunch on a stony beach on gorgeous Flagstaff Lake, a stiff breeze was driving whitecaps ashore. Once again, I decided not to swim, and maybe that was a good sign: It was the first week of September and maybe, just maybe, my endless days of swampy sweating were finally coming to an end.

To the southwest loomed the Bigelows, the first "real" mountains since Katahdin (though I'd found bumps like Whitecap and Pleasant Pond plenty steep and challenging). Patches had told me "the Bigs" were beautiful, but I could see in Awol that they were also as jagged as cougar teeth, as were Crocker, Spaulding, the Saddlebacks, Bemis, Old Blue, Baldpate, Mahoosuc, and others down the trail.

I had now finished the "easy" part of Maine, and the training wheels were about to come off. In the next 100 miles, I would be climbing or descending 11 of the 20 steepest half-miles and nine of the 25 steepest miles on the Appalachian Trail.

"The AT since Gorham (N.H., about 17 miles from the Maine state line) has been as challenging as the trail anywhere," Awol observes in his memoir *after* he's finished the legendarily challenging White Mountains of New Hampshire.

On a whim, that morning I'd decided to count the number of NOBOs I passed. The final tally blew me away: 51, not including day hikers. That number included many hikers I'd not just met, but spent at time with on the trail—Mudpuppy, Ninja Roll (a Louisianan who wrote "Laissez le Ninja Roll!" in every logbook), cheerful German Refill, who had road-walked most of Shenandoah at night, and Tumbleweed and Shiv, the honeymooning, organic-farming couple from Florida with whom I'd camped near Unaka Mountain and at Overmountain Shelter in Tennessee. I had already seen many friends and acquaintances, and over the next couple of weeks I would see many, many more.

Beginning to feel like Old Home Week, I wrote in my journal.

*

The nearly 2,000-foot climb up to the plateau of Little Bigelow Mountain doesn't make any "steepest" lists, but it felt like a long slog for late afternoon. I was good and tired when I stumbled into the Safford Notch Campsite after 23 miles and 3,700 feet of climbing.

While I pitched my tent someone up the hill had cranked up a tinny AM radio talk show, shattering the peace of the woods and setting my teeth on edge. After getting water from the trickle below the camping area, I walked up the hill until I zeroed in on the sound.

"Hey man," I said to a large, black-bearded guy, "is that your radio?" He nodded without a word. "Would you mind turning it down a little, please? Thanks."

As loud and opinionated as I can be, I will often avoid confrontation over such things, as when I chose to pack up and walk to another shelter near dark when Bad News and her pal interrupted my quiet enjoyment of South Mount Wilcox Lean-to. I made my request in a neutral voice, with a smile, then turned around and headed back down to my tent, hoping the guy wasn't as mean as he looked. Somewhat to my surprise, he turned the radio off. *Ahhhh*....

As I passed her tent, a German woman who'd set up near me gave me a conspiratorial thumbs-up.

"Thank you for doing that," she whispered loudly. "That was a *terrible* noise!"

*

The temperature when I rose at 5 the next morning was a wakeup call. It was still above freezing, but not by much. The sun was out, but it was breezy and only got cooler as I made the 1,900-foot climb up to Avery Peak (named for AT pioneer Myron Avery), including—wait for it—the 25th steepest mile on the AT.

I made good time, and once on top, I was rewarded with spectacular 360 views of Flagstaff Lake and endless miles of nearly unbroken wilderness.

After a short dip and steep, short climb, I was atop Bigelow Mountain. The tread remained chunky and challenging for the next two miles as the trail dropped, then rose to the summit of South Horn. Looking at Awol's elevations, it appeared that I had just a mild ascent before a long, fairly steep downhill down to ME 27, where I planned to hitch into Stratton for a resupply.

As it turned out, the descent was just barely faster than the 2,700 feet of climbing I'd done since starting. Steep, rocky, rooty, and featuring many hidden PUDs, it made for slow going. I reached the road at 11:30, which meant I'd been traveling less than 2 mph, and that included a relatively flat runout across Stratton Stream.

Once again, the hitchhiking fairies were with me, and I only had my thumb out for perhaps five minutes before an older woman in a brand-new gray SUV stopped.

"We're local," she said. "We like to support the hikers."

She told me about a recent experience she'd had at the lodge on top of Mount Greylock in Massachusetts. She and her husband were eating at the ledge when she noticed a tall, dark-haired hiker. He was, she said with a girlish giggle, an "*extremely* handsome young man." They watched in amazement as the hiker ate what seemed to them an impossible amount of food in a stunningly short period of time.

"It was so funny," she said, "when he told us his trail name was Tapeworm."

Tall, dark, handsome—that was definitely the Tapeworm I knew. We'd leapfrogged a little in central Pennsylvania and shared a ride up to Lehigh Gap from Palmerton. She was amazed at this coincidence, the kind of magical serendipity I assured her was quite common on the AT.

"Does he *always* eat that much?" she asked.

"Well, I only saw him eat once, and that time he accidentally dropped his cooking pot and spilled half the contents into the dirt right in front of a shelter in Pennsylvania," I said, remembering how I'd scooped it up with a long-handled shovel to deposit it in the woods, just in case any bears turned up. "But his reputation for appetite was how he got his trail name."

My driver nodded. "Well," she repeated, "he was *very* handsome."

She dropped me off in front of the White Wolf Inn, where I ate a big, leisurely lunch and charged my phone. While eating a piece of pecan pie I talked to Jody, then checked in with my sister to see how my mother was doing. It was clear that when I finished the trail, I was going to have to go to Colorado and see what was up.

I wasn't particularly thrilled with the selection and high prices at Fotter's Market just across the street, but I was too lazy to head back up the road to see if the Flagstaff General Store was any better. As I was packing up my food bag in front of the Stratton Motel, which had a $25 bunkroom, I was happy to see Dragon Head, a young engineer from Denver whom I'd spent time with in Pennsylvania. Last time he'd seen me I was sweating and shivering in the heat of mid-day at a shelter where I'd collapsed from as-yet-undiagnosed Lyme disease. I was glad to see he was now hiking with a female companion.

I toyed briefly with the idea of bunking in Stratton, but hating to waste such a beautiful day—sunny and 70 degrees—I decided to head out. I walked for perhaps a half mile before a charmingly accented couple from Montreal stopped to ferry me the rest of the way to the trailhead. They were section hiking in the area, but peppered me questions about thru-hiking.

"We would like to do this someday," the woman said.

They gave me some grapes, chunks of watermelon, and cheese for the road.

For NOBOs, the trip into Stratton is a major milestone, as the trail crosses the 2,000-mile mark less than a mile south of ME 27. For me, that meant only that I'd walked 189.1 miles from Katahdin. I never even saw the assemblage of stones laid across the trail to announce the frontier.

The trail wasted no time in turning steep and rocky on the five-mile climb to north and south Crocker mountains. It took me two-and-a-half hours to reach the north summit (NOBO mile 1995.7; SOBO 193.4) and I was completely drenched in sweat when I got there.

But I was psyched to be descending what looked like a brutal climb from the Carabassett River valley to South Crocker, which encompassed the 12th steepest half-mile and 13th steepest mile on the AT. I could see a thin line of blue smoke rising from the trees in Crocker Cirque for a long, long time before

I finally hit the campsite at 5:40. I was tapped out, having climbed some 5,700 feet over 17.7 miles.

All my talk about scaling back mileage in the Whites, but today I figured out maybe I need to do that here in S. Maine, I wrote that night. *It's pretty brutal, tons of PUDs, steep, rocky. It's not like I have to be anywhere, so I'm going to start aiming for 17-20s.*

THIRTY:
SAND AND GRANITE

September 2016: Carabasset River to Andover, Maine

The trail was rocky but not egregiously steep for a mile down to the South Branch Carabassett River, which I was able to ford by hopping from one blocky white boulder to the next. Turning back, I could see that it would be quite a dangerous crossing in a wetter year or earlier in the season.

The ascent of Sugarloaf Mountain—home to the Sugarloaf Mountain ski resort, which I'd seen across the valley the day before—began with a crank that was very nearly as steep as the lunatic descent I'd hobbled down the night before, and included, in fact, the 14th steepest mile and 16th steepest half-mile on the entire AT.

Once I'd cleared that rocky ladder, the trail climbed into a bergschrund (German for "mountain cleft") studded with tough spruce-fir krummholz (Deutsche: "crooked wood") and offering incredible panoramic views to the south. Relieved when the trail leveled out offering actual dirt and duff on which to place my sore feet, I practically skipped along until I reached the utterly unexpected 500-foot knob that was Spaulding Mountain. But like a mother who buys ice cream because she feels guilty for yelling at her kids, the trail soothed me with another spectacular view up top.

I ate lunch down by Orbeton Stream (SOBO mile 207.0), where a hiker told me that the upcoming Saddleback range wasn't too bad and it was "smooth sailing" after that until Bemis Mountain. But it all began with the 26th steepest half-mile on the AT, which spilled out onto a relatively level ridge before surging to the top of Saddleback Junior. I was continually awed through southern Maine and New Hampshire by the sweeping, unobstructed views from various tree-less summits, and the Saddlebacks were no exception.

But Maine's brutally steep, rocky ups and downs were definitely kicking my ass, and I was tired enough after descending Junior that I decided to call it a day after just under 17 miles. I set up my tent at the Redington Campsite (SOBO 212.4), which I was to have all to myself that night ... or at least there were no *people* around.

Somewhere nearby, on July 21, 2013, a 66-year-old NOBO hiker named Inchworm, aka Geraldine Largay, from Tennessee, stayed at Poplar Ridge Shelter (SOBO mile 209.7), less than three miles north of my campsite. Two days later, when she did not arrive at a rendezvous point, her husband reported her missing. Authorities finally called off one of the largest search-and-rescue efforts in Maine history after about a week. But nearly every 2016 AT hiker heard the news in May when Inchworm's remains were found about two miles off the trail.

"In somm trouble," she had written in a text message to her husband that never sent, still stored in her phone. "Got off trail to go to br (bathroom). Now lost."

Inchworm set up her tent and waited for someone to find her, and after 26 days, died of starvation and exposure. She had dutifully followed the supposed "rule No. 1" when you get lost—stay put—and it had killed her.

Some 1,500 pages of documents released by investigators indicated that Inchworm may have had a poor sense of direction, which would explain how she got lost while taking a bathroom break. But I was disturbed by the thought that she just sat there, waiting for someone else to save her. She wasn't injured, and could easily have hiked to a mountaintop to find cell reception, or followed a draw or stream to the next inevitable road crossing.

There are many dangers on the trail, but if you are the kind of person who can get turned around that easily, or you don't know how to use a compass, you really shouldn't be out there. The trail in that part of Maine travels through dense forest and over many mountains, but it's not *that* dangerous or easy to get lost. Inchworm's tragedy can be laid at the feet of her lack of skill and refusal to take charge of her own salvation when it should have been clear she had no other choice.

Sort of a downer day, I wrote that night. *No reason, unless just cumulative fatigue. Or maybe Inchworm now haunts this section of trail.*

Not that I believe in ghosts....

*

I rolled out at 6:20 the next morning, knowing that a BoDMoFo was on the breakfast menu. The march from Redington Campsite up to The Horn (4,032 feet) included the 19th steepest half-mile on the AT, but it didn't seem too bad so early in the day.

To my delight, the trail remained above treeline from the summit of The Horn all the way to the top of Saddleback Mountain (4,120 feet) and for a mile or so beyond. Both peaks were fantastic (*The Saddlebacks kicked ass*, I wrote later, *but in a good way*) and the weather was gorgeous, warm, clear and calm, even on top. Remarkably, throughout my hike, the weather had cooperated on every major summit I'd reached, with the lone exception of Unaka Mountain.

The walk down the other side took me off those exhilarating granite crowns and back into "standard-issue forest." Given that it was a holiday weekend, I couldn't help feeling a little disappointed that there was no magic when I got to ME 4, which led to Rangeley nine miles to the west.

Rangeley is considered a great trail town, but I had just done a resupply in Stratton (just an OK trail town, in my opinion) and I was strangely loath to hitch too far from the trail, so I skipped it. In general, I wasn't too interested in towns. But in hindsight, I wish I would have more carefully studied Awol's descriptions, which might have led me to time my town stops so that I visited the best trail towns.

On top of the mountain, I changed clothes and once again pulled my frequent stunt of setting my pack on the pinch-valve of my water bladder—I learned a couple years later (duh) that the valve had a lock—which left me waterless for much of the morning. I stocked up at a stream, but never quite caught up on my hydration. Somehow, I still made decent time, and I was thrilled to reach my expected destination, Sabbath Day Pond Lean-to (NOBO mile 1959.4; 229.8 from Katahdin) at 2:30.

There was a hiker sprawled out on the shelter floor, snoring loudly, but I tossed out my sleeping pad and hung up my clothes and tent to dry while eating some lunch. As I sat there flipping through the logbook, a young guy with dark hair and glasses ambled in.

"Oh, you're Pony? I've heard a lot about you," said Jeff, who was still awaiting his trail christening. "You've been moving pretty fast."

That seemed odd, since I'd been traveling solo and over the past week had been averaging only between 18 and 19 miles a day. But, according to Jeff, people had been talking about me and he'd been "chasing" me. Go figure. An ultra-runner, he had given himself the ambitious goal of finishing the trail in under 75 days, an average of 30 miles a day. He certainly looked fit, and his pack was enviably light. I never did find out if he made his goal.

After Jeff left, I turned back to the logbook. I truly loved going through the logbooks along the entire trail, reading every entry whenever possible, though somewhere in the mid-Atlantic I'd stopped signing every one. I came across an entry from a NOBO named Ninja Hoops who wrote that she'd camped on a tiny sliver of beach on Long Pond, about three-tenths of a mile south of the shelter. With the comatose snorer showing no signs of letting up, I made a snap decision, sloppily tossed my gear together, then headed down the trail wearing Crocs.

Sure enough, I soon came to a 15-foot path that led down to a short, narrow beach that looked just big enough for a couple of one-person tents. After poking around in the woods nearby I found a less exposed spot to pitch my tent that offered a spectacular view of the pond.

I hadn't been swimming in a while, but now I waded far out across the clean, sandy bottom and dunked myself repeatedly. Stripping off my clothes, I swirled and wrung them until the drippings were as clean as the cool, clear water of the pond. The skies were blue, the air was warm, and there was not the faintest breath of wind, making for an almost perfect swimming experience. Back on shore, I draped my clothes on a rickety little table someone had constructed and lay on the sand to soak up the beneficent rays.

I rinsed out la ropa—Spanish for "clothes"—and it actually DRIED in the sun! I wrote later, marveling at the prospect of putting on dry gear the next morning.

The place was a mini-paradise. I watched a huge blue heron patiently stalking fish for more than an hour, after which I not only heard, but *saw*, two red-eyed loons ducking under the water and resurfacing no more than 20 yards away; I had no idea they were so big. And if a couple of very eager leeches did their best to attach themselves to my ankles, well, I was too happy to care; I plucked them off and tossed them back in the water with all good wishes.

Sitting there in my skivvies, I felt like the proprietor of my own personal Shangri-La as many hikers stopped by and heeded my advice to take a dip, including SOBO flippers Spud and Rude, Sunshine (who had last seen me suffering from Lyme disease in Pennsylvania), Sphagnum PI, a sharp, funny biologist from Iowa who I met in Virginia, good ol' Goodtalk, and two enthusiastic young women who went by The Yogis.

With the exception of the reeking poop-log and plops of toilet paper my nose detected near my tent (I gave them a proper burial, cursing the inconsiderate dolt who left the mess), it was a perfectly magical afternoon and evening. The sky was a screaming asylum of sharp stars that night, and I fell asleep with the haunting laughter of loons and the velvet-soft lapping of water in my ears.

*

The next morning dawned cloudy and muggy. As I strolled through the woods past Moxie Pond (NOBO mile 1957.2; SOBO 231.9), I heard the splashing of some very large critter. Scurrying back to a place where I could see through the trees, I spied the massive black shadow and sprawling antlers of a bull moose about 50 yards away. It was a great start to another challenging day in Maine.

After dropping steeply to Bemis Stream, I had the dubious pleasure of grinding back up to Bemis Mountain (including the 40th steepest half-mile of the AT). Unlike the previous days' spectacular mountains, the trail to Bemis was mostly enclosed by trees and unexceptional, though at least it leveled out after the first brutal slog.

I'd begun to worry about the condition of my pole tips, which I'd replaced all the way back in Harpers Ferry. They'd been showing signs of pending collapse and sure enough, one snapped off just before I reached the summit of Bemis. On top, I shrugged off my pack, put on my rain coat against the chilly mist, and went to work, wrapping the tip in a blob of duct tape, which I hoped would remain intact until I got to Andover, where I planned to resupply and spend the night. Somewhere along in here, I ran into Sequoia, whom I'd last seen in Hot Springs, N.C., and Alasdair, an English bloke I'd met at Pine Grove Furnace in Pennsylvania.

The summit of Old Blue, crowned with tight, low spruce and fir, was shrouded in mist when I arrived. Having read that there was no cell phone reception at the bottom of the steep descent to South Arm Road, I called up the Pine Ellis Hostel in Andover to see if they could pick me up.

"You're on top of Old Blue now," said the woman. "It'll take you three hours to get to the road."

"*Three* hours? It's only 2.8 miles."

"Trust me," she said.

I had a hard time believing that I would slow to a pace of less than a mile an hour, no matter how steep and rocky the descent. I suggested she pick me up in two hours.

The woman sighed. "Well, you sound young"—?!—"so I guess maybe you can make it. We'll pick you up at 3, but if you ain't there and we have to come back, I'll have to charge you double for the ride."

"Fair enough," I said, thinking, *Me, young?*

The descent was tough, to be sure, as I wrote later, *steep, then ridiculously steep. 'Sweating' rocks were slippery and I fell several times.* (What's that you say? You *demand* to know how it compared to other parts of the trail? Well, I'll tell you: it included the 8th steepest half-mile and the 22nd steepest mile on the AT. You're welcome.)

After clambering down the seemingly vertical final half mile to the road, I checked and saw that I'd made it in an hour and 25 minutes, plenty of time. But for unknown reasons (*Inchworm, is that* you?), I had an unshakeable premonition that there would be a problem with the shuttle.

A cluster of exuberant hikers who had just finished slackpacking the even steeper segment to the south, including Moody and Wyman mountains, lay sprawled on their sleeping pads across the little-used strip of asphalt, waiting for a shuttle from the storied Cabin hostel. Among them was a shirtless C# (C-sharp), whom I'd spend time with back in Shenandoah, who was strumming happily on his ukulele. After a short time, a shiny black pickup drove slowly around the bend. The crew gave a whoop, loaded up, and headed out.

While I was sitting there by myself another hiker tumbled out of the woods across the road. It was Sage, whom I'd run into several times along the trail. He, too, was slacking.

"How was it?" I asked, having noticed the rather nasty profile of the next 10 miles.

"You know," Sage said, managing a weary smile, "just... shitty."

Shitty, translated: Steep, rocky, slippery, up and down, exhausting. In short, typical southern Maine.

We chatted while I waited for my shuttle. The truck from The Cabin came back and picked up another load of slackers and soon it was after 3 p.m.

"What the hell?" I grumbled. "I had a weird feeling this wouldn't go right."

It was eight miles into town, which neither Sage nor I had any intention of hiking. But we had no phone service and during the time I'd been sitting by the road I'd seen just two vehicles, the shuttle and a logging truck.

"Aw, man, I really don't want to park it here for the night," I grumbled.

"Don't worry," Sage said. "Someone will come along."

Soon, someone did. A large pickup driven by an older man cruised blithely past at about seven miles per hour. His wife waved cheerily as they rolled up the road and around the bend, ignoring our outstretched thumbs. I was getting more and more annoyed. I'd actually had the foresight to call the stupid hostel from the mountaintop, and still I was stuck out here in the middle of nowhere. Just then, we heard a faint rumble from around the corner. Soon the big red pickup that had just drifted by was coming back down the road, in reverse.

"Don't get much traffic out here," the driver said. "We got up around the bend and decided maybe we ought to offer you a ride, if you're willing to ride in back."

And *that's* what they mean by magic....

THIRTY-ONE:
FAMILIAR FACES

September 2016: Andover to Mahoosuc Notch

When we got out of the pickup in bustling downtown Andover, Maine, population 900, Sage headed off to pitch his tent in a field behind the Little Red Hen Diner and Bakery, a hiker gathering place.

I wanted to clean up and do laundry, so after slamming two quarts of Gatorade, gobbling a bunch of Oreos, and buying some Sam Adams Oktoberfest at the Andover General Store, I walked about a half mile to Pine Ellis Hostel. It was another of those kinda-sorta hostels that non-hiking people have established in their homes along the trail.

"I'm sorry, we don't have any room, unless you want to pitch a tent. That's $10," said the cranky old woman who greeted me when I stepped inside the dowdy kitchen.

"Oh, I already called to reserve a bunk. From the top of Old Blue," I said. "You were supposed to pick me up at 3 on South Arm Road but I never saw you."

"What's your name?"

"Pony."

"It says here we already picked you up."

I stood there blinking for a moment. "Uh, no. Unless there's another Pony."

After a further moment of confusion, the woman said in that case, she'd be happy to take my money. And if that *other* Pony showed up, she said grumpily, well, he'd just be out of luck. Needless to say, this was not my favorite hostel (it didn't help when, two days later, they tried to charge me for the shuttle-ride-that-wasn't). But I loved being in Andover, where I was reunited with at least a dozen people whose company I had enjoyed somewhere along the trail, including:

The Dude, the Houston accountant who sponsored two "Dudefests" along the trail, who I dubbed "The Most Popular Man on the AT" and with whom I've since become off-trail friends; Sequoia; Honey Badger, my occasional companion in Shenandoah; Greyhound, who recognized me from our meeting on the observation tower at Clingman's Dome all the way back in March (and who had later traveled with Patches); Terrible Lizard, the smart and snappy redhead who'd watched the hailstorm with me and my crew at Abingdon Shelter in Virginia; The Dutchess from the Netherlands; Owl, who with Southwind (who had left the trail in Massachusetts) had seen me half-dead in PA; Tapeworm from Pennsylvania, who had *so* impressed the woman who picked me up in Stratton with his handsomeness; and others.

Once I'd claimed a bunk, I bagged up my laundry and tossed it in front of the ancient, wobbling washing machine, where three other heaps lay waiting for ablution. I showered in the main house, grossed out by the dank humidity and residual odors of a residential bathroom routinely being used by 20 or 25 unrelated people.

Rummaging through the hiker box, I found a roll of red duct tape that appeared to have perhaps 20 feet left. Back in the bunkroom, I pulled out my own supply of thicker silver duct tape. Then I began scouring my kit for something small, rigid, and appropriately shaped, which I could place on the end of my tip-less pole and wrap with mounds of tape. I soon settled on the hard-plastic cap from a nearly empty Aqua Mira bottle, grabbed the tape, my pole, and a bottle of Sam Adams, then headed to the front yard for a little MacGyver session.

Setting the cap on the end of the pole, I wrapped the blood-red tape around and around until it felt stable. Then I wrapped it in several more layers of the thick silver tape and tightly collared it with another wrap of red. I knew the trail would immediately start eating away at the tape, and this way, once I saw the base layer of red tape exposed, I would know it was time for a rewrap.

I hung out for a while in the front yard with Squarepeg, a guy about my age who was hiking the trail for the third time, and Terrible Lizard, who continually cracked me up with her wry humor.

"I'll tell you one thing I didn't expect when I started," she deadpanned. "All these men hiking in little ladies' short-shorts."

I walked back into town with a couple of hikers and ate a fat corned-beef sandwich, a salad, a cup of vanilla ice cream, and more Gatorade at the general store. When I was finished, I wandered down the block where I found more than a dozen hikers hanging out at picnic tables outside Mills Market. The Dude was there, as were Sage and Tapeworm. I regaled the whole table with the story of Tapeworm's elderly admirer in Stratton ("He was *so* handsome!"). When a clerk from the market came out to say they were selling off the day's last pizza for cheap, I bought two pieces and gobbled them down.

Back at the hostel, I pored over Awol and noticed that I only had about 240 miles left to go and, barring any nasty surprises, my hike would be over in less than three weeks.

The idea of finishing is surreal, I wrote in my journal. *I've been like the lost troop all this time and the idea of coming to the end just seems so strange.*

I felt sad, too, knowing that my finish in Vermont would be a notably pallid affair compared to the glorious triumph of those steady-on NOBOs who earn their final reward at the summit of Katahdin, the noblest, most challenging mountain on the entire Appalachian Trail. I'd experienced post-trail blues after hiking the Colorado Trail, and now I began to wonder what life would be like after my AT epic.

That evening, feeling strong, I made an executive decision: I told the ladies I'd stay another night, and pay for them to slackpack me for the 10 miles between the two roads into Andover, which Sage had described as "shitty." That would give me a nero and another day to stuff my face before moving on.

*

I got dropped off at East B Hill Road at 7:30 a.m. The first miles to the top of Wyman Mountain were standard-issue Maine—tricky footing and lots of green tunnel, but thankfully, the 1,700-foot climb was gradual. But the descent to Sawyer Notch was crazy steep (including the 8th steepest mile and 15th steepest half-mile). You truly can't imagine what a crank all these violently upturned bits of trail really are.

In normal circumstances I would have agreed with Sage about the climb from there to Moody Mountain—which entailed the 9th steepest half-mile and 15th steepest mile—but as I was unburdened by my full pack and had a mere 10 miles to hike, I practically pirouetted through my day. Purists may sniff at slackpacking, but my first experience with it (besides Katahdin) was brilliant. It would not be the last time I would avail myself of such services on the final leg of my hike.

I was back at the hostel by early afternoon, which gave me plenty of time to relax, recover, and eat. Pummeled by Maine, I had trouble believing New Hampshire could be much harder, but I was doing my best to store up energy for the final push through the legendarily difficult White Mountains.

That night, I pulled everything out of my pack and considered whether I needed it. With regret, I chucked the lonely Mountain Hardwear gaiter whose mate I'd lost in Millinocket and thinned my medical kit to the bare bones. But I also I decided to pack a pair of tall wool socks that Tapeworm was leaving behind, so it was probably a wash, weight-wise.

And I took the opportunity to order a new pair of Altra Olympus 2.0 shoes online, to be delivered to White Mountains Hostel near Gorham, N.H. I had erred badly in going back to the Hokas.

I know this trail is tough on feet, and pain is part of the deal. But the Hoka squeeze is killing me. I feel like there are fiery little BBs in the ball of my R foot all day long, and if anything touches the side of the joint the pain is brutal, I wrote.

The worst was when I ran into the occasional, but inevitable, "stick-jam"—when my left foot pinned the end of a stick at just such an angle that it drove directly into the sore spot as my right foot swung past.

*

Maine wasn't about to let up, and not long after I was dropped off at East B Hill Road the following morning, I was grinding breathlessly toward the summit of Baldpate, a climb that included the 13th steepest half-mile on the trail and 17th steepest mile. The first part of the climb was unexceptional, but as I climbed higher, the mountain grew less stingy.

Wow, I love Baldpate. Gorgeous granite spines with views much of the way up, though I couldn't see much through the wind and fog, I wrote. *The descent was the same, wide open above treeline and I loved it.*

Besides that, I'd had another great reunion on top when I ran into quiet, sandal-hiking Five Star, whom I'd met first in Virginia and run into again at the monastery campsite in New York. He was in good spirits, but looked haggard.

"In New Hampshire and Maine," he said, "it's like you have to make five times the effort for half the miles."

I don't know if I'd say the AT's northernmost two states are literally *10* times more difficult than the rest of the trail, but I'd certainly go as high as four, maybe five, times as hard.

Just before noon I reached Grafton Notch, where the air was muggy and hot. With few views to interrupt the green tunnel, the long, 2,500-foot climb up Old Speck was arduous, and I was glad to have the distraction of Dostoevsky's *Crime and Punishment* cued up on my iPhone to distract me.

I took a break at Speck Pond Shelter (NOBO mile 1917.3; SOBO 271.8) at mid-afternoon, where I talked to some NOBOs and the site caretaker about the famously challenging obstacles that lay just ahead on my path, Mahoosuc Arm and Mahoosuc Notch.

The Arm not only presented the 10th-steepest mile and 6th-steepest half-mile of the trail, but most of its mile-and-a-half length consisted of long, sloping, slippery slabs of granite. The Notch isn't steep, but is referred to by some as "the hardest mile of the AT," "the most fun," or both. It's essentially an obstacle course of enormous boulders, some the size of houses, that have tumbled down from the steep cliffs on either side for eons.

"It might rain tonight," said the caretaker, a vigorous young woman who was busily shoveling mulch from the composting privy. "The Arm is always slippery, but it's way worse if it gets wet."

That, and the fact that I'd hiked less than 15 miles and was still feeling good, was enough to make up my mind.

The climb to the top of the arm went quickly, but the descent was slow and painstaking as I navigated my way down the endless series of slick, humid rocks. Relying heavily on my poles, I busted the other tip. My duct tape-bottle-cap jury-rig worked out OK, but it slipped much more easily than a graphite tip or rubber cap (which I learned not to use on the Colorado Trail because they pop off too easily in mud and become litter).

I spent more time than I would have liked on my butt, whether I was scooting down some tricky spot or sitting down, hard, after a slip. Although cognizant that it violated Leave No Trace principles, I did what many hikers do and orangutaned my way from tree to tree to aid my descent. All told, it took me two hours to travel less than 2.5 miles up, over and down the Arm.

I pitched my tent in a well-used stealth spot just below the trail just north of the Notch, where I was happy to see the Japanese couple whom I'd met in New York. A couple of hours later Happy Feet, a woman I'd chatted with at Speck Pond, arrived, giddy and amazed at having survived the descent of the Arm.

"That's the craziest thing I've seen on the trail so far," she said.

"I'm just glad I didn't have to do it the other way," I replied, imagining that brutal slog.

Happy Feet chatted amiably as she set up her tent and I squatted nearby cooking ramen noodles on a rock. Eventually, she made a proposition—no, not *that* kind of proposition; to my knowledge, she wasn't plagued by mosquitoes (see chapter 20).

"So, everyone says it's more fun to go through Mahoosuc Notch with a buddy or two," she said, standing arms akimbo above me as I wiped my cooking pot clean. "Would you like to go through together tomorrow?"

I sensed that Happy Feet had more than fun on her mind. Certainly, from the descriptions I'd read, the Notch was full of opportunities to get hurt, and it would be a nightmare to be stuck down there by yourself (though hikers were going through all the time). Hiking with her would probably slow me down, but I also wanted to be helpful.

"Sure," I said. "I usually get a pretty early start, if that's OK."

"I'll be ready."

THIRTY-TWO:
HO(S)TEL NEW HAMPSHIRE

September 2016: Mahoosuc Notch
to White Mountains Hostel, N.H.

As I was falling asleep in my tent near the mouth of Mahoosuc Notch, I heard the most peculiar sound I'd experienced on the trail: A frantic, persistent flapping, as if a giant fruit bat were careening around inside a Hefty bag. Unzipping my tent, I shone my red headlamp around the area, finally echo-locating the sound as coming from Happy Feet's tent. Then the sound stopped as suddenly as it had started.

The next morning, I was up before it was light and packing up when Happy Feet emerged from her tent.

"Did you hear that last night?" she said.

"Yeah. What the hell was it?"

She said a bird had flown up between her tent and rain fly and couldn't find its way out in the dark. She was frantic inside the tent but didn't want to make noise, for fear of waking the Japanese couple or me.

215

I was ready for an even earlier start, but I waited for Happy Feet and we finally got going at 7 a.m. I had stowed my poles in anticipation of needing my hands, and almost immediately we entered the topsy-turvy funhouse of the boulder-filled gully known as Mahoosuc Notch.

Moving through the Notch was slow, but not difficult, as I stretched, leaned, and scrambled over boulders and across deep, shadowed chasms that exhaled air a good 20 or 30 degrees colder than the ambient temperature. In several places I assisted Happy Feet, grabbing her pack or extending a hand when she wasn't sure of herself. The "trail" through the notch is marked with blazes, but they're not always easy to see and should be considered suggestions rather than strictly directions. I was thrilled that I got us off track only once.

My Colorado roots had prepared me well for this kind of maneuvering, which was sort of like a mile-long, horizontal bouldering problem. The notch was a ton of fun, but, to me, nowhere close to the "hardest" mile of the AT. After about an hour, the obstacle course apparently over, I bid Happy Feet goodbye.

"Thank you for helping me through," she said. "I would have been a lot more nervous without you. I'm sorry if I held you up; you could probably do it in a half hour! You're like a mountain goat!"

As it turned out, there was still a bit of tricky terrain to navigate. By the time I realized it, Happy Feet was out of sight, but I was sure she'd be fine.

Having focused on the notch, I was oblivious to what lay beyond, which turned out to be a tough, slow series of ups-and-downs, including, immediately, the 14th steepest half-mile on the trail, up to Fulling Mill Mountain, followed by marches up Goose Eye Mountain, Mount Carlo, and Mount Success, the descent from which is the 11th steepest half-mile. Maine: Steep, steep, steep, start to finish.

The Notch was a blast. The rest of the day ... ugggghhh. A million little climbs, lots of steep, lots of chock-a-block, lots of slippery slabs and just so tiring, I wrote that night.

Still, the remainder of the day was not without its rewards. I'd been thrilled to see so many toads and frogs all along the trail in Maine, but that afternoon, I came across the most magnificent specimen I'd ever seen. Not long after crossing into New Hampshire, movement on the dry, leaf-strewn slope above the trail caught my eye. I stopped to see a fist-sized black frog covered with bright green speckles, as if someone had spilled a vial of green glitter on her back. Although most frogs along the trail tended to bound away from humans at great speed, this one stayed still long enough for me to get a spectacular photo.

Then there was the pleasure of still more reunions: Castaway, a Boulder native I'd talked to all the way back in Tennessee; Bearwall, formerly Darkness, who earned his new trail name when he faced down a charging mama bear on Watauga Lake Dam; Trailtalker, a woman I'd walked with briefly in New Jersey; and Kaleidoscope, the young Ecuadorian-American woman with dark hair and a brilliant smile, whom I'd first met at Groundhog Creek Shelter at the foot of Max Patch Bald in Tennessee (and, in my opinion, the most beautiful living thing I'd met on the trail, bears, frogs, moose and deer included).

I staggered into Gentian Pond Campsite Shelter (NOBO mile 1902.6; SOBO 286.5) at 3 p.m. after a mere 12.3 miles, the first day since I was sick in Pennsylvania that I'd badly undershot my goal for the day. Though I'd averaged only 1.5 mph for the whole day, I was exhausted. After dumping my pack in the empty shelter, I picked my way down to a gurgling gully below the pond to dunk my head and rinse the sweat from my sodden clothes. Then I kicked back and flipped through the logbook, noting that hikers frequently saw moose on the pond in the early morning. I couldn't complain, having seen two moose in Maine, but I crossed my fingers, hoping to see more.

Just as the sun slipped behind the peak to the west, two young section-hiking guys hauling ginormous packs arrived. After meeting the weird old guy wearing nothing but long underwear in the shelter, they wobbled across the precarious stick-and-stone dam between pond and gully and set up their tents on a rocky promontory. They then set about gathering wood and soon the pleasant smell of camp smoke brought a smile to my face.

Not long after, a couple of teenage girls appeared around the corner, followed shortly thereafter by a young teenage boy and an even younger girl. They immediately claimed spots in the shelter and the older girls divvied up chores like (mostly) friendly sergeants—getting water, hauling out dinner makings and stove, hanging up wet clothes.

They older girls were The Diva and Zabumafu, 17-year-old twins, their 15-year-old brother was Flying Hubbinator, and the youngest, Flying Piglet, was just 12. They were hiking the trail alone, supported by their mother, Big Mama, who would meet them at road crossings, handle their resupplies, and all that.

They were home-schooled members of the Church of Jesus Christ of Latter-Day Saints from Florida, where their father is an English professor at the University of North Florida. But they took pains to explain that they weren't *that* kind of Mormon. Their parents, they said, were intellectual, liberal, and adventurous.

The kids planned to hike to Katahdin before flipping back to Vermont and hiking SOBO to Pennsylvania. The older girls were in charge, but everyone did their share of the work and they seemed to get along.

"Sometimes we fight," Flying Piglet said. "But usually we're too tired."

"Tell me about it," I said, my throbbing feet pressed against the sloping ceiling of the shelter. "Most days I don't have the energy to fight off an insistent housefly by the time I stop walking."

Flying Hubbinator and I talked *Lord of the Rings* for a good long while, and I waxed loquacious about William Faulkner when one of the older girls mentioned that America's greatest novelist was her father's specialty.

"Oh, my dad would *love* you," Zabumafu said, in a tone suggesting that perhaps she'd heard enough about the denizens of Faulkner's fictional Yoknapatawpha County to last a lifetime. She preferred Jane Austen.

Those kids turned out to be some of my favorite shelter company along the trail.

*

The siblings were still nestled deep in their sleeping bags when I rolled out early the next morning. Alas, no moose greeted me on either Gentian Pond or Dream Lake up the next hill.

I headed into the day still feeling tired, but happy that I only had about 12 miles and just three "bumps"—Wocket Ledge, Cascade Mountain, and Mount Hayes—to go before I would stroll right up to White Mountains Lodge and Hostel in Shelburne, where I'd called ahead for a reservation.

Though hardly easy, compared to the rest of southern Maine it was a gentle day. To the relief of my Hoka-tortured feet, there were even long stretches of soft, smooth tread here and there. After a final road walk across the Androscoggin River I reached the hostel at 11:30.

A dark-haired woman waved through a kitchen window, gesturing me toward the open garage. There I found racks stacked with filthy, battered hiking boots and shoes and a dozen packs hanging in orderly rows from wall pegs. The wall itself was nearly covered with colorful graffiti left by countless hikers, and I smiled to see many names I recognized.

A young guy emerged from the house and explained the routine: take off shoes, hang up pack, change into "town clothing" provided by the hostel, and toss laundry in a basket for washing.

Although it was a little more expensive than The Barn, a famous hostel just up the road in Gorham, I knew I'd made the right choice. It was thanks, in part, to hostel owner Marnie's welcoming, well-organized approach that I made a snap decision to take, at long last, my very first zero in over 2,000 miles. It didn't hurt that cold, rain and wind dominated the forecast for the following day, particularly since I was now headed into the White Mountains, widely considered the most difficult part of the AT.

I must have enjoyed myself on my day off, because the only entry in my journal was a single sentence pondering whether I should slackpack the next section and come back to the hostel for a second night. There were lots of fun people in the house, though I neglected to write down most of their names; I was pleased when Happy Feet arrived late in the day, having made her own way through the last bit of the obstacle course known as Mahoosuc Notch.

I spent a good deal of time talking to Marnie. She had worked in the fashion industry and apparently made a fortune by inventing some kind of two-sided tape, which allowed her to stop working and buy the hostel a couple of seasons before. I asked her what winter was like in New Hampshire.

"Actually, I don't stay for the winter," she said. Ah, I thought: A snowbird. "I go back home to Minnesota."

OK, so not quite a snowbird.

Marnie's son Ben was helping at the hostel while taking classes in wilderness medicine in Conway, 35 miles away, and she had hired a couple of other hikers to help out. The bunks were made up with real sheets and blankets and 20 people could squeeze in around the enormous table in the dining area.

After I showered, one of the staff shuttled me and a couple of other hikers into town, dropping us at Gorham Hardware & Sports. Their website URL, "nhhockeyshop.com," says much about their priorities, but they also cater to hikers and I was able to buy two new tips for my poles, for less than half of what I'd paid for my last pair back in Harpers Ferry.

I sat cross-legged on the floor and replaced the tips. Then, becoming almost misty-eyed with gratitude to the jury-rigged tip that had served well enough to get me out of Maine, and remembering how even the "filthy orc rags" worn by Frodo and Sam in Mordor were revered in Tolkien's great quest story ("No silks or linens, nor any armour or heraldry could be more honourable."), I lovingly stowed the now-useless wad of red-and-silver duct tape and bottle cap in my jacket pocket, unwilling to toss it just yet. Did I mention how worn out I was?

Then I walked down the street to a sports bar, where I ate a giant plate of spaghetti, drank a beer, and failed in my efforts to ignore the college football game on TV (Penn State vs. Pittsburgh). After a strawberry ice-cream cone, I milled around the White Mountain Cafe & Bookstore before walking back to the shuttle rendezvous point.

That night, I transcribed a poem that I had spent a good deal of time writing in my head over my final days in Maine. Titled, "An Ode to NOBOs at Shelburne, N.H.," it was a response to the many hikers I'd spoken to, or whose shelter logbook entries I'd read, who were astonished and dismayed to discover that "Maine is kicking my ass!"

Dear NOBOs:

You've come through the Whites
—a feat, by all rights—
Now Maine, and the end is in sight.

But the terrain in Maine
Is truly a pain.
It's rooty, it's rocky
And all chocky-blocky.
It's slippery, it's slabby—
Not New Hampshire grabby.

So yeah, it's a pain
And an energy drain.
But the views?
They're insane!
So fret not, for at least
Your pain's not in vain.

I also was thrilled that my new, feet-saving Altra Olympus 2.0 trail shoes had arrived. I retired the Hokas, which—to their credit—surely would have lasted me until the end of my hike. But they just weren't wide enough for my newly expanded feet. Wearing the Altras around the hostel, I felt like I was walking on clouds ... *ahhhhh.*

*

As predicted, the next day was nasty and rainy, with a high in the mid-50s, a low near 30, and wind gusts up to 30 miles an hour. I luxuriated in a breakfast of some sweet heavy casserole, eggs, orange juice, and coffee, then flopped around the house doing nothing, then napping, then doing nothing again. I was just grateful not to be starting the Whites in a tempest.

Sometime that afternoon a remarkable hiking duo arrived: 74-year-old

Sojourner and his 10-year-old golden retriever, Theo. Sojo had been dreaming of hiking the trail since he was 12 years old, and by the time I met him he had less than 300 miles to go.

But I worried about Theo, who wasn't allowed in the house. I went out to the garage to see him several times and he looked plumb worn out, even depressed. There was harsh talk around the dining table when Sojo wasn't around, as some hikers criticized him for pushing his dog too hard. I shared their concerns; our dogs will follow us to death, and it's our responsibility to watch out for them. Thinking about Mahoosuc Notch and the coming difficulties of southern Maine, I was one of several hikers who talked to Sojo about Theo's wellbeing.

"I'm only doing 10 miles a day," he said, "and it's been less in New Hampshire."

I explained that southern Maine was just as hard, and expressed my concerns for Theo.

"I promise you I'm always looking out for him," Sojo said. "At this point, he's in better shape than I am."

I adore dogs. I happily greeted every dog I saw on the trail (so long as he or she wanted to be greeted; it's always their prerogative to say "no"), which helped calm the ache of missing my own three dogs and one cat. That said, I think it's a rare canine who truly enjoys a long-distance hike. Lean, lithe, younger athletic animals who are neither too big nor too small—think border collie or cattle dog or a Vizsla like Huckleberry, whom I'd met down south— may be OK, but believe it or not, humans are better built for long-distance travel than dogs (indeed, research has found that so long as they can follow tracks, humans can hunt down any animal on earth on foot). And personally, it would break my heart to see my dog suffering in the cold or rain, or collapsing in exhaustion at the end of each day.

Sojo and I had a good conversation, and I had no doubts about the deep love this former attorney and Yale graduate had for his partner. But I hoped that our conversation helped him see Theo through other eyes. As it would turn out, it was Sojo, not Theo, who had to be hospitalized in Maine. But they did finally make it to Katahdin on Oct. 27, averaging just over six miles a day for the next many weeks, a pace friendly to old Theo. Good boy!

THIRTY-THREE:
WHITES MAGIC

September 2016: White Mountains Hostel
to Mount Washington

After talking it over with Marnie, the cool and knowledgeable owner of White Mountains Lodge & Hostel (which she sold before the 2017 season; the name was changed to the Rattle River Lodge & Hostel), I decided to slackpack the next section of the trail, a 21-mile NOBO journey from Pinkham Notch back to Shelburne. The day would include some 6,000 feet of climbing over the Wildcats, Carter Dome, and Mount Moriah, including—*ladies and gentlemen!*—the No. 1 steepest half-mile and the 4th-steepest mile of the entire AT, from Pinkham Notch up to Wildcat E.

"Most people bring a light pack and do it in two days," she said. "But you'll be fine. Just be sure to bring a headlamp."

Marnie's son Ben dropped me off at Pinkham Notch on his way to a wilderness first-aid class in Conway the next morning. It was 7:45 when I started walking, later than I would have liked. But the previous day's storm was long gone and the weather was clear and cool, headed toward the mid-70s in the valleys.

After rambling a short way along the flat, rock-strewn Lost Pond Trail, the AT plunged straight up into dense forest. Even burdened only by a daypack filled with water, food, a rain coat, gloves, and a warm hat, climbing 2,000 feet over the next 1.7 miles was brutal. The "trail," such as it was, was marked by too few blazes, and I got off into the weeds—or rather, the trees—about halfway up the mountain.

In good spirits and feeling strong after my zero, I refused to countenance the idea of descending hard-fought elevation to find a blaze. Instead, I checked Guthook to see where I was. Then I started bushwhacking my way back to the trail. The bushes whacked back with glee, as I scrambled up a rocky promontory, waded through tangles of low, grasping fir, and I took repeated slaps across the face from whip-like branches.

After a half hour of slashing and grunting through this obstacle course on literally the steepest part of the trail, I came upon a blaze. I looked like I'd tangled with a particularly irritated wildcat kitten, my face, arms, and legs crisscrossed with scratches. This is what's known as Type 2 fun—terrible at the time, "fun" in memory only, particularly if you have fellow sufferers with whom to talk about it. And my day had just begun.

After marching up and over three more Wildcat peaks (D, C and A—the trail graciously bypasses B) I descended to Carter Notch Hut (NOBO mile 1875.6; SOBO 313.5). Feeling pressure because of my late start and time lost to bushwhacking, I decided I could wait to see what the New Hampshire hut scene was all about. I was uneasy about the huts, anyway, as Awol's memoir had made their system for thru-hikers sound complicated, at best.

The Appalachian Mountain Club has for more than a century operated a series of huts for hikers in the White Mountains. Fully staffed, each hut offers meals, cold running water, composting toilets, and cozy bunks for people who want to hike in without hauling a huge pack. The cost to stay overnight at each of the eight huts is more than $110 for non-AMC members—in other words, a big "no" for most on a thru-hiking budget—and reservations tend to be snapped up by wealthy Bostonian types.

For most of the hut region, stealth camping is either prohibited or discouraged (and always banned within a quarter-mile of any official camp site or hut). However, hut staff (who call themselves "croo") will take pity on a certain number of hiking bums and offer "work for stay," through which they can do assigned chores—anything from washing dishes to reorganizing shelves—in exchange for leftovers (when available) and sleeping overnight on the dining room floor. The huts also sell bars, candy and, famously, soup.

Skipping right past the blue blaze to the hut, I stopped beside a tiny brook to take on water before starting the brutal grind up to 4,832-foot Carter Dome (including the 5th-steepest mile and 7th-steepest half-mile section of the AT). As I squatted there like a caveman, I heard two SOBO hikers approaching.

They didn't see me and I didn't call out, but it was Kizmit and Green Blaze, two young hikers who had left Marnie's hostel the previous morning during the storm. I would encounter them several times over the next week, and Kizmit would become my final, brief taste of trail family as I pushed toward the end of my hike. After my old-home journey through Maine, where I sometimes counted more than 50 NOBOs a day, things were thinning out, and I saw only a few more hikers all day.

The climb to Carter Dome was grueling, but at least I didn't get off track. I felt as fleet-footed as Legolas the Elf when he sprinted across snowdrifts on the knees of cruel Caradhras in Tolkien's great quest story. The tread was knotty and knobby, the climbs steep, but at least there were periodic majestic views of the storied Mount Washington massif to the southwest.

I reached my final summit of the day, Mount Moriah (4,042 feet; NOBO mile 1884.9; SOBO 304.2), at 4:30 p.m. The skies remained spectacularly clear and though I faced six miles of long, steady downhill to the Rattle River, I was now confident I'd make it back to the hostel well before dark. But even with my new shoes, all that ground-pounding had added up, and the descent seemed to take forever. I rolled out onto State Route 2 in Shelburne right at 7 p.m., then walked the half mile to the hostel.

If I subtracted my foolish meandering on Wildcat, I could plausibly claim to have done the 21 miles (and a walloping 6,000 feet of climbing, including not just that crazy steep first climb, but also the 17th, 18th and 55th steepest half miles and 7th steepest mile segments of the trail) in 11 hours, so I felt pretty good. But Marnie told me about a couple of young hikers, one male, one female, who had made it back in under *seven* hours in 2015.

"You did great," she said. "But what in the world happened to your face?"

I sheepishly explained my foolish bushwhack of Wildcat E. Upstairs in the bathroom, I surveyed the damage: dozens of scrapes and scratches scored my arms, legs, bridge of my nose, cheeks, and forehead. To be honest, I thought it made me look rather cool and rakish.

To my ravenous delight, Marnie made dinner for everyone that night—an incredible enchilada casserole, seven-layer dip, chips, and corn—a treat that wasn't included in the price of a night's stay. For that and other reasons, I think the White Mountains Lodge & Hostel was the best overall accommodation experience I had on the entire trail.

I went to bed early and slept hard that night, knowing that I was in for a second straight 6,000-foot day, only this time in the space of 15 miles, and bearing a fully-loaded pack.

*

I started walking SOBO from Pinkham Notch at 8 a.m. after being shuttled by Mellow from the hostel. The weather was once again spectacular—a good thing, as I intended to get up and over Mount Washington, at 6,288 feet the highest peak in the Northeast U.S. and famously home to the "worst weather in the world," including the highest wind speed ever measured on earth (234 mph) until it was dethroned by a 1996 hurricane.

The first five miles were pleasant enough, rolling uphill, sometimes steeply, through open forest alongside a series of crashing white streams and rivers. Then I hit what is surely among the most sustained, steep slogs of the entire Appalachian Trail, the 2.6-mile, 2,800-foot grind to the summit of bony, 5,367-foot Mount Madison, including the 3rd-steepest mile on the trail.

There is no relief and not much fun until you hit treeline after a couple of miles,

I wrote in my journal. *Then above treeline the rocks start … and never stop.*

From there to the summit it was purely a rock-hop/scramble, but the openness offered breathtaking views to the north and east. As I was picking my way up like a mountain goat, I noticed two tiny splashes of color moving on the rocks below. The next time I looked, they had gained on me; who could these speedy SOBOs be? I got my answer a half a mile below the summit, when Green Blaze, a young, compact guy recently mustered out of the Marine Corps, who had a big smile, hustled by me. A quarter mile later Kizmit, a super-fit young woman from Mississippi, did the same.

I loved the scrambly final ascent to the summit of Madison, where the view was even more spectacular. Despite a sturdy breeze, the sun was out and no storms lay on the horizon. A young couple with a baby in a backpack snapped my photo, then I made quick work of the steep, stony descent to Madison Springs Hut.

Kizmit and Green Blaze were hanging out on the warm, sunny deck when I arrived. I went inside and waited a couple minutes before a young croo member deigned to stop washing dishes behind the counter and muttered a sullen, "Help you?" I bought some soup, broccoli something or other, which did not impress me, and paid a couple dollars each for three leftover cookies. I was far from taken by my first hut experience.

But a friendly section hiker named Icebeard, who thru-hiked the trail in 2002, came in and gave me a fair sampling of what turned out to be sound advice about hiking the Whites (dang if I can remember what he said, but I do remember that he was spot on).

I was already approaching 4,000 feet of climbing by the time I headed out at 1 p.m. Hulking Mount Washington, with its tiny ribbon of road, glittering with cars, dominated the view to the southeast. But mounts Adams, Jefferson, and Monroe still lay between me and that august summit; the remaining five and a half miles to the top were intermittently steep, and persistently rocky.

Literally 8 miles of almost exclusively rocks from Madison to Washington, I noted. *I now understand why SOBOs dismiss NOBO whining about PA rocks (but PA is still a bitch).*

It is a tradition among thru-hikers to stop and moon (look it up, kids) the smoke-belching cog railway that cranks up the western ridge of Mount Washington. But I was hiking alone and the trains this late in the day had no passengers, so I didn't see much point in airing out my butt for a laugh. I did see chunks of coal scattered across the hillside, evidently hurled by passengers at all those exposed hiker asses.

I reached the summit of Washington at 4:40 p.m. on an astonishingly perfect day. Having heard that 90 mph gusts forced the closure of the mountain just a few days earlier, I was grateful for my good fortune. Even so, the late afternoon breeze quickly cooled my sweaty shirt and shorts and I threw on a rain jacket before dodging inside the snack bar for a PowerAde and two semi-stale donuts. I didn't think to ask anyone to take my photo at the summit.

Then, despite the cluster of buildings and signs and cars and many people, I could not for the life of me find the trail leading off the summit. I could see my destination about a mile below, Lakes of the Clouds Hut (NOBO mile 1854.7; SOBO 334.4), and the shiny ribbon of trail leading up to it, just not where it left the mountaintop. After wandering to the eastern side of the summit, I began picking my way back across a field of large boulders, thinking I'd intersect with the AT somewhere.

As I navigated the rocks, I suddenly, irretrievably lost my balance. My poles plunged into a yawning black gap and I teetered forward, slamming the middle of both thighs onto the sharp edge of a block of granite. I yelped, more out of shock than pain, and managed to arrest my fall only after bending both poles.

Pushing myself upright, I saw thin lines of blood where the rock had given a little warning nip to my thighs. Though I wasn't really hurt, I would bruise up later, and I experienced an involuntary shiver as I peered down into the gap, imagining how much worse it could have been. There I was, less than 200 miles from finishing, and my hike came close to ending with the most idiotic of missteps, after I got "lost" on top of a famous summit, swarming with people. Duly chastened, I picked my way back to the top where I soon spied a rather obvious sign pointing the way to the hut. How I missed it, I cannot explain.

The 1.3-mile descent included a 1,000-foot drop in elevation, including the

47th steepest half-mile of the trail, but it didn't feel at all steep. Green Blaze certainly didn't find it challenging as he literally ran past me with a smile and a wave.

When I got to the hut it was after 6; counting stops, it had taken me 10 hours to hike just 15 miles and 6,000 feet. I dumped my pack on a stone wall outside and went in, feeling more nervous about approaching the "croo" than climbing Mount Washington. I preferred to be self-sufficient, but now I was dependent upon the kindness of strangers, and if they'd already taken two work-for-stay hikers—the limit, according to the sullen dude at Madison Springs—then I would have to keep walking to … somewhere. The descent from Washington was mostly tree-free for many miles and camping was technically banned.

As it turned out, the two-hiker limit was flexible, and the young woman I talked to at the front desk was very friendly, even enthusiastic. She'd already granted work-for-stay privileges to a hiker of my vintage named Roll Tide (guess where *he* was from) and Green Blaze, who had also petitioned favorably on behalf of Kizmit, making me No. 4 for the night.

"Yeah, you're cool," the croo member said. Having thru-hiked a few years earlier, she grokked (look it up, kids) my anxiety and confusion.

As Green Blaze, Roll Tide, Kizmit and I waited in the foyer, other croo members soon appeared with plastic buckets and bowls and giant kettles full of leftovers for us to eat—beef tips, some kind of pumpkin soup, cheese, bread, juice, and more.

"You're lucky," said one. "We're closing this hut up in less than a week and we don't want to have to pack any food out."

Helicopters drop heavy supplies for each hut at the beginning of the season, but after that, croo must strap on hideous-looking traditional wood-and-canvas packs (why?) a couple of times a week to pack out trash and return with perishables and other supplies. Talk about mountain goats; I'd seen one croo guy blasting up toward Washington faster than I was coming down.

As we ate our leftovers, some 90 paying guests began filtering into the dining room, looking and smelling considerably fresher than we did. Kizmit declined to participate in the smorgasbord, choosing instead to bundle up and cook her own dinner outside.

"She's just like that sometimes," said Green Blaze, who had met Kizmit in Millinocket and been hiking with her ever since. "She can be sort of shy."

After we'd eaten our fill, we brought the empties back to the kitchen, where I stuffed my face with at least half-a-dozen biscuit-like lemon cookies offered by the croo. They instructed us to stay in the riff-raff—excuse me, entry—area or go outside while the paying customers enjoyed dinner. I went outside to shoot a photo of a spectacular sunset, then hung out with Roll Tide and Green Blaze. Kizmit came in after a bit but didn't seem interested in conversation, except for a few whispered remarks to her hiking partner.

After dinner the croo set about entertaining the guests with goofy skits and small-group discussions about White Mountain-y stuff. They asked Roll Tide if he would answer questions from guests about thru hiking; guess he looked most respectable among us.

I poked through books and struck up a conversation with Kizmit. A gym rat from Jackson, Mississippi, she had graduated from Mississippi State University with a degree in wildlife management. She'd completed a NOBO thru-hike in 2012 with her beloved dachshund and this year had hiked NOBO to Damascus, Virginia before flipping up to Maine, where she met Green Blaze. She hoped to get back to Damascus by Thanksgiving.

"Dang," I said. "It's going to get cold."

"I know, and I don't even like cold weather," Kizmit said. "But I really like solitude."

She said she had enjoyed Green Blaze's company, but was considering going her own way. He had candidly admitted to me that he was completely self-absorbed and knew that Kizmit didn't respond well to his blunt, even harsh, way of communicating. He was super social, where she was happy to go days without seeing people. She was 30, he was 24. Both were extremely strong hikers, as I'd already seen.

"I just need to hike alone again," she said with a sigh.

The longer the croo entertained the guests, the more agitated I got. I'd just hiked two of my toughest days, in succession, and I was ready for bed. Hiker midnight (generally agreed to be 9 p.m., though some say it's as early as sunset) came and went, and still the four of us waited like dutiful servants for our work assignments. As soon as the paying guests headed off to beddy-bye, we were put to work doing dishes, including detailed scrubbing of pots and pans, right down to scraping away tiny specks of black carbon that had accumulated through the summer, in preparation for the end of the season. The work was not hard, and the company was great, but I was exhausted when I finally flopped down for the night.

I'd had two flawless days for the Wildcats and Washington, but a cold front was blowing in. It was already cold by the time the orange ball of sun sank out of sight, and later I awoke beneath a dining table and heard 50 mph gusts rattling the windows.

I don't love hut-indenture, I wrote. *But I'm so glad to be inside as the wind howls on Mount Washington....*

My first night in a White Mountains hut would also turn out to be my last.

THIRTY-FOUR:
PRESIDENTIAL PEAKS ...
AND VALLEYS

September 2016: Lakes of the Clouds Hut
to Mount Garfield

Those first two monster days in the White Mountains caught up to me on day three.

The skies were gray, but not particularly threatening, and the air was chilly when I woke early. Not caring about breakfast and not wanting to wait, I was walking by 6:30, putting an end to my lone episode of hut indenture.

Climbing Mount Washington as a SOBO involves 6,000 feet of steep, rocky, descent. For NOBOs, reaching the summit means slogging 12.5 miles to gain some 5,000 feet, a long slog indeed. I was glad to be descending that long, long ridge.

With wind and rain in the forecast, I eyed the sky warily all morning as I trundled down the rocky road past the summits of Monroe, Franklin (hey, wait a second—he wasn't president!), Eisenhower, Pierce, and Jackson. I'd bundled up against the morning chill, but soon stopped and stripped in the middle of the trail, exchanging my gloves, coat, and long pants, for a long-sleeve Merino wool shirt and shorts.

I planned to hike to about 19 miles to Zealand Falls Hut, which would entail less than 2,000 feet of climbing. But the tread remained gritty, rocky, and often slippery as the cloud-wreathed hulk of mighty Washington slowly receded behind me.

When two modest climbs up the flanks of Pierce and Jackson completely thrashed my legs, I knew the bill had come due for my 12,000-foot, 37-mile traverse of the Wildcats-Carter-Moriah and Madison-Washington. Despite the distinctly downward trend of the trail, my pace continued to flag throughout the day.

Descending precipitous stony Webster Cliffs (33rd steepest half-mile; 11th steepest mile) required constant concentration and occasional scrambling. Increasingly exhausted, I cranked an ankle three times, cursing myself out loud for not paying attention. But the views were good, despite the Mordor-like gloom that continued to build in the west.

By the time I staggered out of the woods at the bottom of the cliffs, I knew I wasn't going to make it to Zealand Falls. Stopping by the highway at Crawford Notch, I flipped through my Awol guide to see what my options were. I could have a bunk at the Appalachian Mountain Club's Highland Center, three-and-a-half miles to the west on US 302, for an exorbitant $54, while the Crawford Notch Campground, an equal distance to the east, offered cabins for a whopping $75-$95 and tenting spots for $30.

Thirty bucks to pitch a tent? I thought crankily. *No thanks.*

Not only were the prices outrageous, but I'd also have to hitch, and not a single vehicle had passed during the several minutes I'd been standing there. So I decided to walk another seven miles to the AMC's Ethan Pond Campsite. By the time I'd made my decision, the rain had started. I donned my jacket and tugged on my pack cover, knowing both would soon be soaked through, and stumped across the highway.

Despite my obsession with pointing out how very incredibly fantastically phenomenally absurdly *steep* the Appalachian Trail is in southern Maine and New Hampshire, somehow, I'd failed to note the wee 1,800-foot hill before me included a steep grind up the 45th steepest half-mile on the trail. But at least the tread was decent, featuring actual dirt and even occasional runs of log steps placed by members of the benevolent local hiking club.

Despite the brutal hill, gushing spigot of cold rain, and quivering bags of mush that were once my quadriceps, I suddenly experienced one of those occasional, inexplicable surges of energy (or is it lunacy?) that give me strength I doubted I had (like the time I literally *ran* a mile four times running back and forth while portaging a canoe and heavy gear at the end of an exhausting day in the Boundary Waters Canoe Area Wilderness in Minnesota, to the genuine astonishment of my wiped-out friend). I even started singing, blowing rain and sweat from my lips as I wheezed out my favorite songs from the late, great Dan Fogelberg's early catalog, "Part of the Plan," "Old Tennessee," "The Raven," "The Last Nail," "The River," and others.

But by the time I reached the plateau, drenched and shivering, my second wind was utterly blown out and there was no song in my heart. I stiffly splashed through mud and over many a tippy puncheon over an agonizingly long three-quarters of a mile to the turnoff for the campsite, which also offered a shelter. The two-tenths of a mile stumble down a stony path past the pond seemed to take even longer, as the cruel relativity of the trail—the worse you feel, the longer the miles—nearly sapped me of any remaining will to go on.

I had enough presence of mind to fill up on water at the inlet to the pond, as I had every intention of burying myself in my sleeping bag for the next 16 hours. Finally, after a brief, but maddening, climb, I came upon the shelter. I remembered yet again the tormented astronauts in Ray Bradbury's haunting story, "The Long Rain," but at least the rains on that fanciful version of Venus had the good taste to be *warm*....

Although it was just 1:30 p.m., I interrupted what appeared to be some vigorous foreplay between two giggling hikers. There was a good deal of rustling and hurried rearranging from within the heap of their combined sleeping bags when I dropped my pack on the wood-plank floor. Once decent, the two SOBOs introduced themselves as Maggie and I Don't Know.

"We're not making a lot of progress," I Don't Know said, his voice pleasant, though perhaps ever-so-slightly stressed (sorry, dude; I'd be frustrated, too). But I was so cold and exhausted and miserable that I wouldn't have cared if they'd gone at it like lusty orangutans while swinging from the rafters.

Without further ado, I threw down my pad and pulled out my blessedly dry sleeping bag. Staggering back into the rain for modesty's sake, I stripped out of my wet stuff and hurriedly wriggled into dry, warm gear, including hat and gloves. After hanging everything to "dry," I burrowed into my bag and, despite my usual inability to sleep during daylight hours, promptly fell asleep. I didn't wake until 4:30, when two friendly section hikers from Boston arrived, as drenched and bedraggled as I had been. I hoped for their sake my shelter-mates had been bold enough to get it on during my insensate slumber; I wouldn't have begrudged them the opportunity to commit *coitus continuus*.

It had stopped raining by the time I finished eating the first 600 calories I could rummage out of the food bag—candy, peanut-butter crackers, Pop-Tarts. Feeling now merely 80 percent deceased, I staggered back to the pond for more water, hoping I might see a moose. No moose, but hey, at least I was ready for bed (again) at 6:30.

Smart move to pull up short. Hope the legs feel better tomorrow, I wrote before nodding off. *Gonna be a cold night indeed.*

The next morning the ground was glazed with a thin layer of ice.

*

To my astonishment and delight, after a brief reprise of mud puddles and puncheon-hopping the next morning, the next four miles to Zealand Falls were smooth and flat, by far the easiest going since the miles leading up to Whitecap Mountain in the Hundred Mile Wilderness. As I walked beside burbling Whitewall Brook in a valley between steep, jumbled hillsides, I was reminded very much of the Colorado Trail.

The short climb to the hut had given me a taste of the steep, brutal next mile. (Inquiring minds want to know: *How* steep? Why, I'll tell you—it's the 30th-

steepest half-mile and the 24th-steepest mile of the whole AT.) Zealand Falls Hut was beautiful, standing adjacent to its rushing namesake cascades. But I stopped only briefly to use the privy and change into shorts before heading on.

The day warmed up quickly and I found the next few miles to the summit of Mount Guyot pleasant going. That trend continued until the final pitch to South Twin Mountain, which was startlingly steep, but mercifully short. Stopping for a break on top, I ran into Icebeard, the '02 thru-hiker who had given me good advice at Madison Springs Hut, who was doing day hikes in the area. When I told him I might try to get up and over Mount Lafayette before making camp, he warned that it would make for a long, hard day.

"Why don't you camp on top of Mount Garfield instead?" he suggested.

That would mean only a 15-mile day, but it sounded like a good idea.

And lo! When I left the summit of South Twin, instead of climbing, I actually got to *descend* the 3rd-steepest half-mile and 9th-steepest mile on the way to Galehead Hut (NOBO mile 1829.0; SOBO 360.1). Making my way down those slippery slabs actually was more complicated and precarious than it would have been coming up, but my quads, glutes, and calves were grateful for the break.

The trail meandered just three miles from the hut to the summit of Garfield. I could see my breath as I walked in the shadow of the forest, despite clear skies above, and once again, rocks and roots made for slow going. Then there was my EoDMoFo, a 970-foot ascent over six-tenths of a mile (the 4th-steepest half-mile on the AT) of broken, jumbled, blocky, wet trail to the summit. In no particular hurry, I enjoyed the scramble as much as anything I'd climbed since Katahdin.

Coming out on top at 3:30, I silently thanked Icebeard for his continued good advice. The sharp pinnacle of 4,458-foot Mount Garfield is capped with rugged granite, wind-twisted krummholz, and the concrete foundation of an old observation tower. Dropping my pack, I scouted around for the best place to pitch my tent, eventually settling on a narrow patch of damp dirt between the rocky crown and a small, twisted stand of fir.

Scrambling up the last few feet to the summit, I was dazzled by the panoramic view to distant Washington and the Lafayette massif that still lay ahead. I soon returned to my tent, eager to eat and clean up so I could kick back and watch the sun go down.

It turned out to be the coolest sunset I experienced on the AT, as the descending red orb cast the shadow of Garfield onto the sprawling slopes of South Twin mountain to the east and a full moon rose into a golden-red sky. Staring across a gulf of forest where night had already fallen, I imagined my shadow-self gazing back from that ephemeral summit. Perfectly alone, perfectly happy—both of us.

Talk about magic.

THIRTY-FIVE: BODHISATTVA

September 2016: Mount Garfield to Chet's Place,
Lincoln, N.H.

The descent from Mount Garfield was shorter, but no less steep or rocky than coming up. Garfield Pond was still in shadow when I decided to head into the woods to dig a cathole. There were a half-dozen tents and hammocks tucked just a few yards off the trail, so I followed a casual track deeper in.

Much to my dismay, I came upon a "latrine" area where Leave No Trace principles had been utterly abandoned. The area was scattered with plops of toilet paper and many lazy hikers had simply deposited their loads atop the ground.

Stepping *very* carefully, I pushed deeper and eventually found a depression filled with leaf litter, sticks and stones, where I clawed out a cathole and did my thing. I'd alternated burying and packing out used paper on the trail, but in reaction to the inexcusable mess I'd seen, I vowed to pack it out until the end of my hike. It turned out to be no big deal, and I have packed out every shred of TP I've used ever since.

I tiptoed back through the snoozing stealth site and headed down to the pond to refill my water, where I sank ankle deep in black mud. It was as if the trail had to balance each transcendent moment—my night atop Garfield—with a reminder that really, I was just another grungy guy stumbling around in the woods.

*

The climb up to Mount Lafayette (5,260 feet) was steep (including the 20th-steepest mile and the 23rd-steepest half-mile), but I found it exhilarating. The air was cold enough that I hiked wearing hat, coat and gloves; using the rule of thumb that temperature decreases about 3.5 degrees Fahrenheit for every 1,000 feet of elevation, I later calculated from the overnight low in Lincoln, N.H. that the mid-morning temperature atop Lafayette was probably hovering around the freezing mark. I was thrilled to hit timberline, knowing that the trail would not dip back into the forest for the next four miles or so.

Once again, I was favored with an absolutely spectacular, sunny, and mostly calm day on a major summit. Taking in the breathtaking 360-degree view, I marveled at how tiny Mount Washington, adorned with a fluffy cap of cloud, appeared after a little more than two days of walking. Far below I could see Greenleaf Hut, not a favorite of thru-hikers because it is a steep one-mile off the trail. Off to the southwest the AT snaked along the exposed length of Franconia Ridge, reminding me somehow of the serpentine, crenelated Great Wall of China.

While taking a brief break for peanut-butter crackers and water, I spoke to a local hiker who pointed to a miniscule glint on the furthest eastern horizon.

"See that shining silver ribbon right there between the earth and sky? That's the Atlantic Ocean," he said. "The early explorers could just make out these mountains from the sea on a clear day. That's about 120 miles away."

Reveling in the long, awe-inspiring, 4,000-foot descent to Franconia Notch, I realized I'd jumped the gun on assuming I'd seen "the last NOBO," passing at least 10 as they made their way up to the summit. I stopped to talk to the last one I saw before I descended below treeline, an exhausted-looking woman carrying a surprisingly huge pack, given how far she'd come.

"The Whites are just kicking my ass," she said.

"Yeah, no doubt. I've been keeping my eye out for the last NOBO," I said, thinking I was making polite conversation. "You must be near the end of the line."

"Thanks a lot for reminding me how slow I am," she said, face drooping into a desultory mask.

"Oh, no, I didn't mean anything … I just …," I stammered. "I'm sorry, I wasn't implying you were slow or anything like that. I just like the idea of meeting 'the last NOBO.'"

"Well, there are plenty of people behind me," she said, looking up the mountain. "Does it get easier up ahead?"

I hated having to answer the question, but lying wasn't going to help her.

"No," I said. "From here through southern Maine is pretty tough going. But hey, you've made it this far…."

She groaned and turned up the trail.

Once back in the trees, the tread grew tricky and rocky and steep, particularly the last couple miles from 4,459-foot Mount Liberty to the notch some 2,500 feet below, which featured the 6th-steepest mile and 21st-steepest half-mile of the AT.

Getting a little tired of these endless steep mofos, I groused in my journal.

I'd planned the night before to hike about 14 miles and camp by a stream at the foot of the steep climb to the Mount Kinsman, but as I walked I found myself toying with another option: Going to town, then skipping the looming steepness of the Kinsmans and shuttling to the north side of Moosilauke, the purported last gasp of the Whites, the next day.

The previously distasteful idea of yellow-blazing—skipping a portion of the trail via vehicle—had begun to infect my imagination for two reasons. First, I knew a storm was predicted the day after next. Second, a hiker who shall go unnamed had told me in Andover that they and their crew had in Vermont begun unashamedly yellow-blazing here and there, including a bypass of the grueling Baldpates (which Sage—*not* the person to whom I'm referring—had amusingly described as, "You know, just … *shitty.*") and the daunting Kinsmans.

"We were never purists anyway," explained the laid-back yellow-blazer, one of the more engaging people I met on my hike. "Whatever, man; we're just out here to have fun."

By the time I crossed the Whitehouse Bridge over Cascade Brook it was early afternoon and my mind was made up. Instead of continuing under I-93 and starting up the Kinsmans, I turned left and walked nine-tenths of a mile on a paved bike path to the parking lot for the Franconia Notch State Park visitor center.

Along the way, I passed two pairs of NOBOs. One guy, Tuna, advised me to stay at "Chet's," a hostel that isn't mentioned in Awol's guide except, for reasons that remain mysterious, as a black dot on the map for Lincoln, N.H.

"It's a great place, man," he said. "Super chill hangout for hikers."

He also gave me the phone number for Miss Janet, the legendary trail angel who migrates from Georgia to Maine in her custom van each season, seeking to help hikers any way she can. I'd heard about her all along the trail, and was excited for the chance to finally meet her.

On the other hand, Marnie at White Mountains Hostel had suggested I stay at The Notch Hostel in North Woodstock, saying it was much like her place. So when I got to the parking lot, I called the number listed in Awol to see about getting a ride.

"I'm sorry, we're full," said the woman who answered. "I'm afraid you're not going to find anything in town this weekend"—I honestly didn't even know what day of the week it was— "because of the festival."

That was the annual New Hampshire Highland Games & Festival, the largest Scottish culture event in the northeast.

Great, I thought. I pondered hiking back up the bike path and tackling the first part of the Kinsmans as I'd originally planned, but by then I had my heart set on some real food—and yellow-blazing. So I called Miss Janet.

Since meeting her, I've come to think of Miss Janet as a kind of AT bodhisattva who has made a vow to return to the trail year after year until every hiker is enlightened. Not merely a cornucopia of knowledge about the AT, its towns, hostels, restaurants—you name it—she also is a warm, loving, compassionate angel with an uncanny ability to discern what every hiker needs, whether it's a hug or a stern talking-to.

"Where are you?" she said in her lovely east Tennessee lilt.

"At the entrance to the parking lot at Franconia Notch."

She laughed. "Well, turn around. I'm in the parking lot just behind you."

Sure enough, her well-used, heavily stickered forest-green van was in the process of being unloaded by a daisy-chain of hikers, who tossed packs down from the roof rack. Beaming happily, seven or eight hikers posed for Miss Janet's photos and video, many breaking into some currently popular dance that I knew nothing about. The round of hugs went on for several minutes before they saddled up and waved goodbye. I had Miss Janet all to myself for the short ride into town.

"Don't worry," she said when I fretted about finding a place to stay. "I'll take you to Chet's. It's the best place for a real hiker experience, anyway."

I had not confessed my plan to yellow-blaze the Kinsmans. But Miss Janet seemed almost to read my mind and, without prompting, made a suggestion that would prevent me from making a mistake I would regret.

"Hey, why don't you slack the Kinsmans?" she said. "I can give you a ride up there tomorrow morning and pick you up when you're done. It's a tough 17 miles, but you can do it."

And that's all it took to dispel my ill-advised, short-lived urge to shortchange my hike, which I would have indeed regretted later.

Miss Janet first drove me to the grocery store in Lincoln and waited while I did a resupply. Then we drove a few blocks to a plain, low-slung house. When I got out of the van, a guy in a wheelchair rolled out from the garage and Janet introduced me by my trail name, but neglected to tell me who *he* was.

"Hi," I said, shaking his hand. "Uh, and you are…?"

This was Chet, and he was *not* amused. Unbeknownst to me, he likes to grill hikers before granting them permission to stay. He's not interested in section hikers, yellow-blazers, or anyone other than thru-hikers. He whirled his wheelchair to go back into the garage, but Miss Janet stopped him.

"No, he's the real deal. Tell him, Pony."

I apologized, saying I didn't realize who he was, then began tediously recounting my oddball itinerary—Winding Stair Gap through the Smokys in March; home for three weeks; Springer to Franklin, April 9-16; shuttled to Pigeon River April 17; got off at Rockfish Gap May 17 for five weeks; started back June 25; got off in mid-Vermont for a couple of weeks; flipped up to Katadhin August 25; and now here I was.

Chet looked a little taken aback and glanced at Miss Janet.

"Well, I don't think anyone would make up anything as complicated as *that*," he said, waving me into the garage to find a spot there or in the yard out back.

Miss Janet was right, of course. Chet's was a true hiker hangout. Between tenters in the backyard and spots claimed on mattresses, couches and pieces of carpet in the garage, at least 20 hikers were there, and it wasn't even mid-afternoon.

I tossed my pad onto a creaky wooden gazebo in the yard, where clusters of hikers were smoking various herbs, drinking beer, listening to music and playing games. Among them were Turtle, whom I'd met while recovering from Lyme disease in Pennsylvania and Firefly, a woman I'd met all the way back in Carolina.

After showering in the dungeon-like basement of Chet's home, I meandered back into town in search of Mexican food, which I'd been craving for days. On the way, I ran into Sourpatch and a lanky young hiker named Strider, who were on their way back to Chet's. We hugged and chatted for a few minutes. It nearly broke my heart when she told me that Simba, the young Israeli hiker, had ended her hike in Stratton.

"Dang," I said. "I would have liked to see her again."

"You don't say," Sourpatch said with a wink.

"No, it's not what you think…"

"You don't have to explain," she said, grinning. "I get it. I love her too!"

I ate a huge plate of enchiladas and ravaged a basket of chips down to the last grain of salt, licking drops of salsa from my fingertips at Nacho's Mexican

Grille. I had a Coke for dessert before taking a slow constitutional stroll back to the hostel, where I busted out a 12-pack of Sam Adams Oktoberfest for sharing.

Chet's place was festive that night, and he forgave me my initial faux pas when I took an interest in his excellent crew of two dogs and a cat. Sleeping did not go as well as I'd hoped. My stomach grumbled with a case of town-belly, the night was surprisingly cold, and a skunk expressed itself somewhere nearby in the wee hours.

I was up around 5 o'clock. Miss Janet had told me to knock on the van when I got up and she'd shuttle me and anyone else up to Kinsman Notch, but I couldn't bear to disturb her until 7. At her request, I had corralled four other NOBOs who planned to slack and we got underway, only to stop at the Dunkin' Donuts, where I inhaled two donuts and bought coffee. Miss Janet, I learned, is all about top-notch service, not rushing things, and I had to tamp down my natural impatience and just enjoy the ride. We finally tumbled out of the van at 8:20, some two or three hours later than I would normally get going, but I was grateful for the slacking service.

The day before, Miss Janet explained to me that she doesn't always recommend the Kinsman slackpack to northbound hikers.

"All these poor NOBOs think they're 10 feet tall when they get to Hanover," New Hampshire, she said. "They get here and they've done Moosilauke, but they still don't really get it about the Whites; they *can't* get it. They think knocking out 17 miles is going to be no big deal, but even slackpacking, the Kinsmans are *tough.*"

Oddly, according to my journal, the first eight miles were "a joy, just normal-ass rocks and sweet tread," despite the fact that the first seven-tenths of a mile include the 37th-steepest half-mile on the trail. After that, the tread remains fairly sane as the AT trundles along through the forest, up and over Mount Wolf, then down to Eliza Brook.

But from there, it's a steep, 2,000-foot grind to the flat, slabby summit of South Kinsman, including the 24th-steepest half-mile and 18th-steepest mile on the AT. After a short drop, the trail climbs steeply up to North Kinsman.

Typical NH slog—steep, pure rox, 2,000 feet up to a decent flat top above treeline, I wrote later. *My stomach was sour and I burped coffee and donuts all the way up, but I cruised.*

One of the four NOBOs who started with me had blazed past me on the first climb. When I passed him below the summit of the south peak, he looked trashed.

"My caffeine buzz ran out," he said.

Both summits offered good views, though nothing as spectacular as Washington, Garfield, or Lafayette. Once again, I had excellent weather on a mountaintop, but a haze of thin cloud was cutting into the sunlight by afternoon and I sensed the coming storm.

The first mile down was extremely steep (the 53rd steepest half-mile, in fact), stony and slow going. But after that, the trail leveled and smoothed out nicely, making for a long, but fairly gentle runout to the highway underpass, after which I walked a mile down the bike path to the parking lot for a second time. All in all, what would have been a brutal day with a heavy pack was instead just a really gorgeous hike.

Fuck off, purists! Slack-packing is the best, I wrote later in my journal.

Per Miss Janet's instructions, I had texted her from Kinsman Pond Shelter. But she'd warned me she might be heading north that day, and there was no reply by the time I reached the bottom. So I stood at the parking lot exit and put out my thumb.

Fifteen minutes later, not one of the 20-plus cars that had driven past had even glanced in my direction. To my great relief, Miss Janet texted me just then and said she'd pick me up in 45 minutes; she asked about the NOBOs she'd dropped off, and I said I hadn't seen any of them since morning. They eventually got back to Chet's around 7:30 p.m.

THIRTY-SIX:
PARTNERS FOR A DAY

September 2016: Mount Moosilauke to
Smarts Mountain Cabin

Remembering my chilly, skunky stay under the gazebo in Chet's back yard the night before, I laid claim to a strip of carpet beneath a teetering bookshelf in his garage as soon as Miss Janet and I arrived.

Kizmit, the quiet Mississippi SOBO I'd met on Mount Washington, was there, without Green Blaze. She'd finally walked away from him and was now cranking up her mileage. She planned to climb the crazy-steep backside of Mount Moosilauke the next morning.

That was my intention, too. I wasn't thrilled with the forecast for rain and fog, but it was supposed to be warm with no wind. But I sure got an earful from Chet and a couple other hikers when I mentioned climbing Moosilauke in the rain. Most of the comments were variations on the theme of, "*You're gonna die!*"

"You have to understand, you're basically climbing a waterfall. If it weren't dark, I'd take you outside right now and you'd see the white of the water coming down," Chet said. "You're going straight up, and the rocks are slippery. One misstep and *bam*! You're gone."

NOBOs who had just survived the steep descent alongside Beaver Brook concurred, at times in nearly apocalyptic terms.

"Dude, I would *never* do that in the rain," said one guy. "Seriously, one slip and you're dead. Trust me, you do *not* want any part of that crazy."

But Kizmit, who thru-hiked the trail as a NOBO in 2012 with her sweet little dachsund, waved off all these dire warnings.

"Yeah, it's steep, and if you aren't paying attention, you could slip," she said in her charming Southern lilt. "But you have to realize, these guys are freaking out because Moosilauke was their first real taste of the Whites. But you're SOBO; you already know what it's like. They're the ones who don't understand."

Miss Janet, friendly storehouse of reliable information, concurred with Kizmit: You just can't trust NOBOs who have just gotten their first taste of New Hampshire.

"You two'll be fine," Miss Janet said, promising to drive Kizmit and me up to Kinsman Notch in the morning to hike the "last" big climb in the Whites for SOBOs.

*

Awed by my daily Bad News of beauty and challenge in New Hampshire, I'd not really realized how close I was coming to the end of my hike, started six months earlier in the Great Smoky Mountains, when I'd planned to get off trail just before Memorial Day.

After 4,802-foot Moosilauke, rumor had it that the rest of New Hampshire was a cakewalk for SOBOs. And while what I'd hiked of Vermont had been rugged, I knew I'd have to climb no higher than 2,500 feet before reaching Killington. So even if I took a zero somewhere, I would be finished in a week or less.

Dribbling into Vermont won't be like finishing on Katahdin, I wrote in my journal, *but just … wow. How can I be almost done? How will I go back to the World?*

It was warm and misty when Kizmit and I stepped out of Miss Janet's van at Kinsman Notch the next morning at 7:30. Miss Janet took our photos and gave us warm, enveloping hugs before we turned and walked into the woods. Within a tenth of a mile, we were headed straight up the 3,000-foot climb to the summit of Mount Moosilauke, which includes—the moment you've all been waiting for, ladies and gentlemen—yes, the single steepest mile segment of the entire AT (and, as it happens, the 2nd-steepest half-mile). Following the tumble of Beaver Brook, the trail gains 2,170 feet in just 1.7 miles, a grade of more than 24 percent.

But, with Kizmit prodding my old butt up the hill, I loved every minute of it. We were soaked from sweat and heavy mist, breathing hard, yet somehow, we managed to carry on a conversation for a good portion of the climb. She was by far the strongest hiker I'd been around since BASA and Achilles in Massachusetts, and among the strongest I met on the entire trail.

In contrast to my earlier experiences with Kizmit, she proved engagingly chatty. She'd lit her afterburners after deciding to hike away from Green Blaze, after 400 miles together. She liked him well enough, she said, but he seemed to have no filter and could be thoughtlessly cruel. Kizmit, 31, attributed his sometimes-ungentle words to youth and the military, where such behavior is more commonplace.

We talked about our mutual love for animals, wildlife rehabilitation, Mississippi, the Colorado Trail, movies, and more. I learned that she'd adopted her trail name in memory of a baby squirrel she'd found blown down from a nest, eyes still closed. She raised little Kizmit for several weeks, but he died of pneumonia, leaving her heartbroken.

Kizmit's company made the hours and miles of our steep march fly by, and we reached the blustery, fog-shrouded summit at 10:30. Our ascent felt fast, but the fact that we averaged less than six-tenths of a mile per hour tells you how steep it really was. We took photos of each other grinning in the mist before throwing on rain gear to cut the wind and hurrying off the other side. The descent was steep, rocky (including, since you asked, the 23rd- and 16th-steepest mile segments of the trail), and consequently slow going.

I busted out my "backup," $20 Frogg Toggs rain jacket for the first time and soon realized I should have been using it all along. I know it would have soaked through during the kind of torrential downpour I'd endured elsewhere on the trail, but it kept me impressively dry for 15 percent of the price of my fancier lightweight jacket.

Once we were back in the trees, the fog thinned out and we stowed our rain gear. Remarkably, this was the only inclement weather I experienced on any iconic summit along the AT; I had been extraordinarily fortunate.

We spilled out onto remote NH 25 just before 1 p.m. As far as I knew, I was done with the Whites.

"Yes, but you do still have Cube and Smarts," Miss Janet had said offhandedly that morning. Smarts Mountain, at 3,238 feet, and Mount Cube, at 2,909, didn't sound like very daunting obstacles, though one guy at Chet's had raved that the north side of Smarts was as bad or worse than Moosilauke.

Never believe anyone's horrific tales about anything, ever. All the oogie-boogie about Moosilauke was, big surprise, wildly over the top. Chet and the others made it sound like the apocalypse, I wrote later. *Yes, it's a steep, wet, rocky, 3,000-foot slog, but everyone with their hair on fire didn't even have to climb up it! The Whites may be a buzzsaw, but they are an* expected *buzzsaw. Maine is the stump grinder they don't see coming.*

*

Kizmit had a box to pick up at the Hikers Welcome Hostel a third of a mile up NH 25. I'd planned to keep rolling, but I had enjoyed her company and decided to walk with her and, with luck, find a Coke or Gatorade and maybe an ice-cream bar for sale. The fog had burned away and the clouds were beginning to break up overhead when we reached the hostel. We'd hiked less than 10 miles.

My feet and legs were feeling good, but the grinding and grumbling that had plagued my stomach since I woke up seemed to be getting worse, and I began to worry that it was something more than "town belly." I was also now beginning to mourn the end of my hike. As so many thru-hikers had told me,

"Nobody comes home wishing they'd spent *less* time on the trail."

In a snap decision, I decided to call it a day, even though I might lose Kizmit's company.

The hostel owners, Packrat and his wife Alyson, weren't there, nor was Legion, the usual caretaker. But a nice young woman (whose name escapes me) gave us the lowdown: there was a shower, privy, and rattle-trap old washer and dryer out back, and a brand-new, beautiful barn-style bunkhouse, though the electrical outlets weren't yet hooked up. I took a bed in the bunkroom upstairs, so I could charge my phone.

I fully expected Kizmit to roll on, as she had planned to hike another 10 or 15 miles. But after getting her box, we sat outside together, soaking up the sun.

"I really should get moving," she said, audibly groaning. "But I kind of don't want to."

Much to my delight, she made a snap decision to stay the night.

"But if I'm going to make it to Damascus by Thanksgiving, I *have* to step it up," she said.

We got a ride from the caretaker down to Glencliff, where we bought dinner and I did a mini-resupply for the next couple of days into Hanover. Back at the hostel, Kizmit was thrilled to find a DVD of *O, Brother, Where Art Thou?*, a movie she'd talked about during our Moosilauke slog, and we watched it with three section hikers. After they went to bed, I watched a low-budget, yet charming and authentic, movie about the AT, *Southbounders*.

I'll do 20 miles to shelter tomorrow, I wrote in my journal before falling asleep. *Just two short climbs.*

I woke a couple times in the night to continued sharp, grinding pain in my stomach. I got up just after 6 a.m. and decided I was better off skipping breakfast. Kizmit was up but not yet ready to leave by the time I headed out. She'd made the passage of Moosilauke a pleasure, but I sensed her desire for solitude. I knew I couldn't keep up with her, anyway.

"I imagine you'll pass me sometime today," I said by way of farewell. "But in case I don't see you, thanks for the company."

*

Whether it was due to the warm, humid day—highs in the 70s and average humidity of 94 percent—or my sketchy stomach, that day was not much fun.

In contrast to the day before, and despite my previous light day, my legs were trashed by the time I'd scaled two puny-ass, 700-foot climbs, Ore Hill and Mount Mist. Despite a gentle morning rain, I was sweating like a plough horse. It dawned on me that I was running a fever, and I began to worry about a resurgence of dreaded Lyme disease. But after being forced to flee into the woods a half dozen times before noon, I suspected it might instead be giardia or something similar.

Despite Miss Janet's gentle warning, and the fact that it included 54th-steepest half-mile on the AT, I did not expect the three-mile ascent of Mount Cube to be such a grind. Between the intermittent mist and not-so-intermittent green tunnel, the mountain provided little in the way of compensating views, except for Eastman Ledges on the descent. On the other hand, the tread was fantastic, compared to the rest of New Hampshire and most of Maine, providing actual dirt beneath my shoes for most of the day.

My legs continued to burn with exhaustion all the way up Smarts Mountain, slowing my pace. I was genuinely surprised that Kizmit had not yet blazed past me, though it was possible she'd skated by during one of my many cathole-digging diversions.

When I finally reached the top, I was so wasted that I didn't even bother to climb the fire tower on the summit. Instead, I staggered down a short blue blaze to Smarts Mountain Cabin, a grungy old firewarden's cabin that now serves as a shelter.

There were three NOBO guys goofing around there when I arrived. But having read in the logbook that cabin mice were especially persistent, they decided to sleep in the tower. Confident of my highly effective, mouse-resistant Ursack/OPsak food bag setup, I tossed my pad out beneath a window, then popped an Immodium.

I couldn't recall drinking any untreated water in recent days. But whatever the cause of my ailment, it had definitely amplified the difficulty of this 20-mile, 6,000-foot day.

I decided to scope out the privy, in case I needed to find it quickly during the night. I found it in desperate need of maintenance, the "peak" piled up to just a couple of inches below the seat. Despite my iffy condition, I decided to rearrange things a bit and make room for the next few users, at least.

It appeared to be a composting toilet, but so far as I could tell, there was no hatch to access the dung-heap from below so it could be "stirred." Now, oddly adamant about improving the situation, I found a sturdy stick and went topside again. Breathing through my mouth and involuntarily wincing so hard my face hurt, I proceeded to shove the summit of poop, paper, and mulch down until I'd lowered the Leaning Tower of Feces by a couple of feet. My disgust finally caught up with me, and I puked a mouthful of bitter vomit onto the now-reduced pile. Staggering out of the privy, I heaved my befouled feces-stirrer as far down the hill as I could, my good deed for the day done.

A German couple soon showed up at the cabin, followed by an older NOBO section hiker who was beat from the climb up Smarts, which includes (last one!) the 28th-steepest half-mile on the trail. Chuck from Nebraska (I think that was his name; I was so exhausted and sick that I took minimal notes that night) had been on a years-long quest to section hike the entire trail. He had the shellshocked look of a NOBO on his first day in New Hampshire.

"I hope it's not this hard from here north," he said.

I hated to break the bad news. But I knew I would have wanted the truth.

"Well," I said, "I cannot tell a lie. It actually gets harder. A lot harder, I'm afraid...."

Chuck groaned.

I asked him if he'd seen anyone matching Kizmit's description on his way up the mountain. He said he'd seen her pitching her tent at the bottom just as he started his grueling climb an hour and a half earlier; she must have hiked past after I'd reached the cabin. I was sorry not to see her again, but pleased to learn that she reached Damascus on Dec. 7, wrapping up a cold and often solo flip-flop—just as she'd have wanted it—to become a two-time AT finisher. Kudos to Kizmit, my last, brief "trail family." The following May, she bought an old Subaru and headed north with her dog to take a job as a ridgerunner for the Green Mountain Hiking Club.

"I'm SSSSSSSSSSOOOOOOOOOOOOOOOOOOOOOOO excited to be living on the trail all summer and fall (with my own hippy-mobile for my two days off per week) and actually making money for being out there," she wrote me.

Lucky dog.

THIRTY-SEVEN:
... BUT A WHIMPER*

September 2016: Smarts Mountain to Norwich, Vermont

I was no longer in doubt that I had a fever when I woke the next morning in the Smarts Mountain Cabin, though it was lukewarm compared to the fire ignited by Lyme disease in Pennsylvania. With my digestive system still badly askew, I decided not to provoke it with food.

The first pitch of the descent of Smarts was indeed steep, as one hair-on-fire NOBO had informed me back at Chet's hostel. But it wasn't terribly rocky and there were some cool ledges with great views. It would have been a bear to ascend, but compared to the rest of New Hampshire and Maine, a pretty brief bear, which confirmed my theory—and trail angel extraordinaire Miss Janet's experience—that NOBOs entering New Hampshire really aren't to be trusted when it comes to evaluating the difficulty of the last 500 miles of the AT. But they learn soon enough.

---

* See T.H. Eliot, *"The Hollow Men"*

It was another beautiful day for walking, clear and not just warm, but hot, with high temperatures in the 80s and a relative humidity of 85 percent in nearby Hanover. By the time I passed by the Dartmouth Skiway (NOBO mile 1764.5; SOBO 424.6), I had dropped to a mere 1,200 feet, and without consulting my Awol guide, I assumed the rest of my day into town would be a cakewalk.

I was saddened to come upon a sign noting that long-time trail angel Bill Ackerley, aka the Ice Cream Man, had died in May. AT hikers were always welcome to stop by his home just one-tenth of a mile from the intersection of Dorchester Road and the Grafton Parkway, eat some ice cream, use a portable privy, fill up on water, play croquet, or just rest for a bit.

Had I not been ailing, the brief, steep climb to Holts Ledge wouldn't have fazed me, especially given the spectacular views up top. But I was in no mood for even this 1,100-foot ascent, and I grumbled all the way up.

After I descended to Goose Pond Road, the trail began to climb again, and to my dismay, rather steeply. I pulled out Awol and saw that I was in for an even longer slog on the north peak of 2,300-foot Moose Mountain, followed by a short, steep grind to the south peak, before things leveled out and I was truly home free for the day.

Though too tired to swim, I was grateful to come upon a small pond several miles later, where I soaked two bandanas in the water and swabbed my forehead and face. When I'd left Smarts I'd planned to hike 21.9 miles and call it a day at Velvet Rocks Shelter (SOBO mile 440.7). Although feeling weak and overheated, the possibility of a bed and, if my stomach would allow it, actual food, was enough to inspire me to bash out another two miles and collapse in Hanover.

A million years earlier, my mother and I had visited Dartmouth College on a grand tour of New England colleges on my wish list. We'd come in October, and the trees all over town were riotous with autumn color, from deep magenta to fluorescent pinks and oranges. Truly charming and idyllic, Hanover from afar looks like a staged calendar photograph.

In flip-flopping, I thought I'd be drunk on fall beauty by now, but it was not to be. To my disappointment, even the leaves above 3,000 feet had only just begun to turn, and down in town, it still looked, and felt, very much like summer.

Hanover was the first truly bustling burgh I'd seen since flying to Bangor, Maine on Aug. 24. Students walked briskly along the concrete walks that crisscrossed sprawling, five-acre Dartmouth Green, while others lounged in the hot sun, tossed footballs, or flung Frisbees. I plopped down and reclined on my pack to see what Awol had to say about accommodations.

Just across the street was the impressively large building housing the Dartmouth Outdoor Club, which offered a brochure listing hiker services and angels in town. I would have liked to loll around, or even take a nap on the Green. But it was already 4:15, so I groaned back to my feet and walked across the street to the DOC. The woman at the help window handed me the magic brochure and said I could leave my gear downstairs while I went next door to the student union.

Gatorade went down well, as always. As the grumbling and shooting pains in my belly had finally eased somewhat, I decided to risk eating a small container of pasta salad with olives and pesto and drinking some orange juice. All of it was far too expensive.

To my surprise, there were no "hiker cheap" accommodations in this fancy college town. I'd heard that some fraternities offer floors and couches for a nominal fee, but only before classes start. The semester had begun, so I was out of luck. I started systematically sending texts to trail angels on the list to inquire about lodging. My first five attempts went either unanswered or drew swift, "not tonight, sorry" responses. Hot and exhausted, I started to think I'd blown it by hiking past the shelter.

But then I reached a boisterously friendly woman named Jennie, who replied immediately that I was welcome to stay at the rectory of St. Barnabas Episcopal Church in Norwich, Vermont, where she served as priest. The church wasn't far away, and she said she'd pick me up in 15 minutes. I told her I wanted to walk across the Connecticut River into Vermont.

As it turned out, Rev. Jennie saw me trudging along just past the bridge in

Vermont, so I clambered into the back seat—her big, boisterous Weimaraner, Freecee, occupied the front passenger seat. But she sailed right past the church to Dan and Whit's Country Store.

"You *have* to go in here," Jennie insisted. "It's a local legend."

The place was cool, to be sure. Rev. Jennie excitedly gave me the grand tour, even the hardware department. At the end, I bought three more bottles of Gatorade and scored a "hiker's special"—a free day-old sandwich. As we walked back to the car, she pointed out the "ice cream window" at the side of the building, and I couldn't resist buying a scoop of strawberry on a sugar cone.

Jennie provided an equally detailed tour of the rectory, which was roomy, bright and clean. She suggested I take a single room with a queen bed upstairs, as three young NOBOS taking a zero (and here I thought I'd seen the "last one") had occupied three of four bunks in the adjacent room.

I peeled off my sweat-encrusted clothes and took a long, hot shower. I tossed my filthy raiment into the washer downstairs, pleased that there was no line, then slumped into a comfy couch on the porch and watched a fat, white feral cat poking around the garden.

Consulting Awol, I saw that I had just over 40 miles to go. I was not inspired, to say the least. Two days across Vermont landscapes with plenty of PUD (pointless ups and downs) and a couple of 1,000-plus climbs, and then … *what?* There would be nobody there to meet me at VT road 100 when I drifted out of the woods, nobody to high-five with, no breathtaking views, nothing at all….

A wave of melancholy washed over me and I blinked back tears. I knew from previous experience that I would likely experience weeks, if not months, of post-trail blues, and that my body would take time to recover. Psychologically, I was going to miss the pure and simple purpose of trail life. On a typical day, all you have to do is walk, find water, eat, make camp, break camp, and obey nature's calls, nothing more. There is plenty of suffering, as I've described, but it's vastly outweighed by the many transcendent moments, awe-inspiring communion with nature, and the beautiful camaraderie between you and all those people from every imaginable background, who have shared your odyssey for a minute, a night, or a month at a time.

I loved my unexpected flip-flop, which resulted in happy meetings with so many trail friends, but grieved the loss of that glorious peak moment—physically, emotionally, perhaps spiritually—atop Katahdin. I desperately missed my trail family from Virginia and wondered if I'd ever see them again.

*

That night, Yahtzee, a 2015 thru-hiker who was treating his own persistent post-trail letdown by helping Rev. Jennie, cooked up a large vat of soup, using vegetables from the community-supported agriculture collective where he worked during the day. There was also fresh French bread, a sumptuous selection of cheese, and beer.

The young NOBOs arrived at the rectory after a day of bumming around Hanover and we all ate together with our hosts. Afterward, I hauled a bucket of slop out to the compost and washed dishes.

"I've got 40 miles left," I told Yahtzee as I listlessly scrubbed a soup bowl, "but I'm thinking of wrapping it up right here."

"Oh, man, why would you want to do that?" he said, sounding like a man trying to talk a friend out of putting a gun in his mouth.

I tried to describe what I was feeling. My stomach had settled down for the most part, so that wasn't it. But I was tired and sad and I hated the thought of 40 miles of melancholy followed by a lonely anticlimax, then hitchhiking into grungy, uninspiring Rutland, Vermont.

"Tonight, I had good company, good food, a beer, and I get to sleep in a bed," I said. "I just feel like I'm done."

"Listen, man, I think you'll regret it if you skip the last two days of your hike, or take three if you have to. But that's just my opinion," he said. "Why don't you sleep on it, maybe take a zero? If you're still feeling the same way tomorrow, then OK, call it a day."

He was right, of course. My fragile emotional state had no doubt been amplified by fever and exhaustion.

Never make a decision at the end of a hard day, I reminded myself before falling asleep.

But when I woke the next morning, I felt the same way. Four weeks after climbing Katahdin, I knew in my heart that my journey was over. Subtracting the 41 miles I was skipping in Vermont and the 38 miles I "sick blazed" in Pennsylvania, I had walked 2,124 miles since starting my hike on March 13 at Winding Stair Gap in North Carolina, then "started" again at Springer Mountain in Georgia on April 9. Start to finish, my "patchwork" journey had taken just over six months; minus my three extended breaks, I'd spent 115 days on the trail; had I hiked those skipped miles, I would have finished the trail in just a hair under four months.

Somewhere in the night, my subconscious had provided me a literary, if somewhat frivolous, reason to put a pin in my hike in Norwich, Vermont: September 22 is the birthday of Bilbo and Frodo Baggins, each of whom took a very long, extremely challenging walk in J.R.R. Tolkien's *The Hobbit* and *The Lord of the Rings*, respectively.

Of course, unlike Bilbo and Frodo, I hadn't had to deal with orcs or dragons or Balrogs.... *Not* that I actually believe in orcs. Or dragons. Or Balrogs.

But my journey was done.

*

I spent almost the entire, hour-long flight in a Cape Air six-seater from Lebanon, N.H. to Boston craning my neck to stare back at the receding blue ridge of the White Mountains, tears in my eyes. The summits of Washington and Lafayette remained clearly visible almost until the plane soared out over the Atlantic and banked back to the west to land at Logan International Airport.

I'd heard more than one AT finisher say she couldn't bear to fly back home, to unravel all those months of struggle and joy and suffering and pain and sacrifice in the span of a few hours. Had I gone back to Rutland I might have taken Amtrak, but now I just felt drained and I couldn't bear a long goodbye. As Yahtzee had predicted, I felt a twinge of guilt about bailing on those last few miles of Vermont. I promised that someday I'd come back to walk them (and that Lyme-skipped stretch of Pennsylvania), but now I needed to go into mourning.

My 2016 thru-hike of the Appalachian Trail was not a thing of beauty. It was, at best, a patchwork quilt: 140 miles through the Smokys in March; 720 miles to the bottom of the Shenandoahs in April and May; 800 miles from Virginia to Vermont in June and July; and the last 500 through Maine and New Hampshire in August and September.

It was an artless, fractured itinerary, an ugly, lumpy thing compared to the steady, elegant progress of so many friends I'd met between Georgia and Maine—Olive Oil, Kaleidoscope, Patches, Easy-E, Trekkeroni, Two-Pack, BASA, Achilles, Legs and Verge, The Dude…. But it was *my* hike, and I love it as ferociously as a mama bear protecting her cubs.

I am haunted by it, every day.

I expect I will be, until the day I die.

EPILOGUE: CLASS NOTES

Four years after I finished my hike, not a day goes by that I don't think of my Appalachian Trail journey. It haunts me. But it is a welcome ghost, and I fear only the day that I no longer remember.

I have very mixed feelings about the world of social media, but I confess that it helped me stay in touch with hikers whom I otherwise might have lost forever. Today, one of my best friends (despite an age different of nearly three decades) is Lava Monster, part of my Virginia trail family, and I remain in close touch with Patches and The Dude. I have seen Sourpatch 1,500 miles from the AT, maintained contact with Simba, made friends with Constantine, now a Triple Crowner, and turned to many fellow hikers to help with stories for The Trek (thetrek.co). I want to give a huge shout out to Matthew "Odie" Norman, founder and editor of *The Hiker Yearbook*, an indispensable resource for tracking down trail companions whose real names you might never have known otherwise.

I called this book *The Trail Is the Teacher* for a reason. Without getting too woo on you, I honestly believe that any hiker who remains open to the trail's lessons will come away a wiser person. So to wrap up my adventure, I thought

I'd lay out a few of the lessons I've learned, not just from the AT, but also the Colorado Trail, the Foothills Trail, the Pinhoti Trail and the Great Plains Trail.

Not everyone will agree with all these lessons, and as always, Hike Your Own Hike. These are my personal observations, in no particular order, and if they work for you, great; if not, no worries.

Put things where they belong. To quote the Eagles, *everything, all the time*. Miss America offers this excellent rule: You should always be able to find anything in your pack in complete darkness. Put everything in the same place, so you won't panic and have to explode your pack when you can't find something.

Don't talk about miles. My friend Sparkle clued me into this one before my CT hike after hearing me blab about how many miles I thought I could hike a day. If someone asks, don't lie, but hikers aren't impressed by hikers who boast about miles.

Don't talk about pack weight. Thanks again to the wisdom of Sparkle. At the beginning of a long-distance hike, it's natural—in fact, a cliché—to talk about gear. But constant dick-measuring about pack weight is tiresome and, unsurprisingly, seldom appreciated.

Stop criticizing Bill Bryson and Cheryl Strayed. Bryson and Strayed are something most hikers are not: writers, and good ones, at that. Bryson's seminal *A Walk in the Woods* is a funny travelogue that takes place on the Appalachian Trail. Strayed's *Wild* is a deeply personal memoir built around her walk on the Pacific Crest Trail. Neither author claimed to be some badass thru-hiker, or even LASH (long-ass section hiker), but many hikers—who, it seems to me, are just showing their insecurities—like to complain that the two authors didn't even finish their respective trails. No, they didn't. But their books are more insightful about long-distance hiking than most books on the subject, most of which are little better than glorified journals.

All those numbers mean nothing once you hit the trail. It can be fun to plan out a hike, fret about and create spreadsheets for pack weight and calories and miles-per-day; it was for me. But once a hiker takes that first step, the trail makes a mockery of plans and numbers. The upside is, she'll also teach you all you need to know. Forget pounds—if your pack is too heavy, she'll tell you; if you don't have something you need, she'll let you know. Forget calorie counting—are you hungry? If so, eat more. Pretty simple, no numbers necessary.

Most things newbies worry about aren't worth worrying about. It's natural to be nervous, but once you get going, you'll either have the temperament to do this, or you won't. Fretting up front is wasted energy.

You don't "conquer" the trail. Or a mountain. You do not make it your "bitch." You are there at the pleasure of the trail, and no matter how tough, smart, young, cool, hip, or resourceful anyone thinks they are, it has a way of puncturing even the most inflated ego.

The AT isn't always a thrill-a-minute. Unlike, say, the Colorado Trail or Pacific Crest Trail, where almost daily you can count on mind-shattering vistas of astonishing beauty, AT hikers spend a great deal of time in the infamous "green tunnel," where they are often unable to see the scenery for the trees. This can translate into tedium for some hikers. I learned very quickly to revel in what one hiker aptly named, "microgoals"—small borders, horizons, achievements, a swimming hole, *some* marker of progress. This can be a state line, a century-mile mark (i.e. 100 or 500 miles), reaching the next shelter, catching up to a friend … really anything, so long as it helps break the monotony and seeming lack of progress through endlessly monotonous terrain.

Mental stamina is just as important as—maybe more important than—physical stamina. Nothing more to say about this, but it's true.

No, Bill Nye the Science Guy is not hiking SOBO. Not in 2016, not in any year, despite the (admittedly amusing) rumors. That sticker is my proudest souvenir from my hike.

Don't ignore blue blazes. Because the AT can be monotonous, I found it worth my while to saunter a little out of the way here and there to catch a view or take a dip.

Never quit after a hard day. Give yourself a chance to recover some perspective with a good night's sleep.

Keep it humble. Many a big talker has flamed out before Virginia ... or North Carolina ... or Neel Gap (mile 32.9). I watched, bemused, as some 2017 AT hikers took to social media to loudly trumpet their badassery, blithely dismissing experienced hikers who cautioned that the trail is harder than it looks on paper. One such hiker noisily proclaimed he would do a "quick thru" in 80 to 90 days; by the time I stopped counting, he would have had to average *90 miles a day* to make his "quick, 90-day" goal. Another brashly proclaimed that he would "bash it out" in 80 to 90 days. Last I checked, he was averaging 11 mpd, and to hit his 90-day goal would have to average 389 miles per day to finish in 80 (update: he quit shortly after 80, not much past the halfway point, on a pace—remembering that Maine and New Hampshire are a whole different animal—for about 170 days).

Rain gear doesn't work. No matter how much you spend, you will get wet. Even the most stylin' $600 jacket and matching rain pants will fail after 20 or 30 minutes in a torrential downpour—which you should expect—and you'll sweat out from the inside. Embrace the reality of getting wet. If it's warm enough, walk through rain without rain gear; you'll dry faster.

Virginia is not flat. This oddly persistent rumor infects each new AT class. True, many hikers manage to crank up the miles in Virginia, for a variety of reasons. But it's *not* flat.

Shenandoah is not boring. Yes, you cross Skyline Drive countless times. But it's pretty, you're probably going to see bears, and ... blackberry milkshakes. *Mmmmm.*

The north is hard. *Really. Bloody. Hard.* Much harder than you think it's going to be. Miss Janet, the remarkable and knowledgeable trail angel, chuckles at NOBOs who reach Hanover, N.H. "thinking they're 10-feet tall." Having hiked some pretty tough miles, many assume the trail can't get much harder—but they find out soon enough. Dan "Wingfoot" Bruce came up with the rule of thumb that hikers who reach New Hampshire have completed 80 percent of the miles, but only 50 percent of the effort.

You are not home free after the Whites. Every AT hiker has heard about how challenging the Whites are. But in my experience, few expect the equally difficult gut-punch of southern Maine—which David "Awol" Miller and others, including me, think is even harder. And just because parts of northern Maine are flat, don't expect to burn up the miles—the tread can be a killer.

Yes, Pennsylvania really does suck. Smug SOBOs often mock NOBOs for whining about the rocks in Pennsylvania. In one sense, they're right: Rocks are the norm after PA, and considerably worse in NH/ME. But PA *is* a pain, which is why it is routinely ranked as the least favorite state by AT hikers, by a wide margin. You may not have to do much climbing, but what's there is steep, and the rocks are an actual thing, mile after mile of rocky, blocky, choppy, foot-mangling misery. Worse, after Duncannon you are almost always in a green tunnel. And if you hit PA during the summer, when most NOBOs do, the heat and humidity are absolutely brutal. And ticks. Ticks suck.

Do not mess around with Lyme disease. This nasty, tick-borne affliction is endemic to many parts of the trail, especially Pennsylvania, New Jersey, New York, and Connecticut, but really, anywhere below 3,000 feet. You may not be fond of the chemicals DEET and permethrin, but using them for a few weeks beats the hell out of getting Lyme.

Katahdin does not "close" on October 15. It can be closed for extreme weather conditions or environmental reasons any time of year, by order of the park superintendent. *Camping* in the park ends Oct. 22 (until December), but you can still climb the mountain. Check out the website for Baxter State Park to better understand the rules. As of 2017, you need a permit to climb the mountain, but it's no big deal.

Swim. As often as possible. With your clothes on. It keeps you clean and cools you off.

Be mindful of your music. Play music or a book or podcast if you wish, but don't play it so loud it disturbs other hikers or wildlife. Have the courtesy to turn it off, or at least down, when passing other hikers. If you wear headphones or AirPods, I suggest wearing just one so you can hear what's going on around you.

Don't sweat bears. Chances are, you're going to see some bears—consider yourself lucky if you do. Statistically, you have about a one in 80 million chance of being killed by a bear on the AT in any given year, but be smart. Either hang your bear bag properly—dangling it six feet off the ground from a spindly birch tree won't cut it—or use a system that will keep bears from knowing there is even food around, such as a bear canister or an Ursack/OPsak combo.

Bury your *&^%$#!! poop. It's not that hard. Dig a cathole at least six inches deep, at least 100 yards off the trail and 200 yards from water, dump your load, cover (never touch your poop with your spade, if you have one!). Pack out your TP; it's no big deal, no worse than your regular garbage bag. People who crap on open ground deserve to contract Lyme, noro, *and* giardia, then get mauled by a bear.

Grrrrrr…. Now, to calm myself down, I'm going to watch the hilarious video of the Barefoot Sisters singing their AT anthem, "Dig a Hole, Dump Your Load"…

Be courteous at shelters. Don't play music. Don't smoke (anything) near the shelter. Don't stay up late making noise. Don't jump down in the middle of the night on top of other hikers. If you come in late or get up early, be quiet. Golden Rule stuff.

Do. Not. Impose. Your. Snoring. On. Everyone. Else. Everyone snores from time to time on the trail, even the tiniest wisp of a 19-year-old woman (though their snores tend to be what I call "Disney princess snores," more cute than irritating). But if you know you are a loud snorer, do what Baltimore Jack did and *stay in your tent.* You do not have a right to keep everyone else awake. If you ignore this advice, don't be surprised if someone uses your boots as a cathole while you aren't looking…. *Dig a hole, dump your load….*

Don't shake hands. You are filthy. I am filthy. We are all filthy. And as Purple Mist told me, you can touch your own poop, just not someone else's. Fist bump, elbow bump. Wash when you can. Norovirus sucks.

Listen to your body. It's smarter than you are.

Ignore your body. Or rather, think of it as a spoiled child: Sometimes, it's just whining. If you aren't feeling some discomfort every day, you probably aren't doing this right. We coddle our bodies in our "comfy" synthetic lives, and every little ache, pain, or sore on the trail can cause fretting and hand-wringing. Our bodies expect the same coddling on a thru-hike when, frankly, that isn't going to fly. If it hurts in the same place day after day, or it's getting worse, that might be a problem. But if you suffer from equal-opportunity pain and discomfort—a blister here, a sore shoulder there, a tweaky knee one day, a swollen ankle the next—that's par for the course. Walk through it … until you can't.

I will never resupply by mail again. First, the USPS isn't always reliable, even when you pay $20 to get your package there and send it more than two weeks ahead of time ("Usually two or three days" me *arse*). Also, you may be sick of the food you thought you wanted to eat two or three (or 12) weeks ago. And no, unless you dry and pack your own food (be sure to include the cost of the machine and your time), with postage, mailing boxes is probably not saving you much money. Finally, it's great PR to spend money in hiker-friendly communities.

Don't haul more water than you need to. Think about where you're going and where the next water source is. A liter of water weighs one kilogram, or about 2.2 pounds. If you've got a big hill coming, don't haul two or three liters unless you must.

Take zeroes. I know I didn't take enough breaks on the AT. It's a long, long trail, and just because you can bang out 20+ mile days, day after day, for the first 1,500 miles doesn't mean it won't catch up to you in that last 700, mentally, physically, or otherwise.

Be wary of zeroes. I often threw my GI system out of whack with the sudden influx of town food and beer (just one is my rule) and so on. Town costs money. Also, "town miles"—those hiked when heading into town—are waaaaay longer than regular miles.

The trail will provide—but don't *expect* it to. I'm floored by how often some angel or fellow hiker steps up just when you need it. But those who run around complaining about the lack of magic or the quality of magic deserve none.

Consider unplugging. It's fun for spectators that hikers can now document every step along the way. But in their desperate attempts to photograph/video and post everything they are doing, some hikers just might be diminishing their actual experience.

Hiking faster does not mean you are "missing out." Idiocy, fueled by insecurity. You need not match the pace of someone slower than you in order to "smell the roses." Hike your own hike.

But … nobody regrets spending too much time on trail. Revel in the experience, however you wish.

Hold on to your hat (or whatever). If you don't want to lose stuff, you *must* snap, strap, Velcro, or tie it down.

Don't ask, "How far is it to X?" This makes a hiker look incompetent—can't you read a map and compass or even Awol? Also, the answer you get might be wrong or right, and if it's "far," you'll be bummed either way.

If your shoes or pack smell to high heaven, find someone with a car. No, really. Hose the reeking gear down, then put it in someone's car, windows rolled up, in the full sun, for a couple or a few hours. The extreme heat kills bacteria better than anything else I've tried.

You and your travails are not unique. It took me a couple of weeks to get this on the Colorado Trail, but everything you experience on the trail has been experienced, and is being experienced, by others. Ask others how they have dealt with their issues on trail.

Don't talk about controversial things with people you barely know. Just because we've been trained to be boors by social media doesn't mean we have to take it out on the trail.

The trail makes fools of those who judge. Of course, we talk with friends about the loonball using a mop as a hiking stick (apologies to the amazing Jennifer Pharr Davis), the obnoxious loudmouth at the last shelter, or the incompetent fire builders last night. But recognize that your way is not necessarily better than the next hiker's, and the people you mock just might beat you to Katahdin.

Hike Your Own Hike. This cannot be emphasized enough. Don't worry about what anyone else is doing, or compare yourself to others, or act superior to someone who isn't doing it the way *you* think it should be done. HYOH, HYOH, HYOH!

One misstep can end your hike. Don't get complacent. Pay attention.

Help each other. Please.

Be generous. Double please.

Be persistent. Somewhere along the trail, someone mentioned a great quote from the playwright Samuel Beckett: *I can't go on. I'll go on.* Embrace that contradiction every day.

Practice Leave No Trace principles. For real. Study up before your hike.

Give back. Every year the 30+ volunteer clubs who maintain the AT clear downed timber and repair washed out bridges, shelters, or sections of trail, ensuring it's in good working order for this year's hikers. But club membership skews old, very old, and if younger people don't start joining, or at least donating, there will be no trail in the future. I worked with the Appalachian Trail Conservancy's storied, flagship Konnarock Trail Crew for four weeks in 2017 and 2018, and it was a fantastic experience.

GLOSSARY

A list of some trail terms and a handful neologisms (marked with an *) that my mates and I came up with on the trail.

Aqua blazing — Semi-legitimate skipping of the trail by way of canoe, kayak or other self-propelled watercraft (frequently practiced by AT hikers in northern Virginia).

ATC — Appalachian Trail Conservancy. The nonprofit umbrella organization that manages the trail with the National Park Service and other federal agencies. If you love the trail, you should donate to the ATC or volunteer for one of its trail crews: appalachiantrail.org.

AWOL guide — Most commonly used print guidebook to the AT.

AYCE — Acronym for "all you can eat." Hikers love places that offer this, but beware! Easy to overdo it or get a stomach bug.

Bald — Hill- and mountain-tops cleared of trees (some formerly clear of trees).

Banana blaze — Matching one's pace and miles to catch-up or stay with a male love interest.

Base weight — The weight of all a hiker's gear, minus food and water.

Bearanoid — A hiker with excessive fear or nervousness about bears.

Blaze — Painted trail marking. The AT famously uses 2x6-inch white blazes to mark the trail.

Blue blazing — A blue-blazed trail is not officially part of the AT. A hiker may follow blue blazes to water sources, privies, views and more.

The Bubble — The cluster of northbound thru-hikers who leave Springer Mountain from mid-March to mid-April.

Camel-up — Drinking your fill at a water source, so you don't have to carry as much.

Cathole — What you dig when you poop in the woods. Leave No Trace principles say it should be: at least six inches deep; at least 100 yards from the trail; at least 200 yards from water.

Cowboy camping — Sleeping under the stars, no shelter, no tent, no hammock.

EoDMoFo/BoDMoFo* — End of the Day Motherfucker: That too-often inevitable nasty climb you have to complete before making camp. When you were too tired to climb the EoDMoFo, it becomes a BoDMoFo (Beginning of the Day MoFo).

Flip-flop — Hiking the entire AT, but not contiguously. For example, hiking south from Katahdin to Harpers Ferry, then north from Springer to Harpers Ferry.

Flip-flopper — One who flips and flops.

Gap — The low point of a ridge between two peaks … down South.

Green blaze — Hiking while high.

Green tunnel — Nickname for the AT, due to the fact that so much of it runs through densely forested terrain.

Guthook — *Guthook's Guide to Hiking the AT*, a GPS-powered app. Very useful.

HYOH — Hike Your Own Hike: Advice often given to hikers. In other words, do what you want, at your pace, rather than trying to keep up with someone else's idea of what's right.

Hiker trash — A term of pride among hikers who have abandoned the norms of civilization. Smelly, disheveled, battered and loving it.

Hiker hunger — The extreme boost in metabolism and appetite experienced by most long-distance hikers. Curiously, it doesn't kick in for most people for two to four weeks.

Hiker midnight — Some say 9 p.m., others sundown. At any rate, the time by which most thru-hikers have hit the hay for the night.

Hostel — A relatively inexpensive boarding house for hikers. Most offer bunkrooms, some have private rooms as well. Typically, there are showers, a kitchen for use and laundry machines. Most hostels along the AT are clean, warm and hospitable—but not all. Caveat emptor.

Hut — Alternate name for shelters in Shenandoah National Park and New Hampshire.

Lean-to — Alternate name for shelters in some New England states.

LNT — Leave No Trace is a series of seven principles designed to help backpackers and campers think about ways to minimize the impact that their presence has on the natural environment.

Lyme disease — For my money, the single most terrifying scourge of the AT. A brutal and potentially life-altering disease carried by deer (aka black-legged) ticks found in abundance along the trail.

Nero — A day on which a hiker hikes fewer miles than normal, often just until she gets into a town.

NOBO — Northbound hiker, heading in the direction Georgia>Maine.

Noro — Norovirus. A nasty bug that can survive for many days even on dry surfaces, plaguing hikers with diarrhea and vomiting. Washing your hands is the answer.

Notch — The low point of a ridge between two peaks up north.

Pink blazing — Matching one's pace and miles to catch-up or stay with a female love interest.

Privy — A standing outhouse along the trail, of varying cleanliness, capacity and exposure.

PUD — Pointless ups and downs. Hikers often grumble that the AT goes up and over too many hills needlessly. Of course, if they weren't going up and down, they'd have to go around, and that would add miles....

Purist — A thru-hiker who hikes every step of the trail, passing every white blaze and carrying their full pack.

Safety meeting — A euphemism for gathering to smoke weed on the trail.

Section hike — Hiking the trail in sections over many years.

Shelter — Generally, a three-sided log or stone structure with an adjacent privy, water source and fire pit (though not always). There are more than 250 along the Appalachian Trail. Check out Sarah Jones Decker's excellent book, *The Appalachian Trail: Backcountry Shelters, Lean-tos, and Huts.*

The Shennies — Shenandoah National Park.

The Smokys — Great Smoky Mountain National Park.

Slackpacking — Hiking a section of trail without your full pack. This usually requires support from friends with a car or a hostel.

SOBO — Southbound hiker, Maine>Georgia direction.

Stealth camping — Setting up your tent, tarp or hammock anywhere that is not a designated camping area.

Stickjam* — Perhaps inevitable when walking some 5 million steps, this occurs when a hiker's forward foot pins a stick at just the right angle so that it jams into the other foot as it sweeps by, causing pain and sometimes, damage to one's shoes.

Stone (or stick) roll* — When the weight of your foot comes down just right, so that a stone or stick is like a ball bearing that overextends your stride and sometimes sends you sprawling.

Switchbacks — In an effort to reduce erosion and decrease steepness, designers will build trails in a zig-zag pattern up and down slopes. The Appalachian Trail Conservancy has upgraded many miles of the AT to switchbacks, but it's still widely considered the most physically challenging of the North American Triple Crown trails because of its steep—i.e. not switchbacked—climbs and descents.

Thru-hiker — Anyone who completes a trail within a calendar year.

Trail angel — People who do nice things for hikers on a regular basis, such as providing food or rides.

Trail magic — Anything unexpected, provided by non-hikers, that makes a hiker's day a little better, from food to rides to a foot massage.

Trail name — A nickname bestowed upon, or taken by, thru-hikers.

"The trail provides" — A generally true belief that no matter what, a hiker's needs will be met on the trail.

Triple Crown — Earned when one completes the AT, the Pacific Crest Trail and the Continental Divide Trail.

Ultralight — Carrying as little weight as possible in your pack.

Virginia Blues — An affliction of hikers who grow restless, bored or dissatisfied while traveling the 550 or so miles of the trail in Virginia, by far the longest stretch between borders.

Work for stay — Some hostels and huts allow hikers to stay at no charge, in exchange for work.

Yellow blazing — Using motorized transportation to skip part of the trail (named after the yellow dashes on the highway).

Yogi — Mooning around normal people and looking pathetic, in an effort to score offers of free food.

Yo-Yo — Hiking the complete trail in one direction, then turning around and hiking it the other.

Zero day — A day on which a hiker hikes 0 miles. A day of rest.

ABOUT THE AUTHOR

Clay Bonnyman Evans is a freelance writer who grew up in Boulder, Colorado. He worked for seven years as a cowboy around the West before starting a 25-year career as a reporter, editor and columnist for such publications as the *Los Angeles Times*. He is the author of four previous books, including the Amazon bestseller, *Bones of My Grandfather: Reclaiming a Lost Hero of World War II*, published in 2018.

Learn more at **claybonnymanevans.com**

BY THE SAME AUTHOR

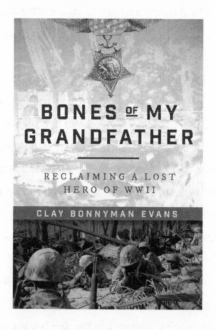

"War, reclamation, and what Tim O'Brien called "the Lives of the Dead" are eternal literary themes for men. Clay Bonnyman Evans has honored that lineage with this masterful melding of military history and personal quest."

—Ron Powers, co-author of New York Times #1 bestsellers
Flags of Our Fathers and *True Compass*, along with
No One Cares About Crazy People and others

In November 1943, Marine 1st Lt. Alexander Bonnyman, Jr. was mortally wounded while leading a successful assault on a critical Japanese fortification on the Pacific atoll of Tarawa, and posthumously awarded the Medal of Honor, the nation's highest military honor. The brutal, bloody 76-hour battle would ultimately claim the lives of more than 1,100 Marines and 5,000 Japanese forces.

But Bonnyman's remains, along with those of hundreds of other Marines, were hastily buried and lost to history following the battle, and it would take an extraordinary effort by a determined group of dedicated civilians to find him.

In 2010, having become disillusioned with the U.S. government's half-hearted efforts to recover the "lost Marines of Tarawa," Bonnyman's grandson, Clay Bonnyman Evans, was privileged to join the efforts of History Flight, Inc., a non-governmental organization dedicated to finding and repatriating the remains of lost U.S. service personnel. In Bones of My Grandfather, Evans tells the remarkable story of History Flight's mission to recover hundreds of Marines long lost to history in the sands of Tarawa. Even as the organization begins to unearth the physical past on a remote Pacific island, Evans begins his own quest to unearth the reclaim the true history of his grandfather, a charismatic, complicated hero whose life had been whitewashed, sanitized and diminished over the decades.

On May 29, 2015, Evans knelt beside a History Flight archaeologist as she uncovered the long-lost, well-preserved remains of of his grandfather. And more than seventy years after giving his life for his country, a World War II hero finally came home.

Bones of My Grandfather: Reclaiming a Lost Hero of World War II is available now in hardback, on Kindle, audiobook and CD, from Amazon.

Made in the USA
Las Vegas, NV
30 May 2022

49554626R00166